Critical Focus

An Introduction to Film

Critical Focus

An Introduction to Film

Richard M. Blumenberg
Southern Illinois University at Carbondale

Wadsworth Publishing Company, Inc.
Belmont, California

Designer: Gary Head

Communications Editor: Rebecca Hayden

Production Editor: Rebecca Hayden

ISBN-0-534-00417-2

L. C. Cat. Card No. 75-17081

Printed in the United States of America

1 2 3 4 5 6 7 8 9 10—80 79 78 77 76

For Julia

Preface

Most film books are either about film history, about filmmaking techniques, or about film appreciation. *Critical Focus,* in contrast, attempts to fill the void that exists among introductory film books by providing one text of wide scope. It includes information about the various sub-disciplines of film study: history, aesthetics, theory, criticism, scripting, filmmaking, and attempts at censorship.

The first two chapters describe some of the general areas of film study and relate film to the other arts. The third chapter introduces terms and ideas necessary for intelligently discussing or writing about motion pictures. Chapters 4 through 11 pay special attention to the evaluative and historical aspects of the narrative, documentary, and experimental film. The filmmaking chapters, in the last part, emphasize the private production film. This emphasis concludes in the epilogue, which is really an essay on my thoughts about the changing American film industry. These comments, together with the appendix on "Careers in Film," will interest people who want to enter the field but find "Hollywood" too foreboding. Finally, there is a glossary of over 325 terms, which should help readers refresh their memories about film language and processes, as well as understand and apply concepts.

Specialists will undoubtedly find that any of the chapters could be expanded into a full text the size of this one. Yet, I have included essential information. The choices of films discussed vary between the classics and recent popular films.

With some obvious exceptions (such as *Citizen Kane* or *The Battleship Potemkin*), films other than the ones I have chosen could be used for examples and the main point would not be lost. In most cases, the concept is more important than the film. I have never included a film to praise it or condemn it.

Critical Focus can be used for introductory courses in film departments as well as for those film courses offered by English, theater, communications, or art history departments. Explanation is due instructors in these fields: the book stresses *film.* When I have had to make a decision about how to examine an attribute of another discipline (such as acting in theater), I have chosen to stress the ways that cinema works in relation to that aspect, rather than the other way around. For ultimately this is a book for people who are trying to understand films and possibly make them at the same time. Specialized books that can broaden, embellish, or add new information to the material presented here are included in the bibliography.

Without the constant enthusiasm of my students at Southern Illinois University at Carbondale, this book would not have been written. In demanding much, they have always made me give more.

My deepest appreciation goes to Joseph L. Anderson. Several years ago, when he was my professor, he suggested the polemic/noninvolved and image manifest/image manipulative distinctions I have borrowed, modified, and made my own. He not only stimulated my thinking about film, but he has been a constant source of inspiration in my teaching. Helping him make a feature film was an exercise in applied history and aesthetics I shall never forget.

Robert E. Davis of the University of Texas at Austin supported my endeavors when he was my chairman, and he helped me with the section on censorship. Frank Paine, of Southern Illinois University at Carbondale, worked long, hard, and expertly to provide me with workable and appropriate still photographs, and deserves a special thanks. David Daly was especially helpful in providing specific information immediately, and in helping me to check and find sources.

Without the efficient and gracious help of Mary Corliss, of the Museum of Modern Art/Film Stills Archive, I would not have gathered the illustrations with as little pain as I did.

To these reviewers, a special thanks: Eric Bickley, Illinois State University; Norman De-Marco, University of Arkansas; H. J. Susser, College of Marin; Orville Wanzer, New Mexico State University; James M. Welsh, Salisbury State College. I have considered all the problems they pointed out, and without their helpful comments I would still be writing. Any faults of omission or detail are mine.

Rebecca Hayden, of Wadsworth Publishing Company, was so continually helpful and so completely supportive that any expression of thanks would be insufficient. She helped make this book.

Brian Williams, as editor of manuscript copy, worked diligently, cordially, and with professional expertise. His many excellent suggestions have made the book better.

Dr. and Mrs. Charles W. Porter III graciously provided me with peace, quiet, and a study. My mother and father were equally supportive. They all helped more than they know.

My wife, Julia, to whom I owe a great debt of thanks, worried through and enjoyed it all with me.

R.M.B.

Contents

Critical
Focus

An Introduction
to Film

Part
One

An Introduction
to Film

Why Study Film?

1

"Quiet, please! This is a take!"

"Quiet on the set!"

"Sound?"

"Speed."

"Camera?"

"Rolling."

"All right. Action."

They are up there in front of us. Images dancing around, changing—moving slowly, accelerating, separating, disappearing. These images and the accompanying sounds catch us up in them—entertain us, inform us, repel us, propagandize us. They can take us to places we have never been and involve us in cultures we have never seen. They can teach us how to assemble rockets. They can place us in a privileged seat at a boxing match. They can show us information about the weather, the day's events, or a distant war.

Film is the basic medium of television, a major tool of industry, and a common aid in education. With so many different uses in our culture, we should pay attention to how film describes our activities. Why is our attention captured? How is our knowledge of the world played with, embellished, or changed?

We know that what we see in a darkened theater is not reality. We know that we suspend disbelief, accept the reality of those images and sounds. Film is photographic, and the photograph is perhaps the closest representation of real objects. But even the cartoon gives us a quality of the real world; it shows us forms in motion.

The term *motion pictures* precisely describes the processes and qualities of the medium. *Movies* implies motion but not other features. *Flicks* also implies motion: the term derives from "the flickers," the name given early motion pictures, which frequently flickered because of mechanical imperfections. Europeans frequently call a movie house a *cinema*—an abbreviation of cinematograph, the British name for a motion-picture camera or projector, which comes from the Greek *kinēma* (motion)—and this word, too, implies movement.

Pictures is only half of "motion pictures," and pics is only half of "pictures." The term *film,* which describes the art of the movies as well as the action of making them, comes from the Old English *filmen* or membrane. The "film" of photographic chemicals on acetate or other substances is what makes the image happen. Both "pictures" and "motion," therefore, go together to make what we see appear authentic. We see things that look the same as what we see in the world outside the theater—and we see them move.

Opposite page: From Milos Foreman's *Taking Off.* (The Museum of Modern Art/Film Stills Archive. Courtesy of Universal Pictures.)

Seeing Movies

Our eyes react almost spontaneously to something that moves. It is this attention-getting characteristic that gives film its expressive potential and that serves as the basic creative tool for the filmmaker. Once they are framed, composed, and removed from the things themselves, the things that move are called *images*. They are reflections of light, the surfaces of objects rather than the objects themselves. Still, they seem real. We see their textures, sense their feel, respond to their energies, and react to what they say. Yet, it is all illusion.

Like painters, stage directors, musical conductors, choreographers, or sculptors, filmmakers mold their raw materials with concentration, selection, and imagination. They shape the unique experience of their work by using the special qualities of the medium. Frequently, they try to expand the known limits of those qualities to form structures not yet tried. Filmmakers not only show events, but they shape their films to help us better understand those events.

We can see some of these attempts in motion pictures that were experiments to find new techniques for showing information. Some of these techniques led to the development of new technology, which in turn suggested to filmmakers new ways of seeing their subject.

When we watch a film, we are seeing events that have been selected for us. We accept what we see, even though we may instantly question it. When we submit to it, we frequently experience a psychological feeling of participation in the actions shown. Although all we see is illusion, much of the time that illusion seems very real.

In the last quarter century, people have increasingly discovered film. Cinema courses are now among the most popular taken, even in the many schools that do not have formal film study programs. Motion pictures have become the art of today, a means of expression that everybody sooner or later experiences.

Within the last twenty years, cinema was seen to have a history. It was seen as the leading contemporary art form, one that owes its existence to the technology that now defines our world. Until a decade ago, many people regarded film as a specialized subject, with about as much value as the study of amusement parks. However, motion pictures as an object of serious inquiry goes back almost to the origins of the medium.

Reviewers and Critics

People who write about how film works are reviewers, critics, or theorists.

Film reviewers may be categorized according to the audience they write for. Reviewers write about specific films, or occasionally about directors or trends, for mass magazines and newspapers. They also appear on television. Examples are Rex Reed, Judith Crist, and Gene Shalot. These reviewers try to write or talk entertainingly as they inform, by being cynical, satirical, journalistic, or highly personal. As the public has grown more sophisticated about movies, the reviewers have increasingly written more about the techniques of a film as well as about the more obvious aspects of plot, character, and conflict. Reviewers can strongly influence the success or failure of a picture.

Read less than the reviewers are critics such as Pauline Kael and Penelope Gilliatt, who write for the *New Yorker;* Stanley Kauffmann, who writes for the *New Republic;* and John Simon, who writes for *Esquire.* Critics write about the social, historical, aesthetic, and political significance of the films they see, as well as about the impressions they create. They are called critics because they usually explain films in depth. Informed criticism can also be found in such specialized magazines and journals as *Film Comment, Film Quarterly,* and *Sight and Sound.*

The writings of film critics provide scholars with original sources for assessing public reaction to a film at the time it came out. Those interested in the sociology of the cinema also find important information in *Variety, Back Stage,* or *Box Office,* trade journals oriented to film exhibitors, which contain news on audience taste, possible box-office grosses, and exhibition practices.

Frequently, as in the case of Pauline Kael or John Simon, critics pose questions or make controversial statements that can stimulate thought and discussion. Their reaction can force film students to look closely at a picture. Critics may also theorize about a film, suggesting possibilities for its structure and content or hypothesizing about a filmmaker's attitude or style.

Theorists

Film theory tries to answer questions about the nature of film. There are theories of criticism, theories of film history, and theories of filmmaking. Film theorists may be concerned with perception, with psychology, or with the psychology of perception. They may try to systematize film so that various techniques can be predicted. They may be interested in a particular problem, such as how truth is conveyed in the documentary film, or how narrative structure is different in motion pictures from that in the novel or the stage play.

Film theorists deal with abstract ideas about film. They refer to particular motion pictures in

whole, in part, or in categories to support their arguments. Film critics, on the other hand, usually base their arguments on the particular movies and deal with concrete ideas about them.

Early Theorists

Some of the greatest discoveries about the potential of cinema came from filmmakers who never considered formalizing their ideas in writing. People such as Auguste and Louis Lumière, Georges Méliès, Edwin S. Porter, and D. W. Griffith found their potential for expression by making motion pictures. Yet, there were also early theoretical writers. American poet Vachel Lindsay wrote one of the first books on film theory, *The Art of the Moving Pictures,* in 1915. Lindsay sensed the peculiar properties of film within the context of such traditional arts as sculpture, painting, and architecture, although his excitement about a "new" art form now appears dated.

Another early theorist was Harvard psychologist Hugo Münsterberg, who in 1916 wrote a book now entitled *Film: A Psychological Study,* which is still a source of many fresh ideas. Münsterberg theorized that film can work like a person's imagination, and his discussion of memory lends psychological support to recent films about the inner mind by such modern directors as Ingmar Bergman, Alain Resnais, and Federico Fellini. Münsterberg suggested that memory and imagination can be conveyed to the viewer by the time and space manipulations of the film. He and Lindsay were among the first to recognize that time in a movie emerges from the action presented in the film rather than imposed by the clock time of the real world.

Russian Theorists

The study of film theory begins in Russia, where, after the 1917 revolution, Lenin declared film to be the state's most important propaganda tool. Little money was available for equipment or film stock, but still genius flourished. Lev Kuleshov set up a film workshop in Moscow, and it attracted such people as Sergei Eisenstein and V. I. Pudovkin, who became great filmmakers and important writers. (Eisenstein's *Film Form* and *The Film Sense* and Pudovkin's *Film Acting* and *Film Technique* are still studied today.) Being without much material to make films, they sat around and theorized about the medium's potential. They looked at D. W. Griffith's 1916 spectacle *Intolerance* so many times that their print finally disintegrated.

Perhaps the greatest film theorist was Eisenstein, an eclectic, creative genius knowledgeable about all the arts, from Chinese calligraphy to architecture, who collected his notions about the potential of film under the word *montage*—the conflict of separate images in a movie to create action or ideas not singly contained in any one of those images. Like other Russians of the time, he saw the creative resources of film to be the ways separate pieces of film could be cut with one another. He described these different ways as various forms of montage. He also hypothesized about how color could be used in film, and he examined conflicts between sound and image. Indeed, his ideas were so rich and controversial that filmmakers and theorists continue to work with them.

Pudovkin also saw montage as a key element in film construction, and suggested that a narrative could be built not only by conflict between images but also by their similarities in line, form, and action. Kuleshov made several notable experiments with the possibilities for putting images together to create effects the original images could not.

The films that Eisenstein, Pudovkin, and Kuleshov made show interconnections between theory and practice; film theorists may suggest ideas and techniques that filmmakers can then experiment with.

Auteur ("Author") Theory

While several important writers have advocated specialized theories of film, montage and the *auteur* theory have had the greatest impact on film study and filmmaking.

In 1948, French filmmaker Alexandre Astruc suggested in an important essay, *Le Caméra Stylo* ("The Camera Pen"), that a film should be made by one person who could control the total creative process, like an author writing a novel. The film's style, content, technique, and plot could then be evaluated according to how they presented the author's vision of the world. Other writers supported this view: film theoretician André Bazin, who established an influential film journal *(Les Cahiers du Cinéma),* and François Truffaut and Jean-Luc Godard who wrote for the journal, formulated *auteur* criticism and explored the theory's possibilities for filmmakers. *Auteur* criticism suggests a literary orientation, perhaps so much that it underrates film's collaborative nature as well as its indebtedness to arts other than literature, such as painting and dance.

Structuralism and Semiology

The theories of structuralism and semiology (or semiotics), which derive from structural linguistics and structural anthropology, attempt to systematize films so that their intrinsic meaning can be found.

Structuralism attempts to describe the works of one filmmaker (and so is indebted to the *auteur* theory), of a *genre* (such as the Western, gangster movie, or musical), or of one film. It tries to show the relationships among cinematic structure, content, film technique, and social or cultural meaning. *Semiology* attempts to translate specific film techniques into signs that, by their interconnections and placement within the film, create an analyzable language system. These theoretical systems involve extremely fine categorization, technical language, and hair-splitting definitions. Among the principal theorists are Peter Wollen (who wrote *Signs and Meaning in the Cinema*) and Christian Metz (who wrote *Film Language: A Semiotics of the Cinema*). Their ideas are in part based on those of the American philosopher Charles Sanders Peirce, the linguist Ferdinand de Saussure, and the anthropologist Claude Levi-Strauss.

The semiologists pay so much attention to "narrativity" that they deal principally with the film that tells a story, and Metz, in fact, offhandedly dismisses the documentary and the experimental film, although they are important types of films and should not be so disregarded.

It is clear that there are various classifications of film theory. There is representational theory, perceptual theory, *auteur* theory, and montage. What eventually is needed, perhaps, is a "field theory," which would assimilate diverse notions about the nature of film and would propose general laws that could help us understand any given motion picture.

History

Film history can help us understand present trends and can take beginning filmmakers through an evolution similar to their own continuing technical discoveries.

Film history has been greatly influenced by the *auteur* theory, and examination of the evolution of form and technique through directors who made significant films is now a standard historical method. Indeed, it becomes primarily a history of directors and only secondarily a history of films.

Technological history shows the development of the medium through advances in equipment —cameras, lenses, projectors, lighting equipment, sound recorders, film stock, and so on. Technological and *auteur* history can be combined to show the evolution of the medium through those who used and developed new devices.

Social history examines the relationships between a film and its audience in regard to: attempts to regulate the medium through censorship, the star system, the studio system, film reviews, exhibition practices, the economics of film, film genres, the effects of film violence, and the uses of film in television. Because the history of a society or culture can be seen through its works of art—and in our century the most popular art form has been the cinema—our values and attitudes, living patterns, use of language, wars, politics, and cultural heroes are all reflected in film. The age-old question of whether society determines the values in its art or whether the art helps to form the values of society also is of interest here.

Particular kinds of films such as the experimental film or the documentary film also have their own history. We could study the history of educational films, television-series films, or genre films such as those about war, the drug culture, blacks, or women.

One reason film history has recently become so important is that so little has been done about examining and classifying the movies of the past. Many films were left to disintegrate or were destroyed after their financial life died, and many films and filmmakers have disappeared. Their rediscovery offers us rich sources for enlightenment. Most of this sorting is being done within the limits of particular individuals, films, or ideas. Hence, there are books and articles on the history of one director or cinematographer, on scriptwriters, and on film producers. There are general histories of the development of film in such major film-producing countries as the United States, the Soviet Union, Japan, India, and the European countries.

There is so much yet to do. The rewards of discovery can make this continuing activity extremely worthwhile.

Filmmaking

Filmmaking is composed of three activities: preproduction, production, and postproduction. Whether we are making an experimental film, a documentary, an educational film, or a feature film, we usually must go through all three activities.

Preproduction includes the work from conception of the idea to the start of shooting the film, whether we are doing it individually or with collaborators.

First, the original idea is expressed as an outline or summary (called a *treatment*), then it goes through several drafts in script form. It must also be decided which kind of film is best or possible (Super-8, 16, or 35 millimeter), which camera, which film stock, which filters and lighting equipment, which actors and crew, which locations, what kind of sets, what shooting schedule—all of which reflect what budget. What type of film we are making will determine the necessity and the scope of these activities.

Production activities are those engaged in during the actual filming. The production manager, who usually controls the shooting schedule, dictates who is to be where at what time, and what equipment, props, and costumes are to be used.

In larger productions, specialists handle the jobs of props, makeup, equipment, costumes, animals, and so on. The continuity person sees that action, costumes, and sets remain unchanged. The director of photography designs the shots according to the director's wishes. The director, as the chief executive on the set, decides how a shot will be taken—everything from the positioning of actors to lighting and the movement of the camera. He makes all the major decisions about the shooting. Other activities are placement of sound and lighting equipment, appropriate makeup, control of electrical operations, and film loading and processing.

The actual filming itself goes slowly, one take at a time, and not always smoothly. The deliberate process of filming each shot is necessary because of all the activities that go into it: camera control, lighting, acting, continuity, and so on. How certain directors or particular films make various events go together is a fascinating subject, and the magic of the filmmaking process can give us insight into the magic of the image on the screen.

Postproduction activities move the film shot during the production stage to a final print, mainly through the process of editing, in which shots and sound are cut together to make the final film. Some people consider editing the most creative phase of filmmaking, and indeed it is one of the most important, since it requires the judicious selection of which shots to use, the focusing of action, and the creation of movement. Film theorists debate whether or not editing decisions are mostly implied in the script (or, in the case of an unscripted film, in the planning). Whatever the answer, filmmaking involves creating works that will satisfy audiences that have experienced all sorts of films and have at least an intuitive knowledge of film language.

To sum up this chapter, film study is concerned with looking at films and classifying them; it examines how audiences grasp what they see and how images are made. It explores the relationships these images have to those from other films. It predicts the future evolution of the form, and reconstructs for motion pictures ideas examined in the study of other arts, philosophy, sociology, anthropology, psychology, history, and technology. Film is totally involving. On the one hand it is a multimillion dollar industry. On the other hand, a film can be inexpensive and as personal as a painting.

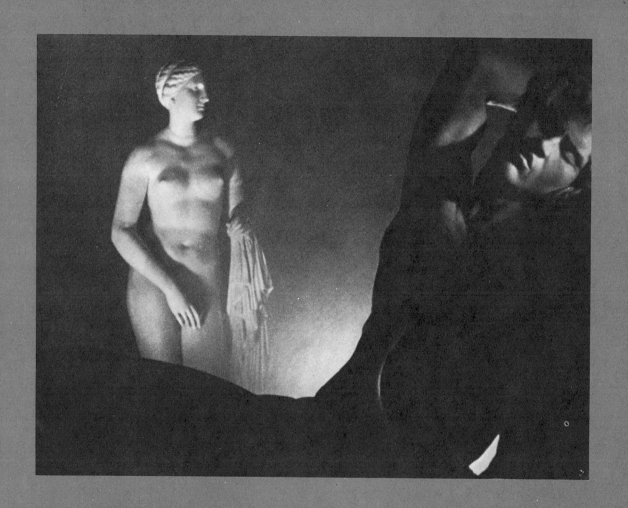

Film and the Other Arts

2

The structure, technique, and content of many films is partly derived from other, more traditional art forms. At the same time, film has emerged as a new art, with its own ways of presenting the world. In this chapter we will compare film with four other art forms: literature, theater, the visual arts, and music.

Film and Literature

Fiction is customarily examined for the components of narration, description, point of view, and character. Let us see how these are used in film; and then we will look at poetry and the essay.

Narration

The narrative film and prose fiction are alike in that both usually tell a story through time and hence they are described as *narrative*. Among the devices used to structure a literary narrative are description, narration, dialogue, point of view, character, setting, conflict, and action. Movies use all of these but in ways different from the short story or novel, for narrative literature is word-oriented

Opposite page: From Leni Riefenstahl's *Olympia, Part One.* (The Museum of Modern Art/Film Stills Archive.)

and movies are image-oriented, and people respond differently to each. Words usually convey ideas in less direct ways than do images. We can read a sentence or a paragraph, linger over it, go back and reread it, and leave it only after it has been thoroughly explored. We can return to a passage time and again. We can put a novel down and days later pick up the story where we left off.

Movies work much more directly. The images usually cannot be pondered during viewing because they are forever changing. Film images convey information immediately and are perceptual in nature. Except for certain experimental techniques, fiction conveys information less directly and is conceptual in nature. Psychologically, words work to cue the reader to concepts or to the meaning of the action they describe. These concepts and meanings move to the senses through the mind by their sound. In pictures, however, concepts and meanings move directly to the senses by shape, color, composition, texture, and motion (ideas we will explore further in Chapter 4). Even such abstract notions as love or evil can be shown directly in film by an image of, say, a woman looking at a man in a particular way or by the appearance of a contorted face.

Description

In fiction, description shows the relationships among people or among objects or explains why a person feels a particular way. Fiction can examine the emotion of fear, for instance, by describing the anxiety of a person facing a lion. A movie, however, can simply show us a person facing the lion; the complex elements of fear are immediately apparent, although it is difficult to analyze them.

The short story or novel molds words to imply concepts. Metaphor can say that "the general was a wall of defiance." Simile can tell us "his face was like a mask." An image, using figures of speech, can create a picture for us: "the dust rolled over the prairie, smothering the wheat and darkening the day." Personification, as in the previous example, can give animate attributes ("smothering") to inanimate objects. Universally accepted symbols can give us depths of meaning. Rain, for instance, can mean purity or rebirth. Snow and winter can suggest death, old age, or despair. Adjectives can give a particular identifying quality to an object: a red stone; a mossy stone; a glassy stone; a wrinkled stone; a cracked stone. Adverbs can give us the peculiar quality of an action: "She walked awkwardly." These and other uses of language are the raw materials of the art of writing.

In fiction, the description of a setting can tell us much about the person living in that setting. In the novel *Washington Square,* author Henry James describes a "heavy" room with overstuffed chairs. This description informs us about the chubby and rather dull young lady who lives there. Movies can do the same thing, of course, but in a much more immediate way. The camera can move within a room to show us various objects that can give us a feeling for the person whose place this is. In this sense, the images serve the purpose of description, even though what they show is more tangible to us than things described by words. In reading fiction (or being told a story, as on radio), we can use our imagination more freely than we can in watching movies. In a book, characters probably look different to each reader, no matter how carefully words describe them. In a movie, detailed pictures of people leave no doubt as to how they look.

Point of View

Point of view describes through whose eyes a story is told.

In the *omniscient* point of view, the narrator knows everything—from what people are thinking to what is going on in places separated from each other by time and space.

In the *first person* point of view, a story is told by one of its characters, "I," who is restricted to places and times that he or she was personally involved in or has heard about.

In the *third person limited* point of view, a story is told by "he," "she," or "it" (as in omniscient narration), but the information conveyed is only that which that person has experienced. For instance, in Ernest Hemingway's short story "The Nun, the Gambler, and the Radio," the central character, Mr. Frazer, is isolated in a hospital room. All that the narrator tells us is either what Mr. Frazer experiences, what is told to him by visitors, or what he hears going on outside his room.

Films frequently mix various points of view, even if one particular point of view generally controls the narration (*Citizen Kane,* described in Chapter 6, is an example). In a scene with two people talking, we frequently see one person through the eyes of the other—that is, from that person's point of view—but also, within the same scene, see both people at once or from the omniscient point of view.

Constant changing of points of view would be confusing in fiction. In film, it works precisely because the images are remembered by sight. The shifting from one to another can be apprehended immediately. Film's ability to shift points of view is one of the major techniques that creates fluidity of movement.

Character

Character in the novel can be given by describing the physical action and the mental processes of persons in confrontation with objects, with other people, or with their own thoughts. Motion pictures do this, too. They take the power of description and show action, whether it is happening in the present, is remembered, or fantasized. In fiction, we interpret character through what we infer. In the movies, we interpret character through what we see.

This distinction is evident when we consider that the two ways we get to know about people are (1) by what we are told about them and (2) by what we observe them doing. When we are told information about a person, we can question it or interpret it. When we see a person doing something, we do not question it (for it is accomplished before our eyes), but we can interpret it in light of what else we see.

A novelist might write: "He struck the stick across the tree trunk with all the anger that was in him. His eyes filled with tears of rage. And then he was relieved. The act made him feel more peaceful." As prose, the words describe an action, tell us the reason for it, explain how the person looked and how he felt. In a film,

we would not be told the action; we would see it. And we would also see the size of the tree trunk, the type of stick, the force of the swing, the tears in the man's eyes, the contortions of his mouth, the sweep of his muscles, and the slump of his shoulders after the event. We would hear the stick hit the tree.

The novelist selects those parts of an action that allow us to interpret the whole action. The film gives it all to us at once and provides for a more immediate type of interpretation. In film, we cannot see all the interior thoughts and feelings. Yet no matter how detailed the description in fiction, it cannot match the direct visual representation of *all* the details that a film can give us.

Film and Poetry

When words are used concisely to express emotions, the result may be poetry. Lyric poetry uses images, figures of speech, metaphors, symbols, rhythm, and frequently meter and rhyme to explore specific feelings. Film can do likewise. For instance, the images and rhythms in the poem "Upon Julia's Clothes" by Robert Herrick (1591–1674) could be translated into film:

Whenas in silks my Julia goes,
Then, then, methinks, how sweetly flows
That liquefaction of her clothes.

Next, when I cast mine eyes, and see
That brave vibration each way free,
Oh, how that glittering taketh me!

The first stanza uses the textures of the lady's clothes to imply her sensuality and the poet's physical attraction to her. The second stanza extends the idea of touch to visual movement,

2.1 Hitler views the Eiffel Tower after taking Paris, in Marcel Ophul's documentary, *The Sorrow and the Pity* (1971). (The Museum of Modern Art/Film Stills Archive. Courtesy Cinema Five.)

then combines both into "glittering." The poem develops the "silk" that "liquefies" into Julia's bodily rhythms, then erotically fuses them.

The meter of the poem is iambic tetrameter ("That *brave vibration each way free"*)*,* and it is rhymed A-A-A, B-B-B. The order of the end-rhyming words helps to create the poem's statement: *goes—flows—clothes; see—free—me.*

All the traditional devices we would expect of lyric poetry are used here both to tie the poem together and to extend its theme. For instance, assonance in the second stanza—"cast," "brave," "vibration," "way," and so on—help mold the poem aurally as it flows toward its final point in the word "taketh." The first stanza works its meter directly, then suddenly flows by means of the word "liquefaction." The silks and the bodily rhythms are metaphors for the speaker's eroti-

cism, and the rhythm of the whole poem moves slowly, then fast, then more excitedly and very fast.

The images this poem suggests could be translated into film, as follows:

1. Several quick dissolves of close-up views of silk.
2. Slow dolly back to show Julia, who is dressed in silk, which flows more and more fervently in the wind.
3. Dissolve into soft-focus view of Julia nude.
4. Through lighting and a special lens, further soften the figure until there is only a kaleidoscopic glitter.

The rhythms created by cutting, camera movement, and the objects photographed could be similar to those in the poem. Here, however, direct images have replaced words to give us a more concrete and immediate experience. The

2.2 Picture and language go together, in Jean-Luc Godard's *Les Carabiniers* (1963). (The Museum of Modern Art/Film Stills Archive. Courtesy New Yorker Films.)

rhythms of the poem are aural; the rhythms of the film are visual. In each case, there is room for possible interpretations.

Film and the Essay

The essay, which expresses ideas and attitudes about particular subjects, is similar to the non-fiction film. The desire to examine, analyze, and investigate events that stimulate the essay writer also can form motion pictures. For instance, French filmmaker Marcel Ophul's *The Sorrow and the Pity* (1971) has the form of a memoir, as it examines the Nazi occupation of France through interviews, archival film, records, and narration.

The essay—including the nonfiction biography and history—might substantiate events with diagrams and still photographs. The motion picture also can do this, but in film, images provide the information our attention is primarily drawn to.

In some of the movies of Jean-Luc Godard, printed words are placed on objects in a scene and words of on-camera interviews appear as printed slogans on the screen, which verbally expand on the images. By letting words frequently dominate the pictures, Godard conceptualizes upon the ways that picture and language can go together to provide sense not fully contained in either of them.

Journalistic essays also are important. Television news film has consistently shown that the images of a battle or of a congressional committee hearing, with conversation and narration included, can give us a very direct sense of involvement. As in writing, selection can form an editorial bias; however, by and large news film can provide a much more direct experience of events than can a written report.

Film and Theater

Both film and theater show actions as they occur before an audience seated in a darkened auditorium.*

In the dramatic theater, our visual attention is caught by movement on stage, by use of spotlights, or by both. In the movie theater, we can see details of objects by seeing them up close. Those same details in the same setting might be fairly unnoticeable in the theater, where all the features are seen from a distance.

The motion picture is able to jump around freely in time and space. Theater is, of course, more restricted, for usually it has only the space of the stage itself to use. Action on stage is created primarily by dialogue, whereas in the cinema the burden of presenting action usually rests in the images.

In the theater, the passage of time is frequently indicated by dropping the curtain or dimming the lights. Film has its own form of curtains and lights in the fade-out, the dissolve, and the straight cut.

In the cinema, both exteriors and interiors can be shown with remarkable fidelity, which gives authenticity to the action. In the theater, part of the visual experience is given through sets that suggest rather than specifically show a location.

In the cinema, a performance is usually cut up into many segments that go together to give the appearance of sustained action. In the theater, action has to be sustained, usually through extended periods of time.

---

*This is true even in arena staging, where the audience more or less surrounds the action. The exception is in guerrilla or street theater, where the audience may physically become a part of the action.

In both theater and cinema, gesture is an important device to create action. In drama, an actor's gesture can reveal much about the character. Yet, because the audience actors are playing to is several rows back as well as near the stage, their gestures and the loudness of their voices have to be exaggerated. In film, by contrast, the microphone allows actors to speak in more normal tones. On the stage, moreover, the action is controlled by the language, whereas on the screen, action is controlled by gesture.

Theater is intimate because we have the physical presence of the performers in front of us. But this presence, seen more or less from the same distance, is always one size. Cinema, on the other hand, exaggerates and diminishes size, and it composes its images according to the same rules governing two-dimensional art forms such as still photography and painting.

Plays and films are similar in that both can present stories. Sometimes stories from the stage are "adapted" for motion pictures, usually unsuccessfully, for at least two reasons: (1) The action in theater generally occurs in only a limited number of settings. When these settings are transferred to motion pictures, they can restrict that free movement from place to place from which film can build its story. In this sense, film can liberate the settings of theater presentation. (2) The dialogue in theater is so important that many filmmakers, in doing adaptations, seem unable or unwilling to cut it down and replace it with images. Too much talk in a motion picture tends to curtail the power of the images. When film adaptations of plays are successful, it is often because the dialogue is matched by satisfactory images.

Film and the Visual Arts

Film images frequently are organized through many of the same compositional elements as

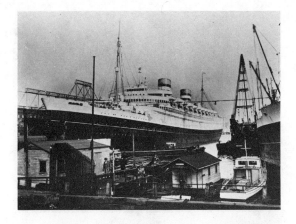

2.3 *Top:* Elia Kazan's *On the Waterfront* (1954) is an example of a representational film. (The Museum of Modern Art/Film Stills Archive. Courtesy Columbia Pictures.) *Middle:* Robert Wiene's *The Cabinet of Dr. Caligari* (1919) is an example of a distorted film. (The Museum of Modern Art/Film Stills Archive.) *Bottom:* Len Lye's film is an example of abstract filmmaking. (The Museum of Modern Art/Film Stills Archive.)

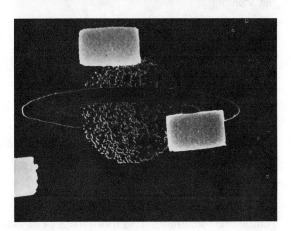

painting, such as line, color, tone, perspective, and texture. Like paintings, film images can be classified as *representational* (looking like the world), *distorted* (looking somewhat like it), or *abstract* (using unidentifiable elements from it).

Modern art has exerted strong influences on both the form and the content of motion pictures. Surrealism, for example, holds that "inner" and "outer" reality can fuse through a work of art to assert a "higher reality" than either, and this viewpoint can be seen in works by Federico Fellini, Luis Buñuel, Roman Polański, and others. In some of their films, dream and reality become so confused that the viewer mistakes one for the other, so that the line between the two becomes obliterated.

Even in more representational films, the organization of objects within the frame shows indebtedness to painting. For example, Michelangelo Antonioni's *Eclipse* (1962) shows how the geometrical forms of modern technological society tend to identify cold, barren, functional, and abstract qualities of life. In several of his pictures, Antonioni visually suggests the environment of the modern world, one of sterility and lack of emotion, by the settings in which he places his characters.

2.4 *Left:* Expressionist Ernst Ludwig Kirchner's 1914 painting, *View from the Window.* (Collection of Morton D. May, St. Louis, Missouri.) *Right:* A scene from Robert Wiene's 1919 film, *The Cabinet of Dr. Caligari.* (The Museum of Modern Art/Film Stills Archive.) Note how both use darkness and light to distort representational forms and assert inner feelings.

The school of art called Expressionism tried to assert the inner feelings of characters through the distortion of representational forms. In one painting by Expressionist Ernst Kirchner, for example, forms are distorted but still recognizable, and large, heavy brush strokes are used to express the inner qualities of both the subject and the painter. The influence of Expressionism on the 1919 film *The Cabinet of Dr. Caligari,* by Robert Wiene, becomes apparent when we compare the sets, which were created by Expressionist set designers, with the Kirchner painting. The settings in *Caligari* reflect the inner state of a mental patient, who is telling the story. All he reports is given in visual distortion through makeup, costuming, and the distorted perspective of things in the frame. The feeling is similar to that in Kirchner's painting.

The Uses of Music in Film

Two aspects of music that are important to film are (1) the performance quality—what one hears —and (2) the form of music; that is, rhythm, meter, tonality, electronic music, atonality.

Movies have been involved with music almost from their beginnings. Projection of early silent movies was frequently accompanied by a piano, an organ, and sometimes a full orchestra. Certain pictures, such as D. W. Griffith's *The Birth of a Nation* and *Intolerance,* had musical scores especially composed to be played with them. During the making of many early films, small ensembles accompanied the actors' performance before the camera, which helped the actors portray emotions and gave their movements a rhythm. For instance, a courtship scene performed to the accompaniment of slow, sweet music would cause the actors to move more deliberately and smoothly.

Certain types of music have been identified as helping the viewer become more involved with the emotions of a scene—for instance, violins during a scene where two lovers meet after a reconciliation. Also, music is used to help prepare the viewer for an emotion. When we hear the snarl of bassoons as we see a young woman walking down a corridor in an empty house, we know that ahead something dangerous is going to happen.

Music can be used in many ways. The musical themes for motion pictures such as *Dr. Zhivago* or *Lawrence of Arabia* repeat themselves in different keys, with different instruments, as the plot unfolds and the heroes engage in different actions. Musical motifs can recall previous scenes for us. Music can also influence the feeling for the visuals, as at the beginning of Orson Welles's *Citizen Kane* (1941), where the music moves as fluidly as the camera while dissolves penetrate the fences of Kane's estate, Xanadu.

Some experimental films, such as Norman McLaren's *Fiddle de Dee* (1947), use music as the basis for choreographing the "dance" of animated forms. In *A Clockwork Orange* (1971), Stanley Kubrick choreographs the movements of his actors to the music of Beethoven. In Bernardo Bertolucci's *The Conformist* (1970), as well as in his *Last Tango in Paris* (1972), the form of the dance dictates the visual rhythms of the camera in several sequences.

In some films, there is a ballet-type relationship between musical rhythm and visual rhythm that supports the playing out of the action. Sometimes there is opposition between the action and the visual rhythms. This is known as *counterpoint,* a term borrowed from music that means two separate melodies in harmony with each other move forward at the same time. In the movies, such counterpoint can be created between picture and music, between picture and visual rhythm, between picture and speech, and between one shot and another.

In counterpoint between picture and music, the purpose is usually to create dramatic tension between the action seen and what that action really means. For instance, in Alain Resnais's 1955 documentary on Nazi extermination camps, *Night and Fog,* the camera smoothly travels along the peace and quiet of the modern, postwar countryside. The music, slow with some high pitches of a reed instrument, supports this peaceful scene. Then, as the camera enters the desolate areas of a former concentration camp, the music becomes confused. It begins to suggest the counterpoint between past and present. The music brings up the awful past and contrasts it with the tranquil present. Usually, however, there are associations, rather than opposition, between picture and music, and counterpoint is saved for moments of deep emotion and for the molding of conflict.

A motion picture can create visual rhythms by establishing a tone or mood at the beginning, then move as an orchestral piece might to a different key and tempo. Ingmar Bergman very often uses musical structures visually rather than audially. *The Magician* (1958), for instance, starts out somberly and slowly in a forest. The rhythms increase as a supposedly dying man is brought into the coach of a troupe of magicians. Then there is a modulation, as the troupe enters a city and sets up to perform for an official. The film paces itself very deliberately. It moves to its climax musically, then extends that climax (as the magician scares the official with tricks while both are locked in an attic), then moves quickly to the end. Thus, throughout the film, the tone or mood of death controls the progression of events and helps pace them.

Horror movies frequently employ electronic music, which has a bizarre and unreal quality that suggests the mystical. Of course, if we have not regularly experienced it, our ears are not attuned to it, but still, when we hear it in horror films it seems right, and we do not question it.

The clanking of machinery or other noises that emerge from the action of a picture occasionally create their own type of music. In Antonioni's *The Red Desert* (1964), for instance, the sound of machinery tells us that the "music" of the sterile modern world is as harsh as its visual forms.

Music, then, has been influential in giving form and meaning to motion pictures. The idea of pitches and tones in movement one with another has helped filmmakers create works whose visual rhythms are supported by the ideas of music.

The time has passed, it is hoped, when motion pictures have to be "proved" to be art. Historically looked at by some critics as a form that has borrowed such attributes from other arts as narrative techniques from literature, staging and acting from theater, visual design from painting, and movement from music, people have only recently accepted film as an art form itself.

Whatever the arts have in common, it is true that they influence each other. Cinema's special qualities—which we will look at in the next chapter—make translating what is borrowed into totally new practices necessary. With so many centuries of evolution, the conventional arts have various histories and critical approaches that can overwhelm the novice to film study. Cinema, however, was born within the memory of people still alive.

Literature, theater, the visual arts, and music began in one way or another in the natural world, and they served the popular needs of culture for expression, ritual, and understanding. As they refined their techniques over centuries, so the cinema, a child of technology, has refined its techniques over decades. The cinema met audience expectations for story, music, reality, and drama, and in so doing has moved into means of expression unique to itself.

Film Itself

3

Like other disciplines, film has its own language, its own terms. In this chapter, we will present the basic vocabulary for analyzing and discussing film.

Visual Language

The basic unit of a motion picture is the *single still photograph* or "frame." In the sound film, twenty-four of these single frames are projected each second, giving a close approximation of real-life motion to the eye. The untrained human eye can perceive an image that lasts three to five frames, or about one-eighth to one-fifth of a second.

The *shot* is any amount of footage given by one single run of the camera. The shot is the basic unit of a motion picture. Shots can be short, with just a few frames, or they can go on for fifteen minutes or more, although either extreme is rare. William Friedkin, in *The Exorcist* (1973), used very short shots of a pasty-looking masked face almost subliminally at the point of the actual exorcism; the shots are cut in for just a split second to replace Father Karras's face as Satan

attempts to possess him, Jean-Luc Godard, in *Weekend* (1967), has a long, twelve-minute shot that travels along scores of automobiles caught in a huge traffic jam; the very length of this shot gives the viewer the feeling of the frustration of the people involved.

Shots are described by movement, camera angle, lenses, and composition, as we will show.

Moving Camera Shots

Camera movement creates visual interest and helps to provide rhythms inside the shot.

A *static camera shot* is when the camera does not move.

The most common types of movement for the camera are pan and tilt shots.

A *pan shot* is any horizontal movement of the camera while it is on a fixed base. A *swish pan* is a pan shot so rapid that only blurred forms will appear in the film.

A *tilt shot* is any vertical movement of the camera while it is on a fixed base.

A *traveling shot* is any shot other than the pan and tilt when the camera actually moves through space. With traveling shots, the viewer experiences *parallactic motion*—one sees new lines of sight continually occur because the camera's eye is moving. There are several types of traveling shots.

The *dolly shot* occurs when the camera is moving smoothly along on a device with wheels

Opposite page: From Federico Fellini's *8½*. A Joseph E. Levine presentation. Copyright © 1963, Embassy Pictures Corp. (The Museum of Modern Art/Film Stills Archive.)

3.1 Pan shot. The camera, on a fixed base, turns horizontally. (Photos by Frank Paine.)

called a dolly, which frequently rides tracks, like a train. This shot gives a fluid, yet dynamic, feeling to the action. A particular type of dolly shot is the *tracking shot,* which occurs when the camera moves parallel to a moving object it is following. An example is the twelve-minute shot in *Weekend,* in which the camera follows one automobile that is working its way past the jammed-up cars.

The *hand-held shot,* an increasingly popular type of moving camera shot, is created when the camera is moved about by the motion of the cameraman. The hand-held shot is frequently used in documentary and news films because, used this way, the camera is more immediately able to react to uncontrolled events. In feature-length films, the hand-held camera gives the viewer a sense of the spontaneous, and some filmmakers believe it makes the events appear more real, for the camera can actually participate in the action.

The *boom shot* or *crane shot* is a dynamic type of moving camera shot. This occurs when the camera is mounted on a specially designed crane that can move vertically or horizontally through wide areas of space.

Other types of moving camera shots are as diversified as a filmmaker's equipment and imagination. Airplane shots and helicopter shots are frequently seen in today's movies. A camera can also be made to fall through space (with a rope attached to it), swim under water, ride a balloon or an automobile. All these devices create visual excitement.

Motion can also be created in the shot by slowing down or speeding up the film as it passes through the camera, then projecting it at the normal speed. An *undercranked* shot (a term carried over from the days of hand-cranked cameras and projectors) allows the film to pass through the camera slower than twenty-four frames per second. When projected at normal speed, this creates *accelerated motion,* sometimes called *fast motion.* Conversely, an over-cranked shot will produce *slow motion.* The speed at which the film passes through the camera is called the *frame-rate speed.*

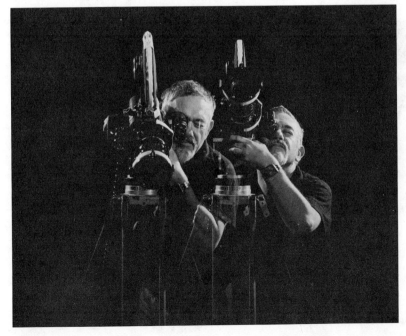

3.2 Tilt shot. The camera tilts up to discover or follow action. (Photo by Frank Paine.)

3.3 Parallactic motion. The planes change as the camera travels in an arc around the nonmoving actors. (Photos by Frank Paine.)

3.4 Tracking shot being executed. The camera tracks forward, following the actor. A crew member pushes the dolly while the camera operator takes the shot. The director instructs the actor, and the script clerk (continuity person) follows the script. Other crew members watch. (Photo by Frank Paine.)

3.5 Hand-held camera with cameraman. (Photo by Frank Paine.)

Camera Angle

The location of the camera in relation to the object it is filming creates the *angle of view*. Shots are described by angle of view as low-angle shots, eye-level shots, or high-angle shots.

A *low-angle shot* is when the camera looks up at the object it is filming. Traditionally, this angle gives the object viewed a sense of superiority.

A *high-angle shot* is when the camera looks down at the object it is filming. Traditionally, the angle gives the object a sense of inferiority.

An *eye-level shot* approximately duplicates the horizontal view either of a person standing or a character in the scene. If a character is seated, the angle of view from which high- and low-angle shots are taken may be from the height of the eyes of the seated person.

An *overhead shot* looks directly (or almost directly) down at the action being filmed.

3.6 Low-angle shot from Orson Welles's *Citizen Kane* (1941) gives dominance to Kane and his friend and associate Jed Leland (Orson Welles and Joseph Cotten), as they assume the responsibilities of putting out a newspaper. (The Museum of Modern Art/Film Stills Archive. Courtesy RKO Radio Pictures, a division of RKO General, Inc.)

3.7 High-angle shot from Milos Foreman's *Taking Off* (1971) shows Buck Henry, insignificant and embarrassed after losing at strip poker. This high-angle shot also assumes the point of view of his daughter who, unknown to him, observes this action from outside her bedroom. (The Museum of Modern Art/Film Stills Archive. Courtesy of Universal Pictures.)

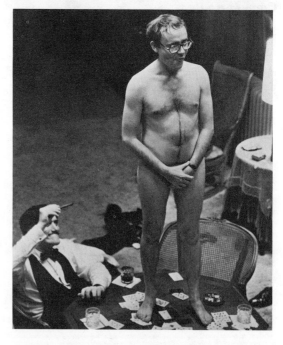

3.8 Normal eye-level standing shot from Mervyn LeRoy's *Little Caesar* (1930). Eye-level shot is taken at height of seated man to suggest, through triangular composition, Edward G. Robinson's intrusion into the atmosphere of the diner. (The Museum of Modern Art/Film Stills Archive.)

3.9 Overhead shot from *Cymbols,* a film by Fredde Lieberman. (© 1975 by Fredde Lieberman. Photo by Frank Paine.)

Lenses

A view can be further modified by different lenses. There are many gradations of lenses, which are described by their length in millimeters, but generally they can be classified into four types: (1) the normal lens, (2) the short focal-length (or wide-angle) lens, (3) the long focal-length (or telephoto) lens, and (4) the zoom lens.

The *normal lens* is used to show objects approximately as the human eye sees them. The main subject is in sharp focus and the environment around it is just a bit hazy. Sometimes one object within a shot will go slightly out of focus, and another object behind or in front of it will come into sharp focus. This manipulation is called *focus-shift* or *rack focus,* and it is used to direct our eyes to the object of major visual interest. Another defining quality of the normal lens is that movement toward and away from the camera is about equal in speed.

The *short focal-length* or *wide-angle lens* gives a wide field of view. The shorter the lens, the clearer the objects in both the foreground and the background. A movie that is a classic example of consistent use of the short focal-length lens is Orson Welles's *Citizen Kane* (1940).

Another quality of the short focal-length lens is that movement toward the camera is rapid, while movement away from the camera is slow. Also, when the angle is very wide, in this lens it tends to distort the edges of the picture. Some specialized types of short lenses, such as the *"fish-eye" lens,* particularly show this distortion.

The *long focal-length* or *telephoto lens* gives a limited field of view. The longer the lens, the less clear the background behind the object in focus. With a very long focal-length lens, a background becomes totally blurred and can seem almost as a "backdrop," with the object flat in front of it.

3.10 Normal lens. From an untitled film in progress by Frank Paine. (Photo by Frank Paine.)

With the long focal-length lens, movement toward the camera is slowed down, while movement away from the camera is speeded up. Near the end of Mike Nichols's *The Graduate* (1967), some of the shots are taken with a telephoto lens of Benjamin as he is running down the streets. This gives the impression that Benjamin is with great exertion getting nowhere.

The *variable-focus lens* or *zoom lens* can change the size and framing of an image instantly. Without the camera moving, the picture can change from a telephoto composition to a wide-angle composition, and vice-versa. Frequently, the zoom shot deceives us into thinking it is a dolly shot, but the two are actually quite different. As we said, the dolly shot is dynamic because it gives us the feeling of movement through space. This feeling, which is due to parallactic motion, is not evident with a zoom lens. In the zoom shot, the object photographed is primary. In the dolly shot, the space the camera moves through becomes a defining quality of the object photographed.

3.11 A wide field of view from *Citizen Kane,* with Orson Welles (standing left) addressing the staff of the rival newspaper that he has managed to hire *en masse.* Notice how the composition is built in depth from an elevated angle to draw us in as observers (through the statues in the foreground) to the power of Kane (whom almost all are looking at) and to the number of professionals at the celebration banquet. (The Museum of Modern Art/Film Stills Archive. Courtesy RKO Radio Pictures, a division of RKO General, Inc.)

What lenses are used and how close the object is to the camera determines whether the shot is a close-up, a medium shot, or a long shot. Consider the example of a camera trained on a standing person.

A *close-up* is a limited view of part of an object or a small object filling the screen. A full shot of just a person's head would be a close-up. A shot of just the person's *eyes* would be an *extreme close-up.* A close-up then, can give us a detailed

3.12 This telephoto shot from Roberto Rossellini's *Rome: Open City* (1945) makes details grainy and flattens out the perspective. Here the camera observes from the distance a child consoling his mother who has been a victim of the Nazis' retreat from Rome. (The Museum of Modern Art/Film Stills Archive. Courtesy Contemporary/McGraw-Hill Films.)

view of an important physical characteristic of a person or object.

A *medium shot* would be a view of the person's body from the waist up or the person seated and filling the frame. In either case, the medium shot can be modified so that it is a close medium shot, a medium shot, or a long medium shot. Of course, there can be overlapping between, say, the close medium shot and the long close-up, but as long as everybody on the film crew or discussing the film knows what one means, it is accurate.

A *long shot* would be a view of the person standing, with at least some surrounding area seen above and below the body. An extreme long shot would show not only the person but some of the setting. An extreme long shot is used at times as an *establishing shot* —the shot that opens the

film (or a scene) and lets us know the time period, the place of the story, and frequently the placement of the characters in the setting.

Composition

The photographic composition of a shot consists of framing, scale, relief, and texture. Framing and scale give information about the detail of composition. Relief and texture give information about the substance of the objects photographed.

Framing refers to the limits beyond which there is no longer a picture. The frame is determined by the *aspect ratio* —the ratio of width to height —of the movie screen. Over the years, various size screens have been used. The standard screen size —the popularly named "golden ratio" —

3.13 A close-up from J. L. Anderson's *America First* (1972). (Courtesy Optos Limited.)

3.14 Medium shot from F. W. Murnau's *The Last Laugh* (1924), in which the former Atlantic Hotel doorman (played by Emil Jannings) is seen eating lunch after being demoted to lavatory attendant. The medium shot lets us make associations between the bowl of soup (and its ironic inscription) and the old man's despair, getting us in just close enough to participate in the emotions of this private moment. (The Museum of Modern Art/Film Stills Archive.)

3.15 Long shot from René Clair's *A Nous la Liberté* (1931), in which money that has been hidden on a rooftop flies around a courtyard because of heavy wind and disrupts a dedication ceremony. Here the long shot permits us to view the chaos as it occurs, especially as the flying objects bring disarray to the formal lines of the architecture and the formally dressed official. (The Museum of Modern Art/Film Stills Archive. Courtesy Contemporary/McGraw-Hill Films.)

had an aspect ratio of 1.33 to 1. With the advent of the wide screen in the late fifties* and its acceptance since as standard, the ratio has become 1.85 to 1. Of course, screens wider than the "wide screen" are used for many pictures today; the Panavision screen, for instance, has an aspect ratio of 2.2 to 1, and Cinemascope is 2.55 to 1.

A shot with more than one person in it is described as a *two-shot* (with two people), a *three-shot,* and so on. A *crowd shot* would show a lot of people.

A shot is framed not only for what it shows within the frame but also what it can suggest outside the frame—for instance, visually, by showing smoke drifting into the frame from the right or, on the sound track, by having the noise of a car pulling up and stopping. Often information outside the frame is brought into the action by use

of a traveling shot or a pan or tilt shot that moves away from the action to the source of the smoke or the car noise. Another device is to widen the shot, using a zoom lens, so that the character photographed becomes smaller while the field of view becomes larger to include the added information. A third way is to end one shot and edit it together with another that shows the additional information.

Scale refers to the relative size of objects in the frame—whether we see the objects in close-up, medium shot, or long shot. It also describes the size of the object being photographed as it appears to the viewer. For instance, a battleship may actually be a three-foot miniature, but the scale it has on the screen may be huge.

Relief is the visual quality given to objects as different light values provide shadows and illumination. This contrast makes for "modeling" in photography, where parts of objects appear to project themselves "out" at us.

Texture adds information to relief by letting the viewer see those distinguishing qualities of the

---

*Actually, the wide screen came in 1926 with Abel Gance's *Napoleon,* but was not adopted until the 1950s, when the movie industry began trying to offer alternate visual experience to television.

Standard screen
aspect ratio 1.33:1

Wide screen
aspect ratio 1.85:1

Panavision
aspect ratio 2.2:1

Cinemascope
aspect ratio 2.55:1

3.16 Four screen sizes, ratio of width to height.

3.17 Texture and relief. Erich von Stroheim's *Greed* (1923). Contrasting textures of the packing material and the huge gold tooth (which Gibson Gowland has bought to hang in front of his office building as a sign of his profession) create a sense of accomplishment and pride for the viewer. The relief dimensionalizes the form and textures of the tooth, making it appear almost alive. (The Museum of Modern Art/Film Stills Archive. Courtesy Metro-Goldwyn-Mayer Inc. From the MGM release *Greed* © 1925 Metro-Goldwyn Pictures Corporation. © renewed 1952 Loew's Incorporated.)

surfaces of things: skin pores, grains of sand, smooth silk. Texture is especially important in close-up views, as well as in objects in the fore-ground of shots.

The shot is the basic construction unit of a motion picture, and the diverse elements of a shot all have to work together to provide what Jean-Luc Godard has called reality at twenty-four frames per second.

Editing

If motion can be created within a shot, it also can be created by placing one shot next to another. Editing refers to the various techniques of creating change through this method. Editing is some-times called *cutting,* which accurately describes the process, for a film editor literally cuts different shots (with a blade, or with scissors) at appropri-ate places and splices them together to create rhythm and to show information.

Transitions

The *straight cut* (or simply *cut*) is the most com-mon way to change a motion picture view. This occurs when one shot ends and another begins immediately.

The straight cut can be used to show that place and time are different from one shot to the next. It can also be used to show an event that a char-acter might have been responding to. For exam-ple, if we see a man working in a garden and hear the sound of a car driving up, a straight cut from the man to the car would show us that new ele-ment in the scene. A *reaction shot* is a straight cut that shows a person in a group reacting to some-thing that has happened or been said. A *reverse-angle shot* is a straight cut to a shot that is the opposite of (180 degrees from) the first shot. A reverse angle frequently suggests the point of view of one of the characters.

A motion picture builds its shots into *scenes,* which show one action occurring in a limited time period, usually in one place—for example, peo-ple sitting around a table and talking. Scenes accumulate into *sequences,* which are structured by time, place, and action, or by character—for example, the scene of people sitting around the table talking, then the scene of one man getting up and walking out of the house, then a scene of him running to a horse and saddling up, while the others rush out to stop him, and finally a scene of him riding through desolate country, on his way someplace. There is a dramatic unity to this sequence. The sequence also ends with a ques-tion—Where is he going? Or, what will he do when he gets there?—and his arrival at his des-tination would begin the next sequence. Except in experimental films, scenes and sequences are important as limiting units within which the edi-tor can construct the story.

There are other transitional devices besides the straight cut: the fade-out, the fade-in, the dis-solve, the wipe, and the iris. Originally these devices were done in the camera, but now they are mostly created by film laboratories.

The *fade-out* is when the image gradually disappears, usually into black; but there are exceptions—for instance, in Ingmar Bergman's *Cries and Whispers* (1972), scenes fade out into red. The *fade-in* is when the picture emerges from black (or from some other color). A *dis-solve* is a combination of a fade-out and a fade-in. As one image disappears, the new image appears superimposed under the old image for a moment as it emerges into clarity. A *superimpo-sition,* which is not a transitional device, is when two or more overlapping images are seen at the same time, and usually does not end a scene, as does a dissolve. Fade-outs, fade-ins, and dissolves produce particular effects when they are fast or slow. A slow fade-in, for instance, can create a sense of suspense; a slow fade-out might create a feeling of remorse, or nostalgia.

The *fade-out* announces the end of a major event and can be seen as a type of punctuation. It indicates the passing of time. After a fade-out, a new image can fade in or appear as a straight cut.

A *fade-in* usually is used to begin a sequence, and its speed can set the tone for the events to follow.

A *dissolve* also is used to show the passing of time. Usually a dissolve makes some type of association between the images fading out and fading in. For instance, *Citizen Kane* uses several quick dissolves with swish pan to show the growing separation between Kane and his first wife. The sequence uses a number of shots of them at the breakfast table. The events in each shot change from Kane and his wife close together at the table, both reading the newspaper Kane owns, to a shot of them at opposite ends of the table, Mrs. Kane reading the competitor's paper. The series of quick dissolves between the separate shots builds a sequence in a few minutes that presents information rich in detail about the matrimonial difficulties of the two.

The *wipe*—once thought outdated, but recently come into use again—is when the new image from one direction or another "pushes" the old image off the screen. It is almost like watching a 35 millimeter slide in a slide projector push another slide off the screen. The *flip wipe* is when the old image turns around, bringing us the new image from on the other side. The wipe is used today to give period flavor to movies, as in George Roy Hill's *The Sting* (1973), in which wipes are used to give a feeling for the 1930s.

The *iris,* which was particularly popular in the silent cinema, is coming back somewhat. The

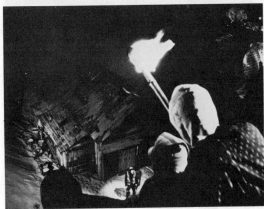

3.18 Reverse angle in Hiroshi Teshigahara's *Woman in the Dunes* (1964). *Bottom:* We see actor Eiji Okada, playing the man trapped in a pit in the sand dunes, surrounded by peasants who will give the man limited freedom if he performs sex in front of them. *Top:* The next shot cuts to this reverse angle showing the reactions of fierce anticipation. (The Museum of Modern Art/Film Stills Archive. Courtesy Contemporary/McGraw-Hill Films.)

iris-in closes a border—such as a circle, diamond, or other geometric form—around a character or object the filmmaker wants to emphasize. It thus serves as a transitional device, and its uses are similar to those of the fade-out. The *iris-out* begins a scene or sequence and withdraws the border from the screen as the shape centering the character or action disappears from the frame. In *The Wild Child* (1970), François Truffaut uses irises instead of fade-outs and fade-ins to create a distancing device for the action, which occurs during the eighteenth century. Iris-ins frequently center their object, hold the attention for a second or two, then move to black (having somewhat the effect of the zoom-in). Iris-outs can do the same thing by moving the opposite way.

The *freeze frame* stops an image for a time, making it appear like a still photograph. This suspends movement in time and space, as at the end of François Truffaut's *The 400 Blows* (1959) where a freeze frame of a boy shows the end of childhood and the beginning of adulthood.

There are also ways to make transitional devices within a shot. One fairly common method is for the camera to pan to a wall and hold on it for a few moments; then the film cuts directly to the next shot, and the wall thereby serves as an in-shot fade-out. Another common method is to cut on the opening or shutting of a door; this action serves as an in-shot wipe.

The transitions that editing creates determine the progression of the scenes or sequences. Thus, editing within scenes is crucial, for the rhythm, pacing, and sense of the movie depend on it. The style of a film often depends on the relationships between rapid cutting and slow cutting, since they create tension and relaxation in the flow of images.

Montage is occasionally used interchangeably with "cutting," "editing," or with "rapid editing." The term in French means "assembling" and is used in Europe to mean editing. However, in this book, we will use montage to refer only to that type of editing practiced by certain Russian filmmakers in the 1920s and 1930s, as we briefly mentioned in Chapter 1 and will describe in more detail in Chapter 5. Briefly, montage may be defined as an intellectual process used to construct a film, building the emotion of scenes by juxtaposing conflicting shots to provide a comment not contained in either—as Bruce Baillie did in his 1965 experimental film, *Quixote,* when he cut a shot of men eating at a club luncheon with shots of pigs eating.

Editing can create motion by using the movement of characters and objects within shots. We can observe this idea by looking at three editing techniques: cuts on action, matching action, and jump cuts.

Cuts on action occur when the cut is made before the completion of a motion. In a scene of a man waving his arm, for example, the editor would cut just before the completion of the wave, then begin the next shot with the wave's final motion. Cut together, the two shots would give the impression of one motion. In addition, the motion of the arm waving would "hide" the cut.

Matching action creates a geographical space that does not necessarily exist in reality. If we were filming a person standing up and exiting from the door of a room, for instance, we would expect the next shot, taken from outside the door, would show us the room or hallway that actually exists. Cheating, however, is a part of movies. The cameraman and actor could travel miles away to another building, set up the camera in front of another door, and the shot of the actor exiting there could be cut with the shot of him leaving his room, which would create a "place" that does not exist but in the movie. We see, then, that motion within a shot can be cut to provide a sense of continuous movement.

Jump cuts jar the audience by cutting out space in the movement of a character or object. If an actor is being filmed running down the street and several spaces through which he runs are cut out of the shot, the result would be an interruption in feeling on the part of the audience. Jump cuts in narrative motion pictures have been considered taboo for a long time. Recently, however, they have been used with some success to provide a feeling of anxiety or frustration for the action. For example, in Stanley Kubrick's *A Clockwork Orange* (1972), the "ballet of destruction" in which the gang of teenagers destroys a writer's house is created through fluid body movement of the actors as well as by means of jump cuts. The opposition, created both by not cutting on action and the fluid body movements within the shots, underscores the violence of the scenes.

Editing, then, creates different sorts of rhythms by cutting together shots in terms of the motion they contain. Editing also builds suspense through parallel action, and it condenses time through the use of the cutaway.

Parallel action (sometimes called *crosscutting*) cuts together two or more actions that occur simultaneously. An example is the action from old serials in which the heroine is tied to the railroad tracks. First we see her helpless, struggling but unable to get away. The next shot shows the train coming. The third shot shows the hero on horseback galloping to the rescue. Shot four shows the train getting close. Shot five shows the heroine struggling against the ropes. Shot six shows the hero, galloping, but at another place (presumably closer to the tracks). The next shot includes the heroine in the foreground, with the train coming in the distance. Shot eight shows the hero riding along the tracks, the train in the distance. In shot nine, the hero finally reaches the heroine and unties her. In the last shot the train rides over the ropes as the hero and heroine embrace. Parallel action is always based on the idea of showing two or more simultaneous actions, in various combinations, one after another. It is most frequently used to create suspense.

The cutaway condenses time by eliminating unwanted space. For example, if a character were driving from one town to another, the director usually would not want to waste film time by showing the whole trip, yet at the same time he might want to create suspense. Thus, he would probably condense time by "cutting away" from the major action and then cutting back to the same character, usually at a different place. The first shot would show the character riding out of town. The next shot would show an action in the town the character is going to. The third shot would show the character's car pulling up in front of a house in that town. The space between the one town and the other, then, has been eliminated by cutting to an occurrence at a different place.

Time and Space

Cinema's ability to contract and enlarge time as well as to create new spaces rests in its use of motion.

Time in motion pictures is in many ways different from time in real life. We run our lives by chronological time, or clock time—that system which lets us organize our actions in the past, in the present, and in the future. Similarly, with space. In the real world, space is either continuous—that is, it goes on and on over the horizon—or it is created by natural or architectural forms (such as a room or the inside of a tent). In the movies, however, time and space are selected for us.

Time

If we were to take a particular flow of time and put a beginning and an end on it, we would initiate a time structure. That is, we would cut events from their total flow in order to organize and understand them.

Any medium of expression that "begins," "goes through events," then "ends" is organized by time. Among the arts, so-called "time arts" include dance, opera, music, the novel, drama, and motion pictures.

Motion pictures specifically manipulate time in order to provide knowledge of events. A film can jump around in time through the use of flashbacks and flashforwards. It can slow down time by using slow motion, or it can speed up time by using accelerated motion and jump cuts. In its use of time, motion pictures are not unlike fantasies, daydreams, night dreams, or hallucinations.

Psychologist Hugo Münsterberg suggested that movies have the capacity to give one the experience of dreams.* French writer Henri Bergson equated the imagination with what he called a "cinematograph," and suggested that, in projecting pictures within the mind, the imagination follows no particular chronological line.†

Bergson also suggested that memory is not a "filing system" into which we can reach and pick out the folder of a particular event that happened in the past. Rather, according to Bergson, memory can bring events to focus at any time, and their presentation to the mind can show things quite different from their actual occurrence in the past. For instance, if in childhood the first

taste of a strawberry was so exciting that we remember it with pleasant feelings, we might recall the taste at the total exclusion of where we were or whom we were with. Eating a strawberry at lunch may trigger the memory and give us that pleasant feeling anew.

Motion pictures can handle time in much the same way as dreams, imagination, and memory. The reason for this derives from the peculiar qualities of the mind and their equivalence in cinematic technique.

Accelerated motion, as in a chase scene, gives the action in much less time than what it really takes. Our minds do this, too. We dream of running, and we get from one place to another in an instant.

Slow motion stretches time. It can show someone running as if through water. The sense of panic at being unable to escape relates directly to our inability to move as fast as we would in clock time.

Jump cuts show us here, then there, then someplace else in quick instants.

Flashbacks are recollections of actions that have occurred in the past. Every time we remember something, we have a flashback.

Flashforwards are projections of something that we hope or expect to happen. We frequently anticipate, or fantasize, events in our minds.

Both flashbacks and flashforwards can be unrealistic. That is, we may totally rework an event from the past, especially if it was unpleasant or if we made fools out of ourselves. We may project this experience into a flashforward, thinking "Next time this happens . . ."

In addition to having these psychological ways of manipulating time, motion pictures have the ability to jump around in historical time. Historical time refers to past events such as the fall of Rome, the Civil War, or the presidency of John F. Kennedy, and to future projections such as an

---

*See Hugo Münsterberg, *The Film: A Psychological Study* (New York: Dover Publications, 1970).

†Henri Bergson, *Creative Evolution,* trans. Arthur Mitchell (New York: Modern Library, 1944).

astronaut landing on Mars, public travel on space-ships, or the year 2000.

Past and future are defined in movies by the "time" that the major character or action exists in. For instance, in George Roy Hill's *Slaughter-house 5* (1972), the central character, Billy Pilgrim, is shown to us typing in the present. The world in which he lives his life, however, is the world of memory—World War II, the bombing of Dresden, his children growing up. It is also the world of the future, which is a part of his imagination and which selects and projects events according to his feelings.

D. W. Griffith's *Intolerance* (1916) intercuts stories that take place during four historical periods: the fall of Babylon, the time of Christ, the Catholic massacre of the Huguenots in France, and the modern period. Whereas the jumps from one to another are controlled by Billy in *Slaughterhouse 5,* the time jumps in *Intolerance* are controlled by the theme that intolerance for ideas and people is a universal characteristic of humankind.

A movie can show us in two hours events that take place over days or years of clock time, and the time that is not needed for expressing the theme is simply cut out. The converse is also true: a movie can take events that occur in only a short time and extend them beyond that time. For instance, the "Odessa Steps" sequence from Sergei Eisenstein's *The Battleship Potemkin* (1925) shows the massacre of the Odessa townspeople by Cossacks marching down a flight of wide steps. The actual massacre probably occurred in something like three minutes, but Eisenstein stretches it out. He cuts in separate events through parallel cutting. He builds suspense by cutaways to other events on the steps. He shows us extended shots of the Cossacks walking down the steps, intercut with shots of townspeople running down them, as well as with

3.19 Cossacks massacre townspeople in the "Odessa Steps" sequence in Sergei Eisenstein's *The Battleship Potemkin* (1925). (The Museum of Modern Art/Film Stills Archive.)

a woman ascending the steps as she goes toward her wounded child. This famous use of *montage* extends time for us by building the action through the growing emotion it contains.

Few movies show the duration of events in the same time as they would actually happen, but two well-known examples are Alfred Hitchcock's *Rope* (1941) and Fred Zinneman's *High Noon* (1952). In *Rope,* Hitchcock attempts to give us a picture in which there are no cuts, instead using fluid camera movement. Actually, there are transitions—they occur when the camera magazine runs out of film and a new magazine has to be inserted—but still the events appear to take place within one shot. Certainly they occur in real time. *High Noon* uses cutaways, parallel action, and other editing devices to present events that take place from about 10:30 in the morning until a little after noon time. The suspense in the film is partly created by constant visual references to clocks.

Experimentation with time, then, is one of the directions in which filmmakers have always moved. Time is definitely a defining quality of the medium.

Space

Space in the movies shows the relationships of objects and characters by referring to the dimensions of height, width, and depth. Since the picture is shown within only two dimensions, height and width, the depth is created artificially by perspective, relief, and scale.

The aspect ratio of the screen gives the filmmaker the frame for the pictures, and this frame not only shows space but also, as mentioned, blocks it out. This unseen space can be suggested by what is shown.

Space can be created in motion pictures by the use of the extreme close-up. For example, a tight close-up of skin can give us the feeling of a universe of sand. Or we can scale buildings down very small in a miniature, let an iguana run through them, and we have thereby created the return of a prehistoric monster.

Space can also be used to provide objects as points of reference for cuts. For example, suppose we have a long room, with a table in the middle, and a vase of flowers on the table. We can shoot into one half of the room, with the table in the foreground. Then we can reverse angle and shoot the other half of the room, also with the table in the foreground. The two shots may be taken in different sets separated from one another by quite a distance, but when cut together, they will give the appearance of action occurring in a single room.

A good way to further examine how space is created in films is to look at the ways space relates to time. When you say, "I'll be there in a little while," the sentence refers to both space and time. "There" refers to a particular space; "while" refers to time, and the amount is determined by space—the distance (space) between you and me. If you are in another town, "while" may mean about an hour. If you are next door, it may mean five minutes.

Another word for "while" is "duration"—the amount of time measured by clocks or calendars. The duration of an event refers to its length in time. Space, on the other hand, is covered—a person travels from one city to another, covering one hundred miles in two hours. The space that the person has traveled is directly related to the time taken to make the journey. We say that the person "averaged" fifty miles per hour.

This *averaging* is just what occurs in a motion picture. An action occurs simultaneously in space and in time. Consider the following example.

A motion picture shot has a particular duration—say, fifteen seconds. That shot contains certain action—say, a man running left to right through the woods. The camera tracks with him, and as the person runs, a certain amount of space is shown—namely, the space he runs through. Now, because normal time in movies is the standard of twenty-four frames per second, a slow-motion shot of the person running would slow time down for us but enlarge the space. Slow motion enlarges the space for us by allowing us to *see more* of it than we would at the normal speed. The space is also enlarged for us by the actions of the body moving. The body's motion creates a space that surrounds it rather than a space through which it simply moves. This is one reason why slow motion seems so ponderous. Thus, film can destroy our notions of normal time and space by weaving one with the other so that both simultaneously project sense.

How we perceive something relates frequently to our experience and to the ways we see.

For instance, the phenomenon of *persistence of vision* allows us to see fluid movement while watching a movie. Actually, there is nothing on the screen half the time we are looking at it. Twenty-four single frames run past the aperture every second during a sound movie. Each one of those single pictures has to be pulled down, allowed to rest for less than one twenty-fourth of a second, then pulled away. The process of changing single frames lasts for about one-thirtieth of a second. During that time, the retina of our eye retains the image just presented to it. Without the phenomenon of persistence of vision, movies would not move fluidly. They would still be "flickers."

In everyday experience, we select what we want to see by focusing on it, and everything else around the object we focus on is more or less blurred. The camera does this too; manipulation of the lens establishes a point of critical focus. But whereas we can instantly focus on any object, the movie camera cannot; it requires preplanning and dexterous manipulation.

Unless we really concentrate on it, we are not aware of any "frame" or peripheral boundaries that limit what we see. That it is there, however, is proved by the fact that we are constantly moving our heads as well as our eyes to look at things. But in a movie theater, we are looking more or less straight ahead at all times (depending on the size of the screen and how close we are to it and depending on whether the shot is a wide-angle long shot or gives us selective focus). Unless the movie is completely boring, our eyes do not wander from the images in motion. We do not notice the frame.

In film as in life, our visual attention is created by motion. There are five types of motion in film: (1) the motion of the objects being filmed; (2) the motion created by any movement of the camera, such as a pan, tilt, dolly, or tracking shot; (3) the movement implied by the use of a zoom lens, or focus shift; (4) the motion created by the frame-rate speed; and (5) the motion created by editing.

Motion creates space and time. It creates space either by having objects move within the frame or by creating static shots by means of the non-moving camera, the film of which moves at a particular frame-rate speed. This frame-rate speed creates space through time.

The freeze frame stops time, although it is still part of the movement of the film.

Time intersects space to create the continuum for the film.

Impulses in Film

Film has many uses. It may be used to show a fictional story, to show "reality," or to make a personal statement. Traditionally, the novel, the short story, drama, dance, or opera have been used to tell a story. The essay, the article, and the photograph have been used to show "reality." Painting, poetry, music, sculpture, dance, and photography have been used to make personal statements. In film study, these three impulses are categorized as (1) the *narrative film* (also called the "dramatic" or "story" film), (2) the *documentary film* (also called the "film of fact"), and (3) the *experimental film* (also known as the *"avant-garde"* or "underground" film).

The Narrative Film

Fiction describes a recognizable or fantasy world by narrating the actions of characters in settings. It relates events played out through time.

Characters consist of protagonists, antagonists, supporting characters, and minor characters. The protagonist or central character is the person who is trying to achieve a goal or who has something at stake. The antagonist is the person trying to prevent the protagonist from achieving the goal, or keeping what is at stake. Supporting characters are generally close to either the protagonist or the antagonist; their actions form a significant part of the drama. Minor characters are used in crowd scenes or simply have walk-on parts; they do not participate in the major unfolding of events.

It is from the relationship between protagonist and antagonist that conflict arises. Conflict, the "clash of opposites," when accompanied by a dramatic question (for example, will the protagonist achieve the goal?), can create suspense. In this sense, the narrative is structured around suspense. The question "What is going to happen?" keeps the reader reading and the viewer looking.

Whether or not the central character achieves the goal, the character is usually *changed* in some way. In classical terms (espoused by Aristotle), this change is called a *reversal,* and it comes about by means of *recognition.* A reversal is a change in fortune or in status. In Mike Nichols's *The Graduate* the central character, Benjamin, changes from letting the adult world act on him to the point where he takes command of his own life. This reversal is created by his recognition that he is his own man and that if he wants the girl, he had better do something about it.

In George Roy Hill's *The Sting,* there are two reversals. One is a trick played against the real reversal. The audience is tricked into believing that Robert Redford is shot, which immediately implies an unfavorable reversal for him. Then, when we learn that the death has been faked,

the audience recognizes that it has been a ruse (to swindle a racketeer) that has worked exactly according to plan. Unless we watch carefully, and see Redford putting a blood capsule in his mouth in preparation for his fake death, it is the audience that is "stung." In this film the major dramatic question (Are Redford and Newman going to succeed with their plan?) creates suspense and forms the action.

The narrative form essentially poses conflict and resolves it along a string of events unified by time. The events themselves are created by *action.* The protagonist or protagonists physically and psychologically react to events by participating in them as well as by trying to overcome them. These actions unify scenes and occur in particular places.

These places, called sets or locations, are the environments that identify the action. A barroom dictates one possible sort of behavior or action—for example, drunkenness—but such action in a church would be unexpected. Thus, conflict can be created by having unexpected actions occur in a place where that behavior is not normal.

Exposition establishes the characters and the conflict. It tells us where we are and who is there. It indicates what the conflict is going to be. For instance, at the beginning of *The Graduate,* Benjamin is introduced to us as a figure coming home by air. His parents' party is a device to let us know what his status is and what his problem is (his future). It prefigures the conflict by immediately posing Mrs. Robinson and his parents as his antagonists.

At the conclusion of a narrative, the action that falls from the climax collects all the pieces, sometimes very quickly. It satisfies all the questions the story has posed. And it ends. Once the resolution to the "sting" has been given, or once Benja-

3.20 *8½*. Face, costume, gesture, setting, and the content that implies the circus makes this unmistakably a Fellini film. (The Museum of Modern Art/Film Stills Archive. Federico Fellini's *8½*. A Joseph E. Levine presentation. Copyright © 1963, Embassy Pictures Corp.)

min and his girl are seen on the bus, there is nothing else to tell. All the strings have been tied.

Structure is the way the plot is presented. *Plot* is the arrangement of actions. This arrangement presents the theme. *Theme* is the meaning or message, if there is one. If there is no message, there is always meaning—that is, new observations about the world or one's self that emerge from the unfolding of events and their resolution.

Style, intimately tied to plot and theme, is the unique ways the materials of the medium are organized to present the filmmaker's vision of the world. (Style also is a technique, such as master scene style or fluid camera style, techniques we will discuss in the next chapter.)

As an example of personal style, the films of Federico Fellini, such as *8½* (1963), *Juliet of the Spirits* (1965), *Amarcord* (1974), and others,

show this director's consistent use of unusual faces and costumes. These objects, which are the content of shots, are shown to us by the manner in which Fellini's camera moves (long tracking shots, with objects between the camera and the person tracked; boom shots that arc slowly through the air; people looking at the camera that dollies past them). One can never mistake a Fellini film for the work of any other director.

The impulse to tell a story is not always enough to satisfy either an audience or the filmmaker. The story is shaped by the unique way that the filmmaker structures it.

The Documentary Film

The desire to show events as they "actually" occur in the world is very strong. Nonfiction books are now more popular than novels. Biography and autobiography are read widely today, as are studies of events and the ways that institutions operate. Film has consistently attracted those people who would like to structure this impulse into a presentational work.

The *representational quality* of film is one major reason why this is so. Motion pictures not only show us objects with remarkable fidelity, but they also show us those objects in motion. The experience of viewing on film the Rolling Stones in concert is more vivid than reading about it. The event seems real because it is seen and heard. It appears to be happening again, in the present.

When we ask, "What are the facts?" we are seeking verification for an observation or feeling. Movie equipment is now portable enough to get to the events and record them. Seeing Dr. Martin Luther King, Jr., deliver his "I Have a Dream" speech many years after its original delivery can still send shivers through us. "What did he look like when he gave the speech?" and "Were there a lot of people there?" can be answered by the film of the event.

The astronauts have showed us the earth as seen from the moon. They have filmed the moon's surface from the distance of only a few feet. These are records that verify events through sight and motion.

The sense of sight is primary. It provides the mind with information that appears indisputable. In the narrative film, we usually overlook the tricks of film magic and accept what is shown as "real." In the documentary film we do not expect tricks other than the most obvious sorts (a fade-out, a fade-in, a dissolve, perhaps a *freeze* frame). We do not like to think in viewing the documentary film that the reality is manufactured for us by the usual techniques of motion-picture storytelling. Indeed, in the documentary film, the appearance (and many times the truth) of the presentation rests in the impact of the content of the images, rather than the way they were photographed or edited.

Many, if not most, documentaries have this apparently spontaneous quality. The events seem to be happening originally, "before our very eyes." We know that the world can never be rendered exactly. We know that film is all illusion. Still, the movie camera does shoot people and objects and reproduces their form and movements in images larger than life.

This seductive quality of cinema forces our participation or our believability. When Michael Wadleigh's film *Woodstock* (1970), about the rock music festival, is shown with multitrack sound on a big screen, the action and the music create strong audience response. This direct response allows us to *experience* the events, as well as to observe them.

Some documentary filmmakers, impelled to report events without editorializing, try to prevent the audience from sympathizing with the people shown in the film. For example, Walter Ruttmann's *Berlin: Symphony of a Great City* (1927) uses a type of montage to equate the film's rhythm with the rhythms of activity in Berlin. Through all this, however, the attempt in the film is to deny direct response to the people shown. The film attempts to say, "This is Berlin. It is just this way on a typical day. Look at it."

Other films, such as Frederick Wiseman and John Marshall's *The Titicut Follies* (1967), about inmates in an institution for the criminally insane, also try to be objective. The people in this film are so pathetic, and some of the procedures shown are so inhuman, that the film draws our feelings into it. The events may be presented objectively, but the human beings seen in those happenings override the direct, objective style. One feels pity, grief, frustration, cynicism, and fright.

The power of motion pictures is perhaps most

clearly expressed in the documentary. Historically, the documentary was used to provide us with a look at exotic people, practices, and places. Viewers who usually would not experience the fascination of an evangelical preacher on tour get a good look at such a person in Howard Smith and Sarah Kernochan's *Marjoe* (1972). People who could not attend the Woodstock rock festival or the Altamont rock festival can vicariously experience and directly observe these events in *Woodstock* and in the Maysles brothers' *Gimme Shelter* (1970).

The documentary also explains how things work by investigating a process. Basil Wright and Harry Watt's *Night Mail* (1936) shows how the mail gets delivered in Great Britain. *The Making of "Butch Cassidy and the Sundance Kid"* (1972) presents an inside view of the tricks and problems that went into making a popular motion picture.

Documentary pictures educate us by presenting information and interpreting that information. Interpretation is the equivalent of editorializing; that is, giving a particular view on a subject. Occasionally, this results in direct propagandizing. For instance, in Leni Riefenstahl's documentary on Hitler, *Triumph of the Will* (1934–36), we are given a glorified picture of Naziism through careful manipulation of the medium.

Because we usually trust the sense of sight more, the documentary filmmaker has a responsibility not to distort events unreasonably. An anthropologist watching a film on the Australian aborigine does not want one of the ritual dances presented in accelerated motion. This would be an editorial comment that would make mockery of the event and detract from its authenticity. On the other hand, when Leni Riefenstahl, in *Olympia, Part Two* (1938), presents the divers in the Berlin Olympics in slow motion, we clearly observe their grace and the perfection of their movements. In this case, cinema has aided the presentation of "reality."

Documentary films used for particular purposes, such as instructional films, almost totally let the events speak for themselves. A doctor trying to learn a surgical procedure would have trouble in the operating room if he attempted to duplicate practices shown in a film that used distorting lenses, accelerated motion, parallel action, and the like. In this case, the event has to speak for itself.

The documentary film relates directly to the audience's capacity to believe. Because the events presented supposedly have actually happened, the responsibility for verifying them on film is great. If the film of the real occurrences is manipulated, the audience has to be told.

The Experimental Film

The experimental filmmaker is concerned with manipulation of the medium as well as examination of "truth." Experimental films, like lyric poetry, are frequently short in duration and long in content.

Some may consider the word "experimental" a misnomer. All films that try to do something not done exactly that way before can be regarded as experimental. Certainly there are narrative films and documentary films that are more experimental than anything else. For instance, Alain Resnais's *Last Year at Marienbad* (1961) distorts time and space so thoroughly by restructuring it by means of cinema that it would be wrong not to call this narrative film "experimental." Stanley Kubrick's *2001: A Space Odyssey* (1968) similarly has experimental parts, especially in the "Star Gate Corridor" sequence. Walter Ruttmann's documentary film, *Berlin: Symphony of a Great City* (1927) is considered an experimen-

3.21 *Last Year at Marienbad.* Shadows in the shadowless garden—the restructuring of time and space. (The Museum of Modern Art/Film Stills Archive. Courtesy Audio Brandon Films, Inc., the 16mm rental distributor in the U.S.A.)

tal film in its attempt to present the rhythms of the city visually.

For our purposes, the experimental film presents emotions to the viewer primarily through visual images, with only minor reliance on words or other sound. The experimental film also (1) investigates the limits of the medium, using untried techniques or devices; (2) deals with subject matter that does not appeal to the general public; and (3) asserts the filmmaker's imagination and private vision through image and technological manipulation.

Limits of the Medium

As the word "experimental" suggests, a film of this type is frequently used to test theories as well as to discover new uses for the medium. In *Symphonie Diagonale* (1921–24), Viking Eggeling attempted to discover visual intervals through moving forms, to test his theory that movies can express intervals visually just as music does aurally. Michael Snow's *Wavelength* (1967) is a forty-five minute zoom shot from one end of a room to another. The zoom travels slowly, stops, moves jerkily ahead, and as it moves, people enter the room. Somebody is murdered; the zoom keeps going. Action happens "under" and "around" the image. Finally, a seascape painting at the other end of the room fills the frame, then the waves in the painting. Snow has used film in an exciting way to examine the potentials of the zoom shot.

Unusual Subject Matter

Perhaps the best known filmmakers dealing with unusual subject matter are Andy Warhol and Paul Morrisey. Their feature-length homosexual Western, *Lonesome Cowboys* (1968), is shot in a fake frontier town that allows the filmmakers to jumble up time and space. Sometimes the action seems to occur in the old West; at other times, it seems to take place today. At one point, as conventional Western action is occurring (although nothing in this film is conventional), tourists come into the picture. Telephone lines appear. The action is improvised and the elements of light, color and contrast are not controlled. The film is a spoof on the myth of the American male's virility. It also spoofs the audience's viewing habits, for the film totally confuses the expectation of the events we hope to see in a Western.

The Filmmaker's Vision

Most experimental films assert the filmmaker's private vision. Maya Deren, who saw suicide as an imposition of the fantasy world and the "death wish" on a person's actions, shows this interconnection in her *Meshes of the Afternoon* (1943), using oblique angles, distorted images, unusual editing, and a twist to the narrative line. Salvador Dali and Luis Buñuel, in their 1928 *Un Chien Andalou* ("Andalusian Dog") mix dream and reality so totally (offending the audience in the process) that, according to Dali, the only way to understand the film would be to psychoanalyze the filmmakers. Oskar Fischinger created a painting in motion (*Motion Painting No. 1,* 1949), in which he expressed not only his feelings through abstract painting, but also the ever-changing relationships between form, color, and music.

The experimental film grows out of the traditions of modern art. At the same time, it deals with documentary and narrative possibilities of the medium and, in particular, with film technique. Many of these techniques sooner or later find their way into larger, more popular feature films. For instance, the use of the super-8 millimeter format, growing in popularity and sophistication, found its way into Dennis Hopper's *Easy Rider* (1969) in the "trip" sequence in New Orleans. Techniques in computer graphics and videotape experiments have resulted in pictures such as Frank Zappa and Tony Palmer's *200 Motels* (1971).

Experimental films have been very important in the development of motion pictures. These films do not represent either a weird offshoot or a totally separate form from either the narrative or the documentary film.

Film is more complex and more technological than any of the traditional arts. The creative impulse includes the urge to experiment. It is within this context that the experimental film can be extremely useful for study.

The Classic Film

As in any other art, a classic is a work that has permanence. Many people feel that because of cinema's comparative youth, only older films can have this quality. Others feel that the word classic is artificial because it seems to mean that the criteria of literary criticism are used to look at film. But, though "classic" may be a term imposed on us, it does direct us to those films and filmmakers whose original ideas have influenced others.

The following attributes conventionally describe a classic of any work of art: (1) it has withstood the test of time, (2) it is rich and varied in meaning, (3) it is unique in vision, and (4) it is innovative in structure, technique, and style.

These conditions usefully describe distinguished films. As the medium increasingly became able to show richer stories more complexly, film structures changed in order to express—and conform to—artistic vision and personal style. Today, for instance, more traditional narrative forms are being replaced by films with less and less literary or dramatically structured plot lines. This general movement reflects original techniques that even-

tually become standard, as happened with D. W. Griffith's master-scene technique, Carl Mayer and F. W. Murnau's fluid-camera technique, and Sergei Eisenstein's montage. Recently, the direct cut to the subjective shot (showing what goes on inside a person's head) has replaced the more traditional cuts to the past (at one time itself an innovative technique) and has produced methods of editing and plot organization that can show more complicated stories. Resnais's *Last Year at Marienbad* showed ways that the human personality can connect time and space into attempts to make sense out of existence. Michelangelo Antonioni's *The Red Desert* (1964) showed that color in film could express emotions that before were expressed mainly through composition, editing, acting, and sound. Jean Renoir, in *Rules of the Game* (1939), showed how composition, camera movement, and dialogue could together create in-depth analyses of people and the social situations they find themselves in.

Some documentary and experimental films are classics, but the word generally applies to narrative films. Among them are those with three kinds of structures: (1) films based on novels or using novelistic structures, (2) films using the techniques of stage drama or of theatrical structure, (3) films with original stories created for motion picture presentation.

Many important films have been inspired by novels: *The Birth of a Nation* (D. W. Griffith, 1915); *The Conformist* (Bernardo Bertolucci, 1970); *Jules and Jim* (François Truffaut, 1961); *The Grapes of Wrath* (John Ford, 1940); *Woman in the Dunes* (Hiroshi Teshigahara, 1964). From stage plays have come *Hamlet* (Laurence Olivier, 1948), *Romeo and Juliet* (Franco Zeffirelli, 1968), and *Who's Afraid of Virginia Woolf?* (Mike Nichols, 1966). Yet original screenplays serve as a specially restricted source for films. Just as there are individual compositions in music and unique paintings in art, so are there movies that emerge solely from the materials of cinema.

Seven critical methods can be used for carefully discovering the impact of any film. Each approach should draw useful information from the classic film.

1. We can look at the historical reasons for a particular film's style, such as the influence of John Ford's *Stagecoach* (1939) on Orson Welles's *Citizen Kane* (1941), or the importance of Vittorio De Sica's *Umberto D* (1952) to any of a number of Ingmar Bergman's early films.

2. We can employ the critical methods of the *auteur* theory and discuss any given film in light of the vision and style of the director, as these are seen in the body of his or her work.

3. We can analyze a film according to the patterns its structures convey or according to a system of both unique and universal signs (including gesture, camera movement, framing, sounds, symbols) the film gives us.

4. We can look at a film in terms of its content alone —how the story is given through character, plot contrivance, metaphor, and levels of thematic meaning.

5. We can analyze the film by the way it presents evidence of the cultural, political, and other circumstances of its time—as social comment or political satire, for example.

6. We can examine the images of each film—its use of lighting, editing techniques, composition, lenses, pacing, and color; in other words, we can look at its technical construction.

7. Using conventional distinctions between form and content, illusion and reality, or structure and freedom, we can identify the associations between a film's expression of theme and its physical action.

Any combination of these approaches is possible in order to discover a film's complexities and to perceive its uniqueness. Whatever a classic film may be, it should be able to provide unusual information through examination by the above criteria. In addition, a film of permanence will always pose its own questions and will always seem fresh.

Film is created by informed manipulation of the techniques and procedures unique to the medium. These manipulations evolve a specific language that we can use to more accurately describe—and hence understand—what we see. Whatever the type of movie—narrative, documentary, or experimental—certain concepts and practices apply. Film is a time-space medium, perceptual in nature, with the ability to express thought as well as show action.

Part Two

The Narrative Film

Style and Technique of the Narrative Film

4

A motion picture that tells a story is called a *narrative film*. It is the kind we most frequently see in our local theaters. Sometimes the narrative film is called a theatrical film, story film, fiction film, dramatic film, or feature film.

Narration, the opposite of description, tells a story through time. Whereas description points out physical relationships of objects in space ("Joe is to the right of Mary and the table is in back of both of them"), narrative ideally shows a story by concentrating on people and objects moving in space through time ("Joe and Mary run down the street after the car"). Narrative shows events formed imaginatively by filmmakers from their experience and observation of the world and people.

Narrative Film Styles

There are four styles of narrative films: thesis, investigative, subjective, and objective.

Thesis Films

In thesis pictures, everything that is shown, the conflicts that are created, and the resolution of the conflicts (usually by one character with whom the audience tends to identify) are arranged to explore and explain a premise. This premise is usually general, such as "Today's young people are basically good," or "Lives lived too formally at the expense of feeling are hollow and meaningless." The expression of plot through character, conflict, and action specifically explores the premise in terms of particular people in unique situations. Movies enrich their major premise with subplots, which become minor premises; the subplots, however, have direct relationship to the thesis and are extensions of it.

For example, in Mike Nichols's *The Graduate* (1967), the major premise is that the cultural values of the generation of the hero's (Benjamin's) parents, when imposed on a young, imaginative person, can lead to loss of freedom of action. Some of the minor premises, which extend the thesis and enrich the plot, are that "maturity does not mean being used for another person's selfish interests" and that "true morality resides in individual choice." The action of the picture leads to this recognition by Benjamin and causes a reversal that supports the second minor premise above. Benjamin has found himself as a unique person by recognizing the picture's major premise and doing something about it.

Investigative Films

Investigative films point up certain problems of existence without offering a specific resolution to

Opposite page: From Ingmar Bergman's *Wild Strawberries.* Courtesy of Janus Films. (The Museum of Modern Art/Film Stills Archive.)

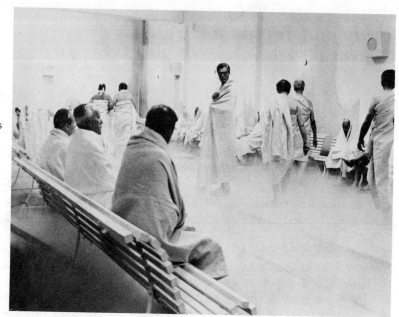

4.1 Marcello Mastroianni, playing Guido, the movie director, in *8½*. This scene in the steam baths shows how atmosphere can be used in the narrative film to blur the border between reality and fantasy. (The Museum of Modern Art/Film Stills Archive. Federico Fellini's *8½*. A Joseph E. Levine presentation. Copyright © 1963, Embassy Pictures Corp.)

them. This type of movie frequently looks at its characters going through their lives, instead of organizing their actions by plot contrivance.

Many of the films of Ingmar Bergman, for example, investigate through the lives of their characters what it means to live in a world in which God has stopped communicating with man. Arthur Penn, on the other hand, has made films that explore social and environmental attitudes (for example, *Bonnie and Clyde,* 1967), that reexamine historical events (*Little Big Man,* 1971), or that probe the psychological reasons for hanging on to life in a world that is basically antagonistic to the individual (*Mickey One,* 1964).

Subjective Films

Some narrative films are subjective; that is, the images are frequently those of memory, dream,

or fantasy. Federico Fellini begins *8½* (1963) with a dream in which Guido, the central character, believes he is suffocating inside a car. With difficulty, he pushes his way out and flies free, floating like a kite out of a tunnel and over the ocean. His friends and others on the beach quickly pull him down to earth by means of a string tied to his leg. As he is falling, he awakens, and we see him in his bedroom at a health resort. This film of a director trying to find material for his next picture in his own memories and fantasies intercuts between "reality" and the "dream mode" to give us knowledge of Guido's private and public selves. The film in this way investigates the creative process while at the same time it points up cinema's ability to show the mind at work.

Many films today intercut "reality" with scenes of fantasy, memory, or dream. Some of the films of Luis Buñuel (e.g., *Belle de Jour,* 1967), of

4.2 Alain Resnais's *Last Year at Marienbad* (1961) consistently uses the dream mode. The use of mirrors and reflections supports the projection of images of the mind. (The Museum of Modern Art/Film Stills Archive. Courtesy Audio Brandon Films, Inc., the 16mm rental distributor in the U.S.A.)

Alain Resnais (*Last Year at Marienbad,* 1961), and of Stanley Kubrick (*2001: A Space Odyssey,* 1968) are in whole or in part involved with showing the dream mode.

Objective Films

Objective narrative films attempt to show events as untouched as possible by the influence of personal attitudes. This approach frequently gives the movie a documentary look, as in William Friedkin's *The French Connection* (1971). In this film mostly short shots build on each other to present a distant observing point so that we can see the events unfold. The political films of Costa-Gavras, such as *Z* (1968) or *State of Siege* (1973), also attempt to do this, trying to hide political bias in the objective style.

Character and Events

Subjective films usually concentrate on character. Objective films usually concentrate on events.

Films of character frequently show or investigate the *motivation* for actions. Such motivation is usually shown to arise from feelings the character has—from the emotions of love, pride, pity, hate, sacrifice, martyrdom, and many others. Most of the films we see are films of character.

Films of events are usually *episodic.* They show characters as instruments in actions that they created or found themselves caught in. The style of these films arises not so much from a straight dramatic line as from playing off one sequence against another. We can see this in George Lucas's 1973 film *American Graffiti.* Here there is no clear hero; the events interweave within the theme of

4.3 In *American Graffiti* the teenage "hop" is one of the events that builds the structure and gives the picture a documentary sense of authenticity. (The Museum of Modern Art/Film Stills Archive. Courtesy of Universal Pictures.)

the activities of teenagers one Friday night in a California city in 1962. Two other examples of films of events are Eisenstein's *The Battleship Potemkin* (1925) and Kubrick's *2001*. Friedkin's *The French Connection* and Francis Ford Coppola's *The Godfather* (1972) are also good examples, although they show that these classifications are not exclusive. In *The Godfather* we follow the lives of the Godfather (Marlon Brando) and his sons, while at the same time we observe the events that force them to act. We see how the Mafia works. In *The French Connection,* we follow Popeye (Gene Hackman) in his attempt to uncover the international drug ring, while we also see the activities of the drug ring revealed in the cat-and-mouse game, which gives us information of smuggling and tailing procedures as well as thematic conflict. Through this mixing of films of events and films of character, the filmmaker's personal view of the world controls the progress of action and provides consistency of theme.

In a picture such as *Bonnie and Clyde,* the events may be seen through the actions of the central characters by means of a *picaresque* structure (in which episodic events are tied through character). For instance, the individual events that lead to Bonnie and Clyde's deaths are connected through scenes showing the characters traveling around in an automobile. These scenes are reinforced with blue-grass music of the period, which helps to cue us to the transitionary purpose of the action. Character is investigated within separate sequences, which accumulate to show events, sometimes in a documentary style.

The relationships between character and event provide the structure for narrative films. Thus, they are among the first elements we must consider in evaluating a movie as a movie.

Films of character are unified by characters confronting obstacles and resolving them to their own good or bad ends. These films are thesis films, and today they are mostly psychological and investigative. The thematic conflict in such films arises from opposition (1) between the characters and their inner feelings, and (2) between characters and the actions of others. Thus, character is central to the conflict.

Sometimes character controls the film's structure, sometimes *events* do. When a character creates events, the picture usually is structured from character. When events control characters, events structure it. Sometimes, in picaresque structure, the two work together.

Films of events are primarily objective; they also can be investigative but usually only superficially. Films of events can be unified structurally by time or place or both, but (except for the picaresque) they are unified by one strong leading character.

Today, feature films frequently use flashbacks or flashforwards that are either subjective (as remembered or fantasized by a character) or objective (as observed by the omniscient camera), and so such films can be governed both by characters and events in ways more related to internal shot arrangements than to traditional literary structures. In George Roy Hill's 1972 film *Slaughterhouse 5,* for instance, the way the images interact with and oppose each other creates the structural unity. The frequent cuts between the violence of the Allied bombing of Dresden in Germany in World War II and "fantasyland" (the world created in the central character, Billy's, mind) shows how Billy is caught between past and future. In *2001*'s "Star Gate Corridor" sequence, the constant forward flow through the universe, with some pauses in fantastic settings, suggests the evolution of man out of time and toward a higher reality than can be provided by worldly experience.

Since the movie can jump back and forth in time and create spaces that do not really exist, it can resemble that interaction in our lives between, on the one hand, how we observe occurrences that actually happen and, on the other, how we fantasize by conjuring up images. Occurrences that we may or may not participate in are *causal* events: one thing happens, and that makes another happen, and so on. However, fantasies frequently do not have this logical order.

Motion pictures of character are usually *image manipulative* when the camera is following the characters, looking at them or observing their interaction in the world. Motion pictures of *events* are also image manipulative. Pictures are image manipulative when their events and actions are composed and related to each other by means of editing.

Pictures or those parts of them that are of a subjective nature are usually *image manifest;* the images themselves assume the burden of presenting information, frequently through camera movement.

Motion

Motion is the defining quality of motion pictures. It provides the frame of mind we have all had in which the whole experience of an activity seems like a dream, or another frame of mind in which we have sat back and watched things around us happen as if we were totally removed from them. Both these types of experiences deal with the psychological problem of *illusion.* Unlike life, motion pictures are all illusion. Among other reasons for illusion *(see inset),* are the fact that we accept both black and white and color as real, that objects and persons on the screen are much larger than they are in life, that the traveling camera shot provides "unreal" fluidity. Thus, objects, people, film, and the camera in motion create a "super reality" in most narrative films.

In understanding what a film means, we have to consider how motion involves both sense and structure. Then we can more directly perceive those elements of a motion picture that seem difficult to describe: pacing, rhythm, visual flow.

To look at a motion picture intelligently we must not let ourselves become so passively acted upon by what is happening that we do not see *how* it happens. As motion is a basic quality of film, it is the obvious element initially to observe.

Two types of motion are most important in appreciating narrative film: editing and fluid camera technique. Today, most movies alternate static camera shots with moving camera shots, and editing frequently works to oppose or support rhythms in moving camera shots.

Editing

The editing style generally used to present a scene involving two or more people is called *master scene technique.* This style organizes a scene into separate shots, which combine to give the appearance of uninterrupted action.

Master Scene Technique   Imagine a scene that involves conversation among four people sitting around a table. In a theatrical scene such as this, the dialogue may pretty well be the action. In order to create interest, to vary image, and to direct response to a main character, master scene technique would open with a long shot (an establishing shot) that immediately gives information about who is where, then intercut the long shot with medium shots and close-ups (reaction shots and shots of people talking). To provide more information about the people, the editor might insert an infrequent close-up of a hand reaching for a glass of water, tapping a cigarette, fidgeting, or the like.

In the master scene method, the camera is usually static. Rhythms are created by object move-

Why Movies Are All Illusion

1. The events we see in a sound movie are projected at twenty-four single frames per second.

2. The phenomenon of *persistence of vision* allows the retina in our eye to retain an image for a split second after that image disappears. This split second gives the projector time to pull down the next frame, and in between frames there is nothing on the screen. Approximately half the time we are looking at the movie, the image we see is in our eye and not on the screen.

3. Even if the events we see in the movie are without movement (as in a freeze frame), movement is still implied, though not noticed, by the frames changing as they run through the projector.

4. The images on these frames are projected by light against a highly reflective surface and hence into our eyes. We are seeing light, not solid objects.

5. The movie frame is a two-dimensional rectangle. Yet most films give us the illusion of three-dimensionality. Occasionally, as a picture takes us out of conventional time and space, a kind of four-dimensionality is created, as in Alain Resnais's *Je t'Aime, Je t'Aime* (1968), in which images of the central character's past are repeated frequently as, caught between present and past by a malfunctioning time machine, he attempts to escape from this nonexistence.

ment or by alternating close-ups and long shots with medium shots. Frequently, but not always, master scene technique depends on dialogue.

A major difference, however, is that in stage drama we see everything in long shot and we can usually select what it is we want to look at. In a filmed master scene sequence, the selection is made for us. This means that a film scene can have people sitting and talking, whereas in the theater the characters are required to get up and move around. On stage most of the people's actions while seated around a table would be barely noticeable, but in the movies selective framing can make them very significant.

Dynamic Editing   Instead of working in a theatrical style, with static images, dynamic editing attempts rhythmically to create emotions similar to those the events portray. It also may on occasion create, through editing, rhythms that oppose these emotions—an effective way of instilling tension and uneasiness in the audience.

Dynamic editing uses synthesis and counterpoint to create a mood. Consider a scene of two lovers walking through the woods hand in hand, with the young lady trying to find the right moment to tell her boyfriend she is pregnant. Simultaneously, as she builds up to her revelation, we are given a warning of danger: we are shown parallel shots of a man with a knife creeping through the woods, watching the pair. To show the love the two have for each other, the film cuts a close-up shot of their grasped hands with a tracking shot moving with the couple from in front. Light music to synthesize the mood suggested by the shots, the action, and the editing gives way to the crunch of the couple's feet on the leaves. The cutting rhythm then changes, counterpointing their apparent mood of tranquility and love with some brief jump cuts and unusual angles, which begin a rhythm appropriate for

the problem of the young lady choosing her words to reveal her situation. Such cutting also prepares us for the shock of the man jumping at them with the knife.

Dynamic editing, then, not only helps express emotions, it frequently sets the pacing of object and camera movement. For this type of cutting to work, the editing has to shape the events and the feelings through external motion and internal motion. *External motion* is created by the editor through image manipulation. *Internal motion* is created by means of camera and object movement, framing, lighting, decor, and color contrast.

Fluid Camera Technique

Fluid camera technique is more easily shown than explained. The 1924 silent film *The Last Laugh* by F. W. Murnau is generally credited with first using the technique as a controlling device. The film demonstrates how fluid camera gives space new meaning, for the camera is used to let the audience experience the space. For instance, in the beginning of the film, the camera assumes the point of view of a guest in the hotel where most of the action takes place. The first scene starts with the camera looking out of the grill of a descending elevator. The elevator door opens and the camera moves into the lobby, then to the main desk, and finally toward the revolving doors and outside to the doorman, who is the main character. Thus, rather than being shown the doorman immediately, in his usual place outside the hotel, we are allowed instead to discover him by going through and emerging from the hotel, which is the space that creates the picture's primary atmosphere.

This dynamic feeling of movement through space is created throughout the film, which, incidentally, uses no titles except in one place. The title begins the "last laugh" sequence, in which

4.4 The doorman enjoying his new status in the "last laugh" sequence in F. W. Murnau's 1924 *The Last Laugh*. The film is perhaps the first example of the extended use of fluid camera technique. (The Museum of Modern Art/Film Stills Archive.)

we are told that the author has taken pity on the doorman, who has been demoted to lavatory attendant. After the title, the camera travels through the hotel dining room, past people eating, and arcs toward a table piled with food. Behind the food we discover the doorman, who has become a millionaire. The fluid camera then extends time as it takes us carefully through the spatial environment of tables of food and people eating, then surprises us with the image of the doorman, a participant in this environment.

What separates movies from other visual arts is that, in film, composition is usually created through motion, as is clear in the fluid camera technique, in which a scene is shown in its entirety in one traveling camera shot. Few pictures can use a traveling shot for each shot in the film; such technique would dizzy the audience and call too much attention to itself. Also, because the action in a narrative film is almost always more immediately important than the technique that shows it, it is usually best for the camera to be hidden in the content. More important, however, is the fact that a motion picture—no matter how exciting its action—builds to its climax by alternating periods of movement with periods of calm, and a constantly moving camera would not allow that respite.

Montage is a type of dynamic editing that can include both moving camera and static camera shots. This device juxtaposes short shots against each other to build scenes that give the picture its dramatic line. The chase beneath the elevated train in *The French Connection* is a good example of montage. The short pan shots of the car, the point-of-view shots from inside the car, the shots of the train it is chasing, and the shots inside the train are edited against each other, creating rhythms that support the forward movement of those objects. The result is we get a dynamic feeling of the chase rather than simply observe it.

Long, fluid camera shots dominate Luchino Visconti's *Death in Venice* (1970). Many scenes in this film are formed by the moving camera exploring the environment in which the action takes place. For instance, the camera travels slowly at night along the extended porch of the hotel where the main character, Gustave Aschenbach, is staying. We move through the faded elegance covered with harsh colors, through the ineffective lighting of the lanterns. We hear a

4.5 *Death in Venice.* The moving camera, having taken us through the environment, stops to show us Aschenbach isolated and lonely. The high-angle shot and selective focusing underscore this impression. (The Museum of Modern Art/Film Stills Archive. Courtesy Warner Bros.)

gypsy song, and we find the hotel environment full of self-contradictions and sadness. Finally, we discover Aschenbach, simultaneously lost and caught in this area through which we have traveled, an area that is an extension of his own emotions and circumstances.

The Discovery Shot

When new information enters into a moving camera shot, this is called a *discovery shot.* There are pan discovery shots, tilt discovery shots, and dolly discovery shots. The discovery shot is one of the most effective ways to dynamically connect information to the space in which it exists. For instance, Arthur Penn's *Little Big Man* begins with the camera slowly panning across a barren Western landscape; then some wisps of smoke come into the frame, and as the pan continues we discover the burning remains of a stagecoach massacre.

Wide-Angle Long Shot

In this technique internal rhythms are created mostly by object or character movement. Although editing techniques and camera movement also can be important, the predominant control derives from the graphic composition of the shot. The wide-angle lens can compose even traveling shots in depth, because the lens can see both distant and near objects about as clearly. Thus, the cinematographer can compose not only with line and color (or gradations of gray in black-and-white pictures) but also with perspective and relief *(see inset next page).*

In terms of audience involvement, the wide-angle long-shot technique is the most objective of the styles discussed here. Because most of the time the camera is at a distance from the action, it permits us to observe more than to be involved. In addition, the composition allows the action to occur within three dimensions, so that it provides almost a stage set playing area. An advantage to this type of shooting is that it allows the audience to choose what it wants to see, even while the composition is directing attention to the point or points of major interest.

Zoom shots can create internal rhythms and quickly move from long shot to close-up or vice-versa to provide immediate information. Many types of zoom shots, however, have become clichés. The movie made for television would probably have a quick zoom into a close-up of Joan's hand as she opens the door or a quick zoom back from a close-up of her hand on the door knob to a medium long shot as she opens the door *(see example in inset)*. The zoom lens is often too easy a way out of a problem.

Something is too easy when it is predictable. There is, however, a fine line between those techniques that are predictable and those that condense time, rearrange space, and generally give information. The audience, because it has viewed hundreds of films with cutaways, parallel action,

discovery shots, quick zooms, and other devices, accepts the information immediately without the cinema getting in the way.

The problem of originality in films may be understood by comparing cinema with music. A musical piece in which the melody runs repeatedly in the same key and in the same tempo, without dynamic variation, would be disastrous. No matter how evocative it is, we would become uninterested in it if there were no modulation, if there were always the required violins at the "right" moment, and if the tempo remained constant. Much of the excitement of music comes from something predictable being given to us in a way we probably could not predict, yet in a way that seems absolutely right. Similarly in movies, our expectations can be set up for resolution, say, by a quick cut to a swish pan rather than by a predictable zoom-in shot. If done properly, the excitement can be such that the trick is not seen; we feel it to be right. Originality, then, means not only using materials in new ways but also in making the experience seem fresh to the audience.

Visual Techniques

The process of creation in films involves the viewer as well as camera technique. In motion pictures, any identification between the audience and the film occurs in large part because of the emotional interaction between the viewer and the events seen. Consider a basic piece of action: "Joan arises and walks to the door." Let us see how it might be rendered by conventional master scene technique, by fluid camera technique, by wide-angle long shot, and by dynamic editing.

Master Scene Technique

1. *LS* [long shot]. *Joan.* (Establishing shot. Places her in easy chair in a room.)

2. *CU* [close-up]. *Joan's face.* (Surprise as she hears an unusual noise.)

3. *MS* [medium shot]. *Joan arising.* (She starts toward the door. Camera tracks with her.)

4. *CU.* Joan's hand on door knob.

5. *MS. Joan as she opens door.*

6. *Reverse angle: CU. Joan's face to show fright.*

Style and Content

As with any other art form, the more we as viewers know about how the materials can be used, the richer our viewing will be. But how can we recall or verbalize the techniques used when (1) they go by so fast we cannot remember them well (and we usually cannot reverse the film) and (2) we get caught up in the "action"? How do we even talk about a film as a film, much less as a collection of thematic relationships of symbols, character, and conflict? How do we sort out the way composition, sound, language, rhythm, cutting, decor, acting, lighting, and other factors work to create the cinematic experience?

The first step is to identify the general cinematic techniques of the picture so that we can observe relationships between its style and content. With some pictures, a particularly striking image or a specific cutting technique can be the starting point, letting us work from particular to general. With other pictures, we can work from the way the conflict among images relates the objective, investigative, or thematic aspect of the movie.

There is an image in Lindsay Anderson's 1973 film *O Lucky Man* that most people who have seen the picture seem to remember. The main character is in a hospital room and sees a man lying in bed, obviously in pain. Wanting to discover the source of the pain, he pulls back the blankets to view the man's body. What he—and we—see is the man's head on the body of a sheep. This surprising, unique, disgusting image is so striking that we as viewers can use it as a basis for observing the style of the rest of the picture. The film's style is to make the unbelievable totally believable, using episodic, loose sequences that have original imagery.

In *2001,* there is a striking cut from the ape man's animal bone flying slowly through the air to the shuttle craft floating through space. This visual contrast suggests thematic conflict between physical and spiritual evolution and organizes the film's external and internal visual rhythms. For example, the contrast of a primitive hand tool (the

Fluid Camera Technique

CU Joan's face as she apparently hears something. Boom up slightly and track with her to the door. Catch what she sees from behind her, using her approximate point of view. Boom down, swinging in an arc to catch her half profile in CU as she shows fright.

Wide-Angle Long Shot

Pick up Joan center-frame, then pan with her to the right as she moves to the door, keeping her center-frame all the way. As Joan opens the door, a glass ashtray in CU at frame right totally distorts what it is she sees, but it does suggest a human form. In center-left frame, at this point, Joan is in LS. She screams.

Dynamic Editing

1. *CU. Joan's eyes.*
2. *MS. The door as we hear a knock.*
3. *CU. Joan's eyes as she responds to the knock.*
4. *MLS* [medium long shot]. *Jump cut in pan of Joan moving to door.*
5. *CU. Joan's hand on door knob.*
6. *Swish pan around the room as Joan screams.*

Here the jump cut (an editing technique) has been added in order to predict a sense of panic and the swish pan (a camera technique) has been added to suggest extreme fright (perhaps even fainting) at the climax. The swish pan, in fact, could replace Joan's scream, rather than support it; it could be a visual representation of the scream.

4.6 Space shuttle floating through space in Stanley Kubrick's *2001: A Space Odyssey.*
(The Museum of Modern Art/Film Stills Archive. Courtesy Metro-Goldwyn-Mayer Inc.
From the MGM release *2001: A Space Odyssey* © 1968 Metro-Goldwyn-Mayer Inc.)

bone) with a space machine (also a tool) jumps us forward in time. The slow-motion movement of the bone soaring through the air is cut with and extended by the ship floating in outer space. This creates rhythms that reinforce the picture's themes of exploration, discovery, and the mind's potential. The cut anticipates the picture's eventual move from physical man to spiritual existence.

In Ingmar Bergman's *Cries and Whispers* color is the film's most distinctive attribute. The picture is keyed to red, which either directly or implicitly controls every image. Many of the transitions are fade-outs to red. All that red symbolizes (passion, death, sexuality) become elements of contrast with the white of dresses and the gold of the props. In addition, the use of clocks and their constant ticking internalizes the themes the picture investigates: the problems of human communication, identity, and death. Rather than

simply becoming an extension of color and time, the characters and their atmosphere recreate universal and personal experiences.

In both *2001* and *Cries and Whispers,* the dramatic line extends from psychological and symbolic relationships among images. This makes the experience *perceptual* rather than *conceptual.* That is, information is directly given and is felt originally rather than pondered during its presentation, as readers might do in a novel were they to linger over or reread a passage.

Narrative Film Technique

To create this direct experience, narrative film style is created from a variety of factors, among them decor and *mise-en-scène,* framing and

4.7 Ingmar Bergman's *Cries and Whispers.* The red room contrasts with red and white of costumes; the clocks tick unremittingly. (The Museum of Modern Art/Film Stills Archive. Courtesy New World Pictures, Inc.)

composition, camera angle, textures and lighting, color and black-and-white film, sound, acting, and costumes, which go hand-in-hand with the attributes of rhythm, pacing, camera, and editing already discussed.

All these factors work in combination with each other. To abstract any one of them would not recreate the total experience. Looking at each, however, can give us a starting point to rebuild the cinematic structure of a picture; we can critically reconstruct the creative experience.

Decor and Mise-en-Scène

Decor is the way a setting is created and embellished by such items as color, props, and costumes, which form the physical environment for the action. By synthesis, extension, or counterpoint, they add significance to the actions carried out in the setting.

Decor can fuse opposites in order to permit characters insight into themselves or to let them recognize something about their relationship with others. For example, if a chubby, good-humored lady were seen in a sparsely furnished, light blue room with a high ceiling and strong vertical lines, the visual opposition between her form and that of the room could force recognition both in herself and in us that she has a weight problem.

If the room is part of the apartment of a young man she has come to meet, the room—seen as an *extension* of him—helps us predict his probable physical characteristics as well as his attitudes. If he enters tall and crisply dressed, our expectations are met and we can feel a sense of panic with the lady. If he enters short, robust, and

4.8 The shabby decor reinforces the old man's despair in this scene from Vittorio De Sica's *Umberto D* (1952). (The Museum of Modern Art/Film Stills Archive. Courtesy of Janus Films.)

equally as chubby as she, our expectations are met in a new way, and humor might result.

The woman is counterpointed by the room she is in. The tension created as she waits and nervously handles a round object, such as a glass ball, helps us to understand her better and supports the conflict at this point.

Decor in motion pictures is created for such physical properties as framing, the use of lenses, lighting contrast, and the kind of color or black-and-white film being used.

Mise-en-scène, a term that originally belonged to the theater and meant "staging," refers to "atmosphere," to the *qualities* of a location or set. Whereas decor is the scenery and props that create the physical environment, *mise-en-scène* is the visual environment as it arises from interaction among people, decor, and objects.

In films using all or part of the style of *cinéma-vérité* (which uses hand-held camera shots, location shooting, and other informal techniques)— exemplified in the United States by the films of John Cassavetes, such as *Faces* (1968) and *Husbands* (1970)—*mise-en-scène* can control both the action and the camera's response to it. Improvisational acting and the hand-held camera in part make this happen. For instance, one scene in *Husbands* takes place in the men's room of a bar, and the restricted area permits the characters to interact with each other as they drunkenly dream aloud. The lavatory equipment and the drab colors reinforce the men's sickness and their fear of "growing old without having experienced life." The actors improvise within thematic limits, and the camera responds with tight close-ups and medium shots. Thus, the rest-room

4.9 A wide-angle shot of Orson Welles, center, in *Citizen Kane*. Here the character is triangularized to show him the victim of circumstances being announced by the financial advisor Thatcher, his ex-guardian (left), and Bernstein, the manager of his empire. (The Museum of Modern Art/Film Stills Archive. Courtesy of RKO Radio Pictures, a divison of RKO General, Inc.)

scene reinforces the plight of middle-aged men caught in common despair.

Framing and Composition

Framing refers to those limits of the image (and hence of the screen) beyond which no picture exists. The screen itself provides the area for composition.

Framing is either static or mobile, depending upon whether or not a moving camera is used.

There are two kinds of composition: formal and informal.

Formal composition refers to traditional ways of creating visual organization through line and color. Because of time flow and shot change, visual organization in film cannot be contemplated at length as it can in still photography or in paint-

ing. Balance traditionally is used to create a feeling of peace through the use of strong horizontal lines. With a moving camera shot, or by means of shot change, vertical elements could contrast with horizontal elements to create tension. In a wide-angle shot, a character can be triangularized, by near and far objects, to show confinement. Flat composition by means of a telephoto lens can be similar in look to a painting, which might be added to the movie for decorative as well as for atmospheric purposes. Formal composition, in short, builds a film from carefully composed images, which extend themselves into meaning by movement.

Informal composition refers to what the camera "sees" rather than to how objects are arranged in front of it. When the movement of characters or objects controls the camera's response, the com-

4.10 This scene from Ingmar Bergman's *Cries and Whispers* has the look of an impressionist painting. (The Museum of Modern Art/Film Stills Archive. Courtesy New World Pictures, Inc.)

position tends to be derived from action rather than from setting, particularly in locations that have been found rather than staged. In informal composition, instead of the composition influencing the action, the action creates the composition by the camera's response to it.

Cries and Whispers is a good example of the use of formal composition. Here color and line create a visual quality that almost dominates the action, as shown by the geometric forms of the rooms of the house in which the action takes place. An opening shot is of the exterior of the house, and the framing shows the house centered in, but emerging from, the fog. The feeling in this and some other exterior scenes is that of Impressionist painting. A dying woman's bedroom is constantly framed to point up the suffocation of the red on the bed as opposed by her white gown and the light from the window.

On the other hand, Dennis Hopper's *Easy Rider* (1969) is in part an example of informal composition. Here the camera on occasion follows and responds to action that frequently moves through, rather than is contained by, found locations. In one scene, the camera follows the movement of the men on their motorcycles and it frames with attention to the action of the cycles.* Other *Easy Rider* scenes are composed by the camera responding to action rather than to the setting or location.

In informal composition, movement predominates over picture; in formal composition, picture predominates over movement.

Camera Angle

Camera angle is directly associated with framing and composition. It refers to the position from

---

*This does not mean the scene was not set up with lights and props. It is only to suggest the informality of found locations in relation to style. *Easy Rider* has other, more formal scenes.

which an object is viewed. As we mentioned earlier, a high camera angle shows the insignificance of the object, while a low camera angle can show dominance. The camera angle normally used in narrative motion pictures is the eye-level angle, which approximates the eye level viewers would have if they were participating in the action.

An interesting use of camera angle is found in the films of Yasujiro Ozu. Many of his pictures are shot from about three feet off the floor, generally looking up at the action. The camera's angle gives us the view of one sitting in the traditional Japanese position on a pillow. (*See* 4.11.)

Camera angle can also approximate the viewing position of a character, as in reaction shots showing a conversation. As one person talks, we are often shown the person being talked to from the approximate angle of vision of the person doing the talking.

Camera angles can let us view a scene from a position where our eyes probably would never normally be—for instance, resting on the ground, under a car, on a railroad track, or high in the sky.

Actually, the "right" angle from which to view a scene is not always easy to find, especially when a film is being shot outdoors or on location. The director and the cinematographer have all of what is in view to select the appropriate rectangle within which to frame the action. But the proper line of sight can increase our response to a film. For instance, a surprising cut to an overhead shot of the murderer stabbing Arbogast in Alfred Hitchcock's *Psycho* (1960) disorients the viewer from the expected horizontal angle and supports the shock and visual thrill of the attack.

Textures and Lighting

Movie images are created by catching light falling in harsh and subtle ways against objects. Shadows that create patterns of light and dark also

4.11 Yosujiro Ozu's distinctive style is seen through low camera angle in *Tokyo Story* (1953). The story builds slowly to show the lack of sympathy given their older parents by the children. (The Museum of Modern Art/Film Stills Archive. Courtesy New Yorker Films.)

support composition and create impressions in their own right.

Textures mold features by light, and they can contribute significantly to theme. By showing the structure of the surfaces of things, textures can help penetrate those surfaces to suggest other meanings. This use is particularly evident in Hiroshi Teshigahara's *Woman in the Dunes* (1964), about a man trapped against his will in a huge sand pit with the woman who lives there. Close-up shots of human skin, of sand, and of sand on human skin, strikingly point up the man's dilemma. They also suggest his movement away from civilization toward harmony with nature. Such shots internalize the conflict, letting the audience sense the frustrations and "trapped" feelings of the man.

If cinema is "painting with light," then lighting can be used to create everything from three-

dimensionality to a feeling of softness for a young woman or dread for a dastardly person.

Key lighting provides the main source of illumination on a subject. High key lighting from a low angle can make a person's face appear evil and malign.

Back lighting (which illuminates the subject from the rear) can create an eerie effect (see 4.13); it can present silhouettes. But when molded with soft fill lights from the side, it can suggest beauty.

Low key lighting provides deep shadows. High key lighting generally makes the object predominant in the frame.

In the narrative film, lighting can substantiate mood, provide clarity for the action, and suggest conflicts through shadows and color. In *Juliet of the Spirits* (1965), Federico Fellini uses all three of these methods, relying quite frequently on the

4.12 In *Woman in the Dunes,* textures of skin and sand show the relationship between people and nature. (The Museum of Modern Art/Film Stills Archive. Courtesy Contemporary/McGraw-Hill Films.)

shadow/color interrelationships. This can be seen in several scenes, but perhaps the most obvious use occurs in shots of the interior of a large building where a Guru is holding forth upstairs. The intermixture between color and shadows points not only to the heroine Juliet's fear at meeting the Guru (substantiated also by a lightning storm outside and the electricity going out), but it visually shows it to the audience. It is, in fact, when color melds with shadow that its meaning becomes extended beyond mere symbolic representation.

4.13 In Alfred Hitchcock's *Psycho* (1960), the house looks sinister; Anthony Perkins, back-lit, visually assumes the eerie qualities of the house. (The Museum of Modern Art/ Film Stills Archive. Courtesy of Universal Pictures.)

Color and Black and White

Color and black and white work in different ways in the narrative motion picture. Occasionally they are used in opposition to each other in the same picture. Lindsay Anderson's *If . . .* (1968) and Dalton Trumbo's *Johnny Got His Gun* (1970) are two recent pictures that alternate black-and-white and color sequences. And in Michelangelo Antonioni's *Blow-Up* (1967), black-and-white still photography is used to counterpoint the color in the film, while at the same time it supports the plot on the psychological level of discovering the artificiality of the physical world.

Black and white is achromatic and extends from deep black through intermediate shades of gray to pure white. The highly panchromatic

black-and-white film stock available today permits color values to be translated into specific shades of gray. Contemporary films such as François Truffaut's *The Wild Child* (1970), Peter Bogdanovitch's *The Last Picture Show* (1971), and Bob Fosse's *Lenny* (1975) contain visual qualities that are intrinsic to their black-and-white presentation. These pictures would not work as well in color.

Black-and-white film best works its particular values on two levels: style and psychological evocation. *Style* includes both a director's vision and the atmosphere that structures that vision through *mise-en-scène,* lighting, editing, camera movement, and other values. The story in the Bogdanovitch film takes place in the past—the early 1950s—when black and white was used for almost all narrative motion pictures. It also attempts to duplicate, within certain limits, the shooting techniques of that period; for instance, no zoom shots are used.

In the same director's *Paper Moon* (1973), the bleak atmosphere of the American Depression years would not have come through in a color film. Color would have made the scenery and the action too pretty. Any attempt to mute color film through filters, lighting, film stock, and laboratory processes would have been involved with trying to work a black-and-white aesthetic in color and hence would have been self-defeating.*

Psychological evocation creates a world, more sensed than seen, from characters' motivations, fears, frustrations, and anxieties. *Mickey One,* for instance, is a fairly complicated picture that deals with the hero's attempt to escape both from an unidentified antagonist (''the mob''), which has put out a contract on him, and his search for identity in an uncommunicative world. Black and white supports Mickey's alienation from his environment. The refined shades of gray that extend the story between somber black and harsh white create a world that is a metaphor for Mickey's anxieties in a way color could not do, for color would make it a different picture.

Color film is chromatic and extends from white, which is produced by reflection of all the rays of the solar spectrum. Color in film is used both in regulating *hue* (a particular tint or shade of color) and *saturation* (vividness of the hue; also

the degree of difference from a gray of equal brightness).

Narrative films sometimes use color simply for commercial reasons. Such pictures are primarily concerned with maintaining the accuracy and balance of the color, not with manipulating it to provide meaning. Films that purposely use color to enrich and extend theme frequently provide a more decorative view of life than do black-and-white pictures. However, both black and white and color are as ''artificial'' as printer's ink or oil paints. It is the expert and controlled use of them that creates the experience of reality, which in movies substitutes for reality itself.

In *The Red Desert* (1964) and *Blow-Up,* Antonioni has created pictures that attempt to use color as perceptual extensions of theme and content. *The Red Desert* is about the oppressiveness of today's technological environment, an environment that is itself a desert. The picture is keyed to the color red. (Good color pictures frequently are keyed to a particular color, which establishes a tone and controls all other hues and colors in the film.) In one sequence, the central character, Giuliana, feeling lost and depressed, is standing near a factory. A cut shows us what she sees—a gray swamp that reflects her particular emotions at the time and plays off the key to red. (In order to achieve this effect, incidentally, Antonioni had the swamp sprayed with gray paint.)

In *Blow-Up,* a photographer in London is also caught amidst the sterility of modern existence. He has lost his personal sense of self and, being a mechanical extension of his camera, he uses people as objects. Except for a public park that he goes to at the start of the film and returns to at the end, this film is keyed to grays (in contrast with the green—for ''life''—that keys the scenes in the park). These grays, seen in black-and-white pho-

---

Bonnie and Clyde (1967) by Arthur Penn is a color picture about this same era, but it is more subjective and investigative. It attempts to use various effects to give the color a ''distant'' quality relating to the historical time of its action. In *Paper Moon,* on the other hand, the black-and-white photography refers partly to the ''look'' of films of that period. Black and white and color, of course, each creates its own cinema universe.

tographs, as well as in dirty streets, are frequently in contrast with lavender, red, and blue—colors that are so "pretty" that they hide the drabness of the surfaces they cover. In one shot, for instance, the camera tracks the photographer as he is driving his automobile. We see a deep red building in the background, then a very blue building, and, as the camera travels, we come upon a drab, gray-brown swamp area. This image supports the photographer's mood at the time; it also contrasts with the brighter hues of the buildings in order to emphasize their artificiality. The city indeed is sterile.

At the end of the picture, a green saturation surrounds the photographer, whom we see in extreme long shot from above. The final statement is made: Life exists, and for a brief moment the photographer has been able to communicate with others by joining them in their imagination (a tennis game without a tennis ball or racquets).

Both still and motion picture photography, through reproducing forms that exist in the world, seem at times to provide a "super reality." Yet in movies it is not so much the *imitation* of what is seen in nature as it is the stylization and formalization of the images "captured," which create the experience of events.

Imitation attempts to duplicate what exists. The problem here is that any duplication is really a reworking of those representational qualities of things that seem authentic. Such reworking *formalizes* an image; that is, it organizes it through cinematic contrivance, giving it its own filmic contour and shape as an image rather than just as action. In terms of color, this shape works to enrich the dramatic line and to dimensionalize the theme at any given point by positing recurring colors and forms as motifs.

This manipulation fashions *style,* which is the filmmaker's particular vision of the world as that world is restructured by cinematic materials.

Such restructuring directly relates the qualities of what is seen. Both black and white and color are different ways to present the surfaces of things so that, when formalized and stylized, they can help us penetrate reality to arrive at richer meanings.

Sound

Sound in narrative motion pictures is created by orchestrating several tracks of sound through any one shot, so as to balance and enlarge the visual experience and to extend it outside the frame. Sound is used for seven purposes: (1) *dialogue,* (2) *narration,* (3) *effects,* (4) *music,* (5) *environment,* (6) *presence,* and (7) *silence.*

Dialogue is the most obvious use of sound. Although dialogue traditionally has been used to provide information about events, people's thoughts, their inner motives, and so on, many filmmakers are reconsidering these theatrical uses and trying to find more cinematic ways to use it.

Many filmmakers correctly assume that motion pictures, as opposed to theater, can present information in nonverbal ways. On the stage, dialogue contains and controls the action. It is primarily from dialogue that actors interpret their roles and stage directors block and orchestrate the physical drama. Most films derived from stage plays still use dialogue as the primary device for action. In pictures not derived from the stage, dialogue is used *as a part of* the action. The differences are crucial, and may be seen in the rule to which directors as different as Hitchcock and Antonioni adhere: When you can show it, don't say it.

Dialogue, as a part of the action rather than as the initiator for it, generally is of the nature of an automatic statement or response. This suggests that talk in film can be put back into its place as a

Color in Film

A motion picture conveys sense through color just as it does through sound. Color in film can provide or enhance meaning—or it can be meaning in its own right. In Federico Fellini's *Amarcord* (1973), the theme of "memory" is reinforced by realistic-appearing images that are tinged with both fantasy and a kind of half-truth of events partially remembered and savored for their high-lights. In this film, Fellini reorganizes episodes from his 1930s boyhood in Rimini, a seacoast town. Taking its theme from the title (which is regional dialect for "I remember"), the film recreates rather than records past situations. Fellini does this by greatly compressing the past into a series of episodes running from spring of one year to spring of the next.

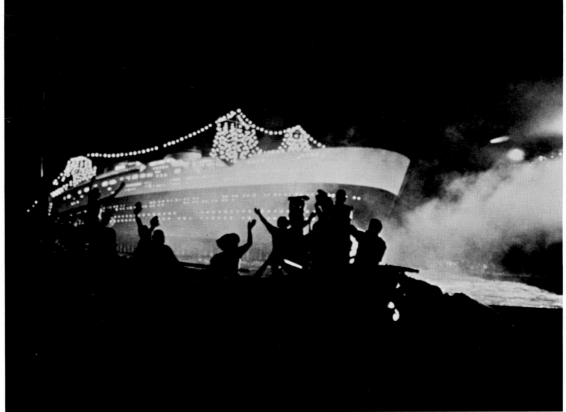

Courtesy of New World Pictures Inc.

Plate I The significance and power of a motion picture image has little to do with its duration. In this shot, almost the entire town has taken to boats and gone out to sea to observe the maiden voyage of the transoceanic liner, *Rex.* The moment is fleeting. As the ship comes into view out of the fog, we get a brief view of its magnificence—a display of power and tinsel. The ship then moves on, carrying its lights with it, illuminating the blues and purples of the sea and the night—never again to reappear.

Plate II   Signor Olivo Olivetti, the local lawyer, acts as an involved observer. Here, near the beginning of the film, he addresses the audience and tries to explain to us the temperament and times. Again it is night, and the lighted archways bring out suggestions of browns and golds. The lights break the street's spaces into fragments that carry through the street lamps running to the back of the composition. The only bright color is Olivetti's red scarf, a touch that adds distinction to his character and separates him slightly from the street he is a part of.

Plate III   Among the town's traditions is the annual high school photograph. Following the lawyer's scene —which ended with vocal derision from unseen youths—we come to the medieval courtyard for the picture-taking session. The somber black costumes, with their fringes of white, contrast with the brightness of the walls. The occasional blue and red counter this, while the flesh color of knees, hands, and faces seems to intrude on the rigid formality. The line of sight of the camera completes a triangle in depth that the contrasts between light and dark emphasize.

Plate IV Color to organize atmosphere is shown here in the town's Grand Hotel. In this epitome of elegance, the whites of the costumes, tablecloths, and chairs oppose the somber colors we remember from the town itself. Here, everything is artificial except for the flowers. Vertical and horizontal lines organize themselves around the dabs of yellow, green, red, and blue. The surfaces, as reflections of things, are more important imagistically than the things themselves. So too with the people in this environment.

Plate V Fellini frequently uses people's faces as the raw materials to create expression. In this shot, the youngsters' faces are lit, as in a Rembrandt painting, with the reds and golds from a bonfire set to celebrate the arrival of spring. All are involved in the same activity, and each one is connected to the other by the glow of the fire. Yet the lighting allows each face, through its shape and contour, to represent a distinct personality. The red costume at left draws our eye to the scene and helps to make the thematic connection with the unseen fire.

Plate VI From Walt Disney's *Fantasia* (1940). A cel is used in making animated motion pictures. It is a painting on celluloid that is placed over a background. One cel is required for each part of a movement. In this example, Disney artists have organized their colors for a most pleasing effect. Peaceful blues and soft yellows and greens provide a feeling of tranquillity. This then fills out the distinctive Disney style —a character whose shape is created through volume.

part of everyday experience. While some information can only be given through speech, little of what we say as we go through our daily lives is really significant. It is this idea with which many filmmakers are now working.

Narration gives us information or observations made by a "voice over" the picture. The voice-over narrator may be totally disengaged from the action, as in most travelogues and informational films. Or the narrator may be a character in the action remembering an event, or commenting on something happening at the moment. In *Little Big Man,* the central character is a man of one-hundred and twenty-two whose telling of his life to an interviewer becomes the visual action of the picture. Occasionally his voice enters to comment on the action. There are many other examples of the involved narrator. The totally disengaged narrator, however, is rare in narrative motion pictures.

Sound effects give authenticity to a film. They are almost always dubbed in. Imagine a summer scene with a man chopping wood in the distance and some horses tied to a post in the middle distance. The people living in the area have been waiting several days for a river boat. Suddenly, from the river unseen over a hill in the background, we hear the boat's horn. The horses whinny and the sound of wood chopping ceases. These three sound effects have enriched the action and have given it definite meaning by carrying the plot forward.

If *music* were to come up at this time, it might be a brass-dominant, fast-tempoed march, used to help sharpen the feeling of anticipation. If, on the other hand, it was bassy, using cellos and a slow tempo, the music might counterpoint the feeling of happy anticipation by *prefiguring* something tragic and unexpected.

Another use of sound is that of *artifact music.* If we followed the man chopping wood as he ran over the hill to the river boat, and the music grew louder and louder, we would expect a band to be playing either on shore or on the boat. Artifact music is music for which a source is suggested; as sound, it can be compared with the involved narrator.

Environmental sound, in this same situation, would be those noises that naturally occur in a particular setting. The sources for environmental sound do not necessarily appear in the image. In the above situation, for example, environmental sound could consist of chickens cackling, sheep bleating, the voices of children playing, and maybe the sound of a man plowing a field. Occurring as it frequently does outside the frame, environmental sound can also extend the action beyond the frame in order to give a more total experience of place.

Environmental sound outside the frame can also be effectively used with the traveling camera, as Robert Altman showed in his *McCabe and Mrs. Miller* (1971). At one point in this picture, for example, the camera dollies past tables full of people in a saloon. As we travel from one table to another, conversation at the previous table remains dominant and folds over that presently being seen. Sound here creates a more realistic physical environment.

Presence is the "feel" of a place. Acoustics are different in various physical situations. The echo quality of a small living room would be different from that of an outdoor location. A voice recorded in a sound studio, then dubbed into a character's action in the outdoors, would not have an accurate presence. Presence also includes "buzz," or the normal sound of surrounding noises, such as insects, electricity humming, or wind.

The difference between environmental sound and presence is that the former distinguishes the action for us, whereas presence is the envelope for sound in a particular setting.

Silence is a part of sound's rhythm and therefore is a part of sound itself. Silences can be very effective. If, in a scene inside a room at night with a woman fearful for her life, footsteps are heard approaching the room, then silence—that silence would create a strong emotion of fear.

Ingmar Bergman's *The Silence* (1963) creates a world of introspection, death, and neurosis by structuring silence as the film's predominant audial quality. Sound enters almost abnormally into the minimally verbal world of his characters.

Sound/Image Relationships   Sound in motion pictures is usually, but not always, synchronous. The test for synchronization is called "lip sync." This refers to the exact simultaneous relationship between the movement of the actor's lips and the words that movement creates. In this test, the direct relationship is between *sound and image.* There are other associations possible between these two.

Asynchronous sound is when the movement that produces the sound is seen barely before or after we hear that sound. In some prints of the film, this effect occurs near the beginning of *Citizen Kane* in a tight close-up of the dying Kane's lips as he says his last word, "Rosebud." The audience hears the word just briefly after the lips form it. This asynchronous effect, supported by an echo quality given the utterance, emphasizes death as "Rosebud" (which motivates the picture's action) remains alive.

Nonsynchronous sound has no direct connection with the image being shown at the time the sound is heard. It is used quite frequently to prepare us for a following shot that jumps in time and place from the previous one. For example, if in a shot of a student sitting in a classroom watching the instructor write on the blackboard, the squeaks of the chalk are erased by a jet engine noise, the next shot might show the student at an airport or on a plane. Another possibility here would be for the nonsynchronous sound to inform us of the emotional or mental quality of the student. If the student is daydreaming, the sound of a jet engine may clue us to the desire to escape this humdrum existence.

There are many other ways nonsynchronous sound may be used. However, to prepare for an action or to prefigure a cut to another time and place are two of the most common usages today.

Parallel sound has a direct thematic relationship to the image, but it does not arise from it. For example, words running through a character's mind may be spoken over the action that character is involved in. Or if one is talking about a distant place or person, that place or person may be shown as the words continue.

Contrapuntal sound opposes the image with information contrary to that seen. For example, a woman is talking about how good her father is to her. As she talks, a shot is cut in showing her father kicking her out of the house. The tension between the image and the sound would give information that would not be contained singly in either. The tendency of the movie viewer is to believe the picture rather than the sound. Thus, we would feel that the woman was lying about her father in order to rationalize her own situation.*

If we think about the use of music again, we can see that it can be used to oppose the feeling of the visual action (contrapuntal sound), to support it (parallel sound), or to be completely different from it (nonsynchronous sound). Music frequently creates a film's *emotional continuum* —the "feeling" expressed and carried forward by

---

*This description of nonsynchronous, parallel, and contrapuntal sound are based on classifications made by Siegfried Kracauer in *Theory of Film* (New York: Oxford University Press, 1965).

the action—and it is not to be underrated. It is, however, always to be carefully balanced with other sounds.

Sound in a narrative motion picture is mixed to provide balance, interest, and excitement. When sound begins to carry a picture, this often means that the visuals are not doing their job.

Acting

Acting styles in motion pictures vary from carefully blocked-out, rehearsed, and controlled performances to those that use improvisational methods. Although an actor's informed and professional performance has to be given, this is only the raw material that film uses to provide its effects. We can never excuse a substandard performance. We can, however, realize that good performances are frequently made from bad ones by editing as well as by shooting techniques.

Acting in motion pictures does not require the sustained performance of stage acting. In a narrative film, a person acts through one shot at a time, and usually through several takes of that shot. This means, for instance, that the actor must reach the same peak of excitement time after time. The actor's action might extend from a shot taken several hours or days before, or perhaps not even yet taken. Also, the actor has to play down both gesture and voice. An inadvertently raised eyebrow may in a tight close-up rise five feet on a large screen and appear grotesque. The actor in films, then, also has to know how tight the framing is. The tighter the shot, the slower and more deliberate the actor's movements have to be in order for them to be accepted as real when cut with other shots in the final picture.

Motion pictures in America are increasingly being considered a director's medium. This is a change in attitude from those days when stars were everything and the public went to the movies to share an experience with a favorite actor. To be sure, there are still actors and actresses who draw people to see them. Yet, with more types of visual entertainment available today, the story and the way it is presented also serve to attract audiences.

Each of the acting styles—the carefully rehearsed and the improvisational—has direct relationships both to camera style and to editing style. These two elements are implicit in any discussion of film acting. A good performance can be created through camera and editing techniques by means of short shots edited with one another. Consider an actor is having difficulty with a long, rambling speech that is supposed to represent an internal disorder. If the speech has to be accurately memorized, and if the actor cannot create the extended emotion through the entire speech, the camera can shoot segments of it with as many takes as is needed to make each segment workable. At the conclusion of each segment, the camera angle would probably change. When edited properly, the speech would appear sustained and would hide the cuts. Further, the variety of camera angles would imply the emotional problem that the words suggest. The performance, indeed, might seem extraordinary.

On the other hand, if an actor has to improvise within the context given above but seems unable to create and extend the emotion, two different techniques might be used. The first one probably would be infrequently used, depending upon the circumstances of lighting and the availability of equipment. This would be the use of "multicam," or multiple cameras. Two or three cameras might shoot the actor simultaneously through several takes. From the high ratio of footage available from these takes, an acceptable performance could be created.

4.14 Costumes reflect differences of personality in Federico Fellini's *Juliet of the Spirits.* The red and white in Juliet's costume (left) imply her conflict between purity and passion, and show her problem in relation to the woman next to her, whose costume reflects both superficiality and passion. (The Museum of Modern Art/Film Stills Archive. Courtesy Audio Brandon, Inc., the 16mm rental distributor in the U.S.A.)

A second way would be the use of fluid camera technique. The camera would slowly travel back and forth and around the actor through several takes. This would permit points to cut in material from the several sound and camera takes. This technique is difficult for the editor but not impossible. It may be the only way to provide sufficient visual excitement. A possible jump cut or two, along with the internal rhythms, would give the audience a sense of disorientation, which would support the emotion the scene conveys.

In the narrative film, acting style is almost always tied to camera and editing techniques. In accurately discussing acting, we should be able to understand the film techniques that significantly help to create the performance.

Costumes

Costumes usually are not considered in motion pictures other than "costume dramas." If they are, they usually are discussed in relation to decor and properties. Yet, the authenticity of costumes influences the believability and orchestration of the images and helps to define character. Just as each character in a narrative film speaks differently from other characters in order to have a distinct personal quality, so costumes have a similar function.

In a color picture, the hues contrast or synthesize with the decor and *mise-en-scène;* they also relate conflict. A woman in a frumpy white dress will appear maternal. But if that woman wears the same dress loosely over her shoulders, with her breasts suggested, the implications of her character can be quite different.

Extending this example into the *mise-en-scène,* the contrast of a white dress in a red room (as in *Cries and Whispers*), or the extension of a red dress in a white room (as in *Juliet of the Spirits*), can create our responses to the woman who wears the dress. The first case strongly suggests the conflict between passion and purity; the second suggests a submission to passion.

The amount of wear a costume has, and whether it is dirty or clean, gives us a further suggestion of character. A long-haired young man wearing a pressed pair of clean jeans and a sparkling white T-shirt shows us something about his character that would be different if the jeans were spotted with dirt and the T-shirt wrinkled with sweat.

Costumes help us better know the person who is wearing them. They aid us in understanding the psychological aspects of the story. In relation to decor, costumes also can extend our observations from the actor or actress into theme.

Most narrative motion pictures are extremely deceptive. Because they attempt to give us a heightened experience, they hide their composition and their contrivance in the action. In order to appreciate and understand the narrative film in terms of the medium that shapes that experience, we must sharpen our sense of sight. We should discover general patterns of the cinematic structuring of conflict, then support our observations with the specific cinematic methods used in the film. As in exploring any other phenomenon, we observe things, describe what we see, and order it in terms of our experience. In this way, we can go through the creative process with a motion picture and emerge from the experience richer and more knowledgeable.

Evolution of the Silent Narrative Film

5

Over eighty years ago, on December 28, 1895, at the Grand Café in Paris, a paying audience for the first time saw incredibly real, bigger-than-life photographic images move on a screen in front of them. One scene, shot from beside the railroad tracks as a train approached a station, was so real, in fact, that it caused some in the audience to jump from their seats.

In this premier program, French film innovators Auguste and Louis Lumière presented scenes that today might look like home movies. They had set up their camera at certain events and simply filmed what happened: a wall being demolished, the Lumières at home feeding their baby, workers leaving the Lumière factory.

But in these films the Lumières did more than just record events. They also saw the narrative implications of their toy. One famous scene of theirs is a small story: As a man is watering his garden, a boy, unseen, steps on the hose, stopping the flow; the man looks at the nozzle, the boy releases his foot, and the man gets a face full of water.

These first films established the possibility of movies showing a story. The Lumière brothers had seen that movement was the key to providing a lifelike representation of the world.

Opposite page: From Georges Méliès's *A Trip to the Moon.* (The Museum of Modern Art/Film Stills Archive.)

Nineteenth-century society, immersed in the challenge of the technological revolution, sometimes seemed obsessed with the idea of motion. As early as 1810, J. A. Paris helped develop a simple toy he called a *thaumatrope*. On one side of a piece of paper, he drew a bird cage; on the other side, a bird. When the paper, which was attached to a piece of string, was rapidly twirled, persistence of vision gave the illusion of seeing the bird in the cage.

After the thaumatrope, other devices were developed to show images in motion, among them the zoopraxiscope, the phenakistoscope, the zoetrope, the mutoscope, and even the "Getthemoneyscope" (which certainly anticipated the economic future of the movies).

E. J. Marey, realizing that a series of shots, made quickly one after another, would show objects in motion, developed a photogun or shotgun camera, a device that quickly exposed several negatives mounted on a circular device. An English-born American, Eadweard Muybridge, produced many scores of people and animals in motion, and his photographs are still used today for motion studies. Thomas Edison and his assistant, W. K. L. Dickson, pioneered motion with the *kinetoscope,* a machine that revolutionized people's entertainment habits, inspiring nickelodeons throughout Europe and America, machines in which, for a nickel, people could see a Hopi dance or a panorama of Chicago.

Partly because of these developments, the movies became a popular form of entertainment.

5.1 Auguste and Louis Lumière's *Workers Leaving the Factory,* a scene from one of the earliest movies, first shown to a paying audience in Paris in 1895. The factory was the Lumières' family factory. (The Museum of Modern Art/Film Stills Archive.)

5.2 One of the first examples of a film showing a story. In this 1896 Lumières' film *Watering the Garden,* a boy steps on a hose, and when the man looks to see what is wrong, the boy steps off the hose, releasing a stream of water. (The Museum of Modern Art/Film Stills Archive.)

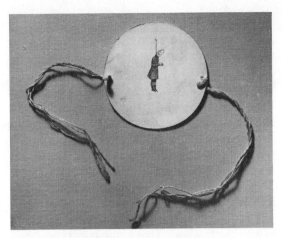 

5.3 Thaumatrope. When twirled rapidly, the man, owing to persistence of vision, appears to be hanging from the gallows. (Photos by Edwin Smith.)

5.4 Kinetoscope. A loop of fifty feet of film provided a private showing for the viewer. (Courtesy International Museum of Photography at George Eastman House.)

Movies were cheaper than most theaters. And because the camera could travel anyplace, whereas most people could not, the movies allowed people a chance to escape drab lives. They provided people speaking many languages with visual information they could all respond to similarly.

The Lumières sensed all these possibilities. Moreover, they perceived that film could present a more real view of the world than could any other form. For instance, they realized that *gesture* could create movement and hence give information. Because they saw that the film and the methods of projecting it could show things bigger and better than life, the realistic movie was born.

But "realistic" and "dream" are two sides to human experience. Realistic shows people acting in the world. The dream mode deals with fantasies, imagination, and memory. The realistic deals with people as objects in the world, and so is sometimes called *objective*. Dream mode deals with the mind and its images, and so is called *subjective*.

Georges Méliès and the Dream Mode

Georges Méliès was a French magician in the late nineteenth and early twentieth centuries who recognized the importance of the dream mode. He saw that the movies could provide the escape from reality that is created by the best magic as well as by the best theater and fiction.

He also discovered many tricks that movies could create. One day, while filming Paris traffic from the roof of a building, he momentarily stopped cranking. When he developed his film, he noticed that a bus had turned into a hearse. This effect, known as *stop motion* (at the time called the "pop on" and the "pop off"), became one of the magical devices in his movies. We see this effect in a film when we see a room full of people who instantly disappear, or an empty room in which people suddenly appear.

Méliès used this camera trick—along with fades, dissolves, superimposition, masking, reverse motion, and accelerated motion—as part of his magic show. In over a thousand films and fragmentary scenes, he showed that film had a language of its own, that it did not have to reproduce the world as it was but could create its own.

Despite these contributions, Méliès's movies most frequently looked like filmed plays. His magnificent and creative sets contained action that happened in front of the camera. He never did liberate his films from the framing that places the audience in its privileged position in a theater.

Perhaps Méliès's best-known film is his 1902 *A Trip to the Moon,* based on the Jules Verne early science fiction novel. Verne's novel provided a connected series of events to which Méliès liberally applied his imagination: scientists make a rocket; at the launch site, they are sent off by (a Méliès film standard) a bevy of young ladies; the moon (which has eyes, nose, lips, tongue) gets closer; the rocket lands like a dart on a dart board; moon people try to catch the scientists; the scientists escape by battling their antagonists, then take off in a rocket that falls off the ledge on which it sits.

Each scene is artificially arranged and is shot separately, with little interconnection. The action and the story together provide the narrative flow. The question of "What is going to happen?" projects the basic story structure.

Méliès's films dealt with the fantasy world but in an objective way. That is, the events occurred in front of the eye. It was not until 1911, with *Baron Munchausen's Dream,* that Méliès produced images that occur within the mind. But by that time such subjective fantasy had been explored by Edwin S. Porter in his 1906 *The Dream of a Rarebit Fiend.* Whereas Méliès showed the potential of the camera to build a narrative through its own resources, Porter developed the possibilities of narrative continuity by means of editing.

Film's New Narrative Possibilities

Continuity, as it developed, showed that an action could extend through more than one shot. (The word also has another meaning in movies: continuity is a shooting script designed to prevent errors of action and in placement of objects from shot to shot.) This action is frequently seen from more than one point of view. Early movies were edited by simply having one photographed scene (with no camera movement) attached to another. Since cranking speed was different with each cameraman, there was no fixed frame-rate speed,

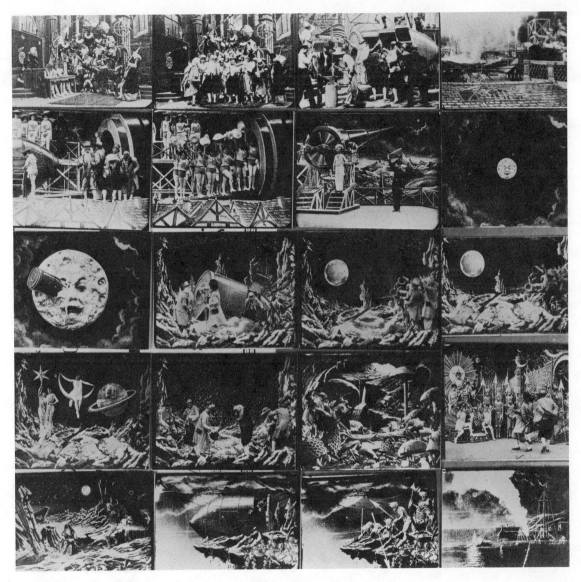

5.5 Several scenes from George Méliès's 1902 *A Trip to the Moon*. Elaborate sets were constructed to convey the fantasy quality. (The Museum of Modern Art/Film Stills Archive.)

and projectionists frequently cranked faster than cameramen, thus speeding movement.

Different frame-rate speeds (slow, normal, and accelerated motion) show us that there is not a one-to-one relationship between the duration of an original gesture and the duration of its representation on the screen. This further suggests a new use of time, one contained within the presentation of a film.

Even with simple editing, curtains did not have to drop, as in theater, to indicate scene changes. No time was wasted in moving from one action to another. The world could be shown with remarkable fidelity.

These qualities of the movie experience presented new narrative possibilities to audiences oriented to the stage or to the novel. The power of words in helping to convey sense was soon discovered. Titles were used to provide dialogue or to indicate time and place. They were also used to comment on action. By and large, however, the picture itself provided most of the information.

Edwin S. Porter and the Development of Continuity

Edwin S. Porter, who had worked for Thomas Edison, extended both the realistic and dream modes in cinema. In *The Life of an American Fireman* (1902), he constructed an exciting though elementary story. Firemen are pictured asleep; then, through the use of a dream balloon (looking like the dialogue balloon in comic strips), Porter shows a fireman dreaming of a lady caught in a fire. The alarm bell rings. The firemen drive their horse-drawn fire trucks through the streets to a house on fire. One fireman goes up to a room in which the woman and her child are trapped. A ladder is placed to the woman's window, and another fireman climbs up it. The

fireman inside hands the baby out the window to his comrade, and he rescues the woman.

Interestingly, there are two differently edited versions of this film, which probably were done by Porter. One version shows the action inside the room; the other cuts back in time and shows the arrival and placement of the ladder. In the second version, intercutting between the inside and the outside of the house shows a pattern of continuity that probably did not exist before. The action is extended through more than one shot, and the shots take place at two different locations.

The Life of an American Fireman also uses *compilation footage*—material already shot and previously used in another film and incorporated in a new film. The shots of the fireman speeding to the scene of the fire were in the Edison archives. They stimulated Porter's idea for the film. He shot the other material around them. Porter thus showed that a movie does not have to have all its shots taken originally for it.

The Great Train Robbery (1903) is considered one of the most important pictures ever made, because of the way Porter used editing techniques to advance the narrative. The film uses several different locations to show the story of a band of robbers who hold up a train and then try to escape with the loot stolen from the passengers and the baggage car. In addition, interiors are cut with exteriors to show events that occur at the same time.

Porter created excitement in a realistic fashion that audiences previously had not seen. The basic action shows this:

Two robbers enter a railroad telegraph office and compel the operator to telegraph a train that it has to take on water at this place.

Bandits sneak on the train as it is stopped.

The attendant in the baggage car loses in a shoot-out as he attempts to prevent the robbers from stealing valuables in a treasure box.

5.6 Bandits forcing the engineer to do their bidding in Edwin S. Porter's *The Great Train Robbery* (1903), the first Western. (The Museum of Modern Art/Film Stills Archive.)

At the same time, two other bandits take over the locomotive. They knock out one of the resisting engineers and throw him off.

The robbers stop the train.

They force the passengers to disembark, with hands high. (There seems to be no limit to the number of passengers as they continue to get off the train and form a line in front of the passenger car.) One of the passengers tries to escape, and he is shot down.

The robbers escape on the locomotive, which is detached from the rest of the train.

They stop the locomotive, then move down a hill and escape on horseback into the mountains.

The telegraph operator, still gagged and bound, is found by his daughter, who, after some melodramatic gestures, frees him.

In a dance hall where a square dance is going on, the robbers make a man dance by shooting bullets at his feet.

The robbers gallop off on their horses away from the dance hall, chased by a posse. Two of the robbers are shot.

The remaining robbers, thinking they have eluded the posse, dismount in a clearing and begin to divide up the loot.

The posse surrounds them, and a gunfight ensues. Some members of the posse fall dead, and all the robbers bite the dust.

The picture ends with a close-up of the leader of the robbers firing his gun into the audience. (Actually, this shot could be used to begin the picture, too, but it is most frequently seen at the end.)

This outline shows several things about the development both of narrative form and of that typically American genre, the Western.

The film builds a conflict between good and evil that relates directly to our concern with law. The realistic action draws us in by the use of suspense—making us wonder if the robbers will get away with it.

The film *shows* events that the audience can react to: the evil of the robbers, as shown by their gagging the telegraph operator; the killing of the engineer, the baggage car attendant, and a passenger; the crass violence at the dance-hall. In this film, Porter showed that cinema has the capacity to build action realistically through several scenes.

Except for the close-up of the robber firing the gun, the film is all done in long shot. Still, the locations seem real (even though this Western was shot in New Jersey); they are not contrived stage sets as in Méliès's artificially arranged scenes.

Also, the camera at a couple of points pans to follow the action, initiating the possibilities for moving camera shots in narrative pictures.

There is also the rhythm created by action extended through several different scenes, as well as a primitive use of parallel cutting. For example, the shot of the daughter freeing her father occurs presumably as the robbers are riding from the place where they picked up their horses to the dance hall. This unseen action, which would take up space and time in the movie, also functions as a cutaway.

Finally, in *The Great Train Robbery* Porter pointed up the potential of the chase, which has been frequently regarded as a dramatic form especially suited to film techniques.

Porter realized that the dream mode too is especially suited to film. Whereas the chase is

The Films of the Lumières, Méliès, and Porter

These filmmakers extended the form of the narrative cinema in ten ways. They showed us:

1. that events could be shown in "real" locations;
2. that locations could be reproduced with remarkable fidelity;
3. that camera angle (as in the Lumières' scene of a train coming into the station) could help create the force of an action represented;
4. that the camera could create events (objective fantasy) as well as simply record them;
5. that conflict and suspense could be built by ordering events through time;
6. that one shot cut with another could create an extended story line;
7. that camera movement could help create events by breaking the conventionally static frame line;

8. that techniques intrinsic to film itself could help create a unique, yet acceptable, way of viewing the world (through dissolves, superimposition, fades, masking, and others);
9. that the form of the chase was uniquely suited to cinema;
10. that the images on the screen could be accepted as being close to those that can occur in imagination, fantasy, dream, and memory (subjective fantasy).

All these ideas point to the evolution of a *film language*. That is, as images were designed through film techniques, audiences grasped them to mean certain things. For example, a cut to another place, then back to main characters situated differently from when we last saw them, shows us that time has passed. It may also show us that certain places that have not been seen have already been traveled over.

5.7 The nightmare floating episode of an ale and Welsh-rarebit lover, in Edwin S. Porter's
The Dream of a Rarebit Fiend (1906), one of the early uses of film for subjective fantasy.
(The Museum of Modern Art/Film Stills Archive.)

defined by physical action, dreams are, of course, internal action—those images that our minds create. In *The Dream of a Rarebit Fiend* (1906) Porter showed the story of a man who loves to drink ale and eat Welsh rarebit—a film that revealed the possibilities of subjective fantasy.

The film begins by showing the central character eating and drinking too much. He then goes home and falls asleep in bed, and Porter shows the ale and the rarebit going to work on his mind: A chair and table disappear. A huge dish of rarebit steams from his head. Three devils jump out of the dish and beat him around the ears. The film then cuts to shots that are the man's nightmare: He floats through the sky, gripping the bed posts, until finally he falls through the

5.8 Mother hears the line go dead as thugs breaking into the house cut the phone wires, in the D. W. Griffith short film *The Lonely Villa* (1909). (Reproduced from the collection of the Library of Congress.)

roof of the house and back into bed. He awakes and understands that he has had a nightmare. The important technique that this film developed, then, was that of a direct cut to the inside of a person's mind. This transition could be accepted by the audience if it was set up properly.

D. W. Griffith: Originator of Modern Techniques

American filmmaker David Wark Griffith is generally considered to have advanced narrative film language into its modern use. His principal contributions are three: (1) He developed to an art the use of parallel action. (2) He broke away from the conventional long shot and developed master scene technique. (3) He refined and shaped the use of *point of view* in narrative films.

Parallel Action

Parallel action (also called cross-cutting, parallel editing, parallel cutting, parallel montage) shows two or more simultaneous events, one after the other. Griffith, who saw its possibilities early in his career, developed this editing device to such a degree that it became known as the "Griffith last-minute rescue." Let us consider two of his early short films as examples.

In *The Lonely Villa* (1909), a man leaves his wife and two daughters alone in the house while he travels to the nearby town. We are shown two thugs waiting for him to leave. After he departs, one of them cuts the telephone wires, and they break into his house. As they proceed through the house, the mother and daughters retreat into room after room. The father in town, trying to phone his family to check on them, hears the wire

5.9 Blanche Sweet playing woman frantically tapping for help as bandits break into the isolated telegraph office, in D. W. Griffith's *The Lonedale Operator* (1911). (The Museum of Modern Art/Film Stills Archive.)

cut just as he is talking to his wife. He rushes to his car, but it won't start, and so he and his friends frantically gallop home in a horse-drawn vehicle. Meanwhile the thugs are getting ever closer to the ladies, and we see them breaking down doors and entering rooms. These shots are intercut with the father riding madly. Finally, of course, the father and his friends arrive "just in the nick of time," and we can breathe a sigh of relief.

In *The Lonedale Operator* (1911), a young woman says goodbye to her boyfriend, a locomotive engineer, and he leaves in his train. The woman locks herself in the telegraph room of an isolated station house. Bandits arrive and force their way into the outer office, then into the inner office. As they are breaking in, the woman desperately telegraphs her trouble. The engineer rushes back on his train, and the shots of his hurried return are intercut with shots of the ban-

dits getting closer to her. Finally, they break in, but the woman holds them back with what looks like a pistol. Ultimately, the engineer and other help arrive, and a tight close-up shows us that the "pistol" is really a wrench. All but the bandits laugh at this deception.

Griffith's use of parallel action points up two important things: (1) Great excitement can be created by the rhythms produced by gradually shortening the shots as they move to the climax. (In fact, in the exciting last-minute rescue that ends *The Birth of a Nation,* Griffith built suspense by actually counting the number of frames in each shot.) (2) Parallel action places the cutaway as a part of the ongoing events of the film. Because it eliminates space and creates action, it advances the visual narrative.

Griffith further extended parallel editing in *Intolerance* (1916), one of the most ambitious

5.10 Two scenes from *Intolerance,* the 1916 film by the master of spectacle, D. W. Griffith. The picture, which was way ahead of its time, intercut scenes from four historical periods to express the theme of intolerance of man to man. *Top:* A scene from the fall of Babylon. *Bottom:* A scene from a modern story of social injustice, in which a man is being erroneously arrested. (The Museum of Modern Art/Film Stills Archive.)

and original features made. *Intolerance* intercuts four separate stories from four different time periods: (1) the fall of Babylon, (2) the reaction of the Pharisees against Christ, (3) the French Catholic slaughter of the Huguenots, and (4) a modern story of social injustice.

In this film, the theme of which is that intolerance continues throughout the ages, Griffith did not simply present one story after another. He cut episodes from one story with episodes from another, offering only the brief transitions of titles and/or a shot of a woman rocking a cradle—an image based upon Walt Whitman's line, "Out of the cradle endlessly rocking." This was given once in titles, and it indicated that human progress toward civilization has not been morally productive.

This advance in parallel cutting—toward creating large episodes tied together thematically rather than by action alone—was way ahead of its time. It was also way ahead of its audience, and the picture failed because viewers found it difficult to follow and because World War I suddenly made the theme of intolerance unpopular.

Intolerance remains one of the most important pictures of film history, and was crucial in the further development of film technique in Russia. It proposed through its form that motion pictures could explore a theme from several different historical perspectives through several different stories. And it showed that cinema had the potential to do this because it could manipulate time and space through editing.

Master Scene Technique

We can observe Griffith's evolution of master scene technique through the importance he gave to the close-up. The close-up was not new to Griffith, but he discovered its potential for conveying specific information and for stressing a point. In *The Lonedale Operator,* as we saw, the close-up was used to provide information that the pistol was really a wrench. In subsequent films, Griffith cut in close-ups at particularly dramatic moments, and alternated them with medium shots and long shots.

This technique opposed the standard method in which everything was seen in long shot. By breaking consecutive action up into several shots, Griffith turned the dramatic possibilities of film away from theater and toward cinema.

In *Intolerance,* Griffith used the close-up to show the result of action. For example, a Persian is shown shooting an arrow. Then there is a cut to a close-up of a Babylonian falling to the ground with an arrow in his chest. In *The Birth of a Nation,* he combined a modified master scene technique with parallel action by cutting a close-up of assassin John Wilkes Booth into the sequence of President Lincoln at his box in the Ford theater.

Through master scene technique, Griffith was able to control the emotion he wanted the actions to portray. He used fade-ins and fade-outs, irises-in and irises-out as transitional devices, and he established the language for them. He discovered that there were many possible camera angles from which to view events. He saw that the camera could record just parts of events and that the editor then could put these separate shots together to give the effect of continuous action.

Point of View

Closely associated with Griffith's evolution of master scene technique is his use of point of view. He further evolved the technique wherein the camera can not only look at events objectively, but it can also assume the eyes of any one of the characters. In *The Lonedale Operator,* for instance, the audience participated with the ban-

5.11 Master scene technique in *The Birth of a Nation* (1915) shows the progression of single events through several shots. (The Museum of Modern Art/Film Stills Archive.)

dits in discovering that the pistol was a wrench. That is, two points of view were combined.

When filmmakers generally held the camera at a distance, the audience could observe only. In most cases, in the scene in long shot, the action was played at the back of the "plane," as if there were a stage apron in front of it, and the audience saw everything from the same distance. The medium shot and the close-up broke through these planes, and the audience, now feeling itself to be right next to the action, could be more involved with it. One result was the development of *film space:* the viewer now could look at objects that were separated from their immediate physical surroundings.

Such isolation, we are told, was jarring at first. When audiences saw a face suspended on the screen in front of them, bigger than life, they panicked or tittered. Very quickly, however, the convention was accepted. Griffith succeeded in accomplishing his rationale: "The task I am trying to achieve is, above all, to make you see."

Within the context of point of view, Griffith also used the flashback (he called this device the "switchback"), as well as the flashforward. For instance, the projection of the future at the end of *Intolerance*—peaceful earth after the millennium—suggests an extension of the Christian ethic into a future where all men will be brothers. Griffith's use of the flashback and the flashforward showed that motion pictures did not have to adhere to ordinary conventions of time and space. Through editing, movies could be freed from these restrictions. The creative opportunities implied by this fact are still being explored by filmmakers.

Another Griffith contribution to the narrative was his use of titles. The drawback of titles is that they can interrupt a visual progression; they can state the obvious, and they can be a verbal intrusion into events given visually. Griffith used his titles to explore the meaning of the events shown. Frequently, these explorations editorialized in the worst propaganda sense—indeed, a good

part of the negative audience reaction to *The Birth of a Nation* was because the titles gave approval to many Ku Klux Klan activities. Still, Griffith used titles as extensions of the images, giving them a poetic dimension. A famous example in *The Birth of a Nation* is within a shot of piles of dead bodies after the waste of a battle. The title "War's peace" accurately extends the feeling the images convey.

Griffith was not the first to use the close-up, the medium shot, fade-ins, and fade-outs, but he rediscovered them and created a special cinematic language from them. His contributions were enormous. He pointed up through his many pictures the narrative possibilities unique to the motion picture medium. He created the form of the "spectacle." For *Intolerance,* he built some of the most gigantic sets ever made, and he used a cast literally of thousands. The world and all of history were his materials, and the camera and the editing table were his tools.

Kuleshov, Eisenstein, and Montage

After the 1917 Revolution, the government of the Soviet Union had little money to spend on such rare commodities as film stock, lighting equipment, and cameras. Yet Lenin had declared motion pictures to be a main propaganda tool for Communism.

The potential filmmakers that gathered in Moscow around Lev Kuleshov had little equipment or film, and so they screened, examined, and criticized movies and developed their own theories about the possibilities of narrative pictures.

D. W. Griffith's *Intolerance* was screened so often that their print literally disintegrated. Kuleshov and Sergei Eisenstein, among others, were particularly enthusiastic about the implications of Griffith's editing techniques but felt that he had not explored the real potential of cutting together shots of different contents. Out of this interest came considerable theorizing about the possibilities of *montage*.

Kuleshov's Experiments

Kuleshov performed several experiments that influenced the creation of narrative films by editing.

In one experiment, he showed that emotion can be created from materials that, individually, do not express that emotion. He took shots of the actor Ivan Ilyitch Mozhukin, in which his facial expression was noncommittal, and edited them against shots of (1) a plate of hot steaming soup, (2) a dead woman's body in a coffin, and (3) a little girl playing with a teddy bear. Audiences viewing the result praised the actor's ability. Through his face alone, they said, he expressed the emotions of hunger, sadness, and joy. Of course, these emotions were created by editing, not acting.

In a second experiment, Kuleshov showed (1) a man walking from the left, (2) a woman walking from the right, (3) the two meeting and shaking hands (after all, this was Russia in the 1920s), (4) a long shot of a building, (5) the couple ascending some stairs. In this experiment, each shot was taken quite a distance from each of the other shots. The building, in fact, was the White House, in Washington, D.C. An important point was established here by Kuleshov: a scene could be created from shots taken in entirely separate geographical locations. When edited together, a new place would arise. Cinema could create places that do not really exist.* This technique became known as *creative geography*.

---

*D. W. Griffith knew this, too: In his 1919 film *Way Down East,* which was mainly shot in New England, he cut shots of New York's Niagara Falls into the rescue of the heroine floating helplessly on a sheet of ice in a river, the hero coming after her, and the falls menacing ahead.

Extending this idea, Kuleshov showed, in a third experiment, that he could create people who do not exist in reality. He took several shots of different parts of the bodies of different women. When edited together, a new woman emerged.

Creative geography is used all the time in motion pictures. For instance, people can be shown in one shot going up the side of a hill by a river. The next shot can show them descending from a hill down into a valley. The actual place of the valley may in reality be some distance from the river. Through creative geography, the movie has placed the valley just over the hill from the river. A new space has been created.

Sergei Eisenstein

The theories, experiments, and practices that emerged from Russia during this time are defined by the word *montage*. The most influential theoretician and director who built his films on montage was Sergei Eisenstein.

The basis of montage is *conflict*. The conflict created between different types of shots cut one with another provides new information—something not contained in either of the shots. The general philosophic system that underlies this is called the *dialectic*. The dialectical form poses something (the *thesis*) against its opposite (the *antithesis*) to produce something not contained in either of them (the *synthesis*). By means of montage, films are built by the collision of shots, rather than strung out in simple sequential order.

In his book *Film Form,* Eisenstein explains montage in reference to the Japanese poetic form, the Haiku.

> An evening breeze blows
>   The water ripples
>   Against the blue heron's legs.

5.12 Rhythmic montage within the frame in *The Battleship Potemkin.* The townspeople of Odessa move to the shore to greet the *Potemkin*'s crew. (The Museum of Modern Art/ Film Stills Archive.)

According to Eisenstein, "these are montage phrases. Shot lists. The simple combination of two or three details of a material kind yields a perfectly finished representation of another kind —psychological." *

The effect of conflict, then, is an emotional response to the juxtaposition of shots. There are five basic techniques of montage.

Metric montage creates its effects by alternating the lengths of film in each shot. The temporal rhythm formed by this conflict can assert specific physical responses. For example, in the famous "Odessa Steps" sequence in Eisenstein's *The Battleship Potemkin* (1925), the shots get shorter and shorter, then oppose longer shots, as the massacre ensues.

Rhythmic montage is structured by conflicting movement in the frame, as in the scene in *The Battleship Potemkin* of two streams of people moving in different directions.

Tonal montage opposes the qualities of shots by contrasting visual expression. For example, low-key lighting and a static camera would express sadness. A scene so composed could conflict with a scene that has high-key lighting and camera movement. A new feeling would be provoked by the juxtaposition—one of irony, perhaps.

Overtonal montage provokes feelings beyond what is shown. These feelings carry over into other scenes and can conflict with others. For example, a feeling of sadness might extend through several scenes and be mixed with a feeling of joy. The two would then help us understand the thematic progression of events. At the beginning of the "Odessa Steps" sequence in

---

*Sergei Eisenstein, *Film Form and the Film Sense*, trans. Jay Leyda (Cleveland and New York: World, 1957), pp. 31–32.

The Battleship Potemkin, joy is created by the action of the townspeople. This tone carries over several scenes until the title *Suddenly,* which begins the massacre by the Cossacks. The tone of terror intermixes with joy and becomes dominant. The two tones extend their sense over the total events of the sequence.

Graphic montage emerges from the various compositional possibilities Eisenstein espouses.

An example would be where two predominant linear structures conflict with one another in different shots, and then are synthesized in a third shot. That is, one scene might show a vertical line, the next scene a horizontal line, and the third scene a cross. Or a high camera angle might be opposed to a low camera angle to produce different graphic values. The possibilities for using montage are infinite. Montage can break up an

5.13 "Odessa Steps" sequence in *The Battleship Potemkin* (continued on next page). (The Museum of Modern Art/Film Stills Archive.)

action to slow down time. It can create movement that does not exist in the objects photographed. For instance, in *The Battleship Potemkin,* shots of three stone lions—one at rest, one arising, and one alert—are cut together to show the lion "reacting" to the battleship firing on the town during the massacre. Today, any juxtaposition of short shots to build an emotion is called montage.

Eisenstein saw montage as the essence of motion pictures and used montage intellectually to build his many films. In his last important work, *Ivan the Terrible* (1943–46), he used color opposite black and white. He also wrote about and experimented with counterpoint between sound and image.

A colleague, V. I. Pudovkin, was sometimes at odds with Eisenstein's ideas of the "collision of

"Odessa Steps" sequence (continued).

shots." Instead, he saw the possibilities for montage in *associative editing* (sometimes called relational editing), or *linkage*. Here, the shots would extend ideas through similarities rather than through conflict of line, action, and movement.

The evolution of narrative film technique reached a high point with the work done by Eisenstein and the other Russians. The idea of montage that grows from Griffith's use of parallel action is to build, through editing, rhythms that give the feeling of the action.

The use of montage created unprecedented experiences for movie goers in the 1920s, and its effects are still felt today in films that use the technique to create emotion and build suspense.

Carl Mayer, the Fluid Camera, and Decor and Lighting

In the 1920s, the narrative technique of fluid camera movement was further developed in Germany. Although Griffith and the Russians used the dramatic possibilities of both decor and lighting, it was also in Germany that significant advances were made in these techniques.

Fluid Camera

Carl Mayer, who had coauthored the script for *The Cabinet of Dr. Caligari* (Robert Wiene, 1919), is directly responsible for initiating fluid camera technique. That he is known as a scriptwriter does not do justice to his contributions. The great detail of his scripts often required the director and cameraman to use unfamiliar techniques. His friend the cinematographer Karl Freund said that "a script by Carl Mayer was already a film."[*]

Moving camera shots had existed for some time. *The Great Train Robbery* has two pan shots: one follows the bandits down off the train engine and the other follows them through the woods. In *The Battleship Potemkin*, a camera trolley was built the length of the Odessa Steps

---

[*]Karl Freund, "A Film Artist," in Paul Rotha and Richard Griffith, *The Film Till Now*, rev. ed. (London: Spring Books, 1967), p. 716.

5.14 In *The Cabinet of Dr. Caligari* exaggerated lighting makes Caligari (Werner Krauss) seem distorted and mad, reflecting the paranoia of Francis, the teller of the tale. (The Museum of Modern Art/Film Stills Archive.)

to provide tracking shots during the massacre scene. Eisenstein even strapped a camera to an acrobat, who, by jumping around, provided shots that, by their erratic movement, helped to convey chaos. But it was not until Carl Mayer that the moving camera became used as an extended narrative technique.

Montage can show events. The documentary-like quality of Eisenstein's early pictures— *Strike* (1924), *The Battleship Potemkin,* and *October* (1928)—seem particularly appropriate for montage.

Fluid camera technique was developed in F. W. Murnau's *The Last Laugh* (1924), scripted by Mayer. This film is primarily a narrative of character, rather than of events. As we indicated earlier, *The Last Laugh* is about an elderly man (played by Emil Jannings) employed by the prestigious Atlantic Hotel who is demoted from doorman to lavatory attendant. Just when we think he has hit bottom in life, a wealthy American dies in his presence. At this point, through the film's only title, events turn about. The dead man has willed his fortune to the last person he talks to. The old man thus returns to the Atlantic and has the last laugh on the hotel by enjoying a huge feast in the dining room.

While planning the production, Mayer asked cinematographer Freund if there were a way to go in one shot from a medium view of a person to a close-up of that person's eyes. Freund suggested that the camera would probably have to be mounted on a "wheeled platform of some sort." Sensing the potential of the camera moving dynamically through space, Mayer rewrote the script to include several of these "dolly" shots.

For instance, in one scene, in which the doorman is supposed to be drunk, the camera was made to assume his point of view and was whirled around the room, with grease on the lens to help create distortion. In the morning, after his drunken spree, a horn player in the courtyard outside his apartment serenades the old man. The camera quickly moves from the horn, out away from it, giving us a visual expression of its sound. In doing this, the camera suggests the irritating noise of the music in the old man's head.

Whereas Eisenstein created rhythms by editing together separate shots, Mayer used fluid camera technique to provide rhythms within a shot. For example, in another *Last Laugh* scene (through the technique of an "invisible" dissolve of one moving camera shot identically picked up where the other ended), we are allowed to read a letter with the doorman as he stands in the office of his boss. We view the scene from outside a glass partition. As the doorman puts on his glasses and brings the letter up to read, the camera dollies toward him, "through" the glass and into a close-up. The film then cuts to a close-up of the letter, letting us read it, as it were, over his shoulder.

The discovery shot is well-suited to fluid camera technique. As we stated, the final *Last Laugh* sequence opens with a long traveling shot that moves past tables of people eating, travels right, then dollies toward a table piled with food, where we discover that the person seated there is the old man. Thus, fluid camera gives us the feeling of space by moving within it, as opposed to montage or to master scene technique in which space is constructed through editing.

Decor and Lighting

Space in movies has to be set and controlled. Studio stage shooting, which allows greater lighting control, emerged in Germany in the 1910s, and *The Cabinet of Dr. Caligari* was possibly the first full-length picture shot entirely this way.

Caligari uses Expressionistic sets and very little camera movement. The central part of the film is a paranoid fantasy told by the character, Francis, who is an inmate of a mental institution (a fact we do not learn until the end of the film). As the story issues from a distorted mind, so the images are distorted by the use of painted sets, weird costumes, unusual spatial relationships among characters and props, and exaggerated makeup and unusual lighting. These distortions add a strong psychological element to the story, something the Germans were to continue to express through the twenties.

Decor and lighting are important techniques to penetrate a person's actions to discover motivations. In *The Last Laugh,* shadows become a part

5.15 *The Last Laugh* shows effective use of exterior and interior lighting (all done in stage studio). *Top:* The old man proudly wears his uniform home, gathering the admiration of his neighbors. *Bottom:* After being demoted to lavatory attendant, he is in the darkness, alone in his new uniform, depressed and hidden in the washroom. (The Museum of Modern Art/Film Stills Archive.)

of the decor and are used as an extension of the main character. Light and dark are also combined in realistic sets of both exteriors and interiors.

The film does not try to examine the reasons for the old man's feelings so much as try to assert them. For example, the doorman's uniform is a status symbol, and because he does not want either his wife or daughter to know that he has been demoted, he steals a uniform and wears it home to his daughter's wedding. As he walks into a courtyard on the way home, his shadow precedes him around a corner of a building. It is straight and strong, and is indicative of his pride. Later, in the depths of the lavatory, when he is wearing his white attendant's jacket, the false light of the place throws harsh shadows into the corners. The decor includes mirrors above the washroom's sinks, and the old man is seen through these, his stooped posture a reflection to himself of his despair. Although his emotions are shown through distortion, they are not imposed on the subject. Rather, they emerge from and blend with it.

Von Stroheim, Chaplin, and Keaton

In the United States, narrative technique was extended during the twenties by means of acting as well as by camera techniques. These can be seen in certain films of von Stroheim, Chaplin, and Keaton.

In *Greed* (1923), Austrian-born filmmaker Erich von Stroheim transferred to the screen the style of Frank Norris's naturalistic novel *McTeague,* about growing paranoia between a dentist and his wife. *Greed* is a huge picture, seen by some in its ten-hour entirety (and never again viewed that way because the film was edited down and much of the footage destroyed). The novel's ability to describe in detail the gradual erosion of the human personality was carefully transcribed by von Stroheim. Real locations were used, both in San Francisco and in Death Valley (where the production company came close to perishing in the desert heat).

Although many other pictures had been made from novels, *Greed* showed that cinema could sustain a long narrative. Using image equivalents for novelistic description, the film builds up over hours, rather than minutes, events that absorb the narrative. Details of the novel were so faithfully transcribed by von Stroheim that total immersion must have been experienced by those who saw the complete film.

The 1920s in American film history are called by some the Age of Comedy. Although comedies were not the only silent films made, Charles Chaplin, Buster Keaton, Laurel and Hardy and others helped to increase the popularity of the medium. They also extended acting and directing techniques in their films. Chaplin in particular had the ability to convey pathos—that combination of the comic and tragic—within his characterization of the Tramp.

When actors take "center screen," decor, atmosphere, composition, camera movement, and editing are influenced by their action. As writer, director, and star, Chaplin, in such a picture as *The Gold Rush* (1925), was able to create an extended narrative from his use of *gesture*. Gesture builds a movie from the physical movements of characters. Whereas stage drama extends from dialogue, movies extend their narrative from gesture.

Gesture is made up of both mime and body movement. Mime occurs on stage and is exaggerated so that the audience, usually sitting some distance from the performer, can observe it. But

5.16 ZaSu Pitts, as Tina in *Greed,* slowly destroys herself by her passion. (The Museum of Modern Art/Film Stills Archive. Courtesy Metro-Goldwyn-Mayer Inc. From the MGM release *Greed* © 1925 Metro-Goldwyn Pictures Corporation. © renewed 1952 Loew's Incorporated.)

as subtle as stage mime can be, it can rarely be as informative of character as body movement on the screen. The movies, through the close-up and the medium shot, can bring us very close to the character. Hence, a small gesture, such as the lifting of an eyebrow, the movement of a foot, or a slight turn of the torso, can create much meaning.

Chaplin mastered film movement. As the Little Tramp, he created a character the lower-class audiences, many of them immigrants, could identify with. In film after film, he showed the Tramp was an inferior being trying to achieve status and love. And in film after film, he won his audiences by asserting his humanity.

In *Easy Street* (1916), the Tramp became a cop. In his attempt to overcome the brute strength of the Boss of Easy Street, the Tramp relied on fate and on the little man's good luck. The Tramp fumbled his way into the chaos of Easy Street and

5.17 At the end of *The Tramp* (1915), Charles Chaplin shows pathos, resignation, and hope through his characteristic walk and costume. (The Museum of Modern Art/Film Stills Archive.)

survived because of his agility and his refusal to be overcome by brute force.

The Gold Rush is set in the freezing Klondike, where each man is on his own and the single woman is drawn to the strong and good-looking. The Tramp falls in love with Georgia, a dance-hall girl. In one scene in the dance hall, he sees Georgia motioning to him. He gestures unbelievingly to himself, "Me?", then discovers that Georgia is calling to a man behind him. In another scene, where the Tramp and Georgia are dancing, Chaplin gets tangled in a dog leash that he has used to hold up his pants, and the dog follows him around the dance floor. The subtlety of his movement and the creation of pathos by gesture shows us the confusion, despair, and hope of a man too ordinary to be loved. At the film's end, Georgia, also on the boat leaving the Klondike, sees him and they declare their love for each

other. But in that America, love was not enough: Georgia is also won over because the Tramp has become a multimillionaire through his luck with a gold claim. Still, it was a happy ending (these endings may have been influenced by *The Last Laugh,* which was very popular at the time). And Chaplin seems to be saying that if we persevere, if we endure and overcome our handicaps, then the rewards will be there. For the many people who thrived on these films, such resolutions were satisfying.

Chaplin showed that film narrative could be built from character and that the individuality of that character could be built from gesture. In one scene in *The Gold Rush* Chaplin has prepared a New Year's Eve party for the dance-hall girls, but no one shows up, and he falls asleep at the table and dreams of performing for them. He creates a dance, "The Oceana Roll," with biscuits at the

5.18 In *Easy Street* Chaplin uses his ingenuity to overcome brute force. (The Museum of Modern Art/Film Stills Archive.)

end of two forks. In another scene, he and a friend, isolated in a cabin, have no food for Thanksgiving, and so Chaplin cooks a boot, eating the leather and twirling the bootlaces like spaghetti.

As we mentioned, the chase is especially suited to cinema, and Chaplin, the Keystone Kops, Harold Lloyd, Laurel and Hardy, and most comedy film actors of the time used the form with many variations. But perhaps it was Buster Keaton who brought the silent comedy chase to perfection. Like Chaplin, Keaton ("The Great Stoneface") often played a man caught up in circumstances seemingly beyond his control. Frequently, as in *Cops* (1922), they were imposed on him by the accident of his being somewhere at the wrong time.

In his films, Keaton played a person not unlike his viewers. Entangled in a web of events, his deliberate attempts to organize circumstances in order to extricate himself borders on the heroic. This is shown in *The General* (1927), in which Keaton plays Johnny Gray, a man with two loves —his girl and his locomotive named The General. When the Civil War breaks out, he volunteers for the Confederacy. The recruiter declares that Johnny is too valuable to the South as a locomotive engineer. Later, complications occur: The General, with the girl aboard, is stolen by the Yankees. Johnny follows in another locomotive. This chase, which occupies over half the film, is brilliant in its invention. One event after another accumulates to show Johnny's frustration and determination.

With all tricks seeming to have been used, a new chase begins. Keaton, now in The General with the girl in tow, heads back to Rebel territory. In this chase, he plays his comedy off his girl.

5.19 Gesture structures action in *The Gold Rush*. Isolated in a cabin in the Klondike without food for Thanksgiving, Chaplin makes a meal from an old boot. He twirls a bootlace as spaghetti and offers his partner (unseen) a boot nail as a wishbone. (The Museum of Modern Art/Film Stills Archive.)

5.20 In *The General* (1927) Buster Keaton (playing Johnny Gray) chases his locomotive, The General, with another train. At one point, he attempts to fire a cannon at the Northerners he is pursuing. (The Museum of Modern Art/Film Stills Archive.)

5.21 Buster Keaton, in *Cops* (1922), caught up in circumstances beyond his control. (The Museum of Modern Art/Film Stills Archive.)

5.22 *Two Tars* (1927), with Laurel and Hardy, in the traffic jam, on the verge of total destruction. (The Museum of Modern Art/Film Stills Archive.)

Although her characterization today stereotypes the "stupid female" at her worst, the young woman does play an important role in the film: She complicates Johnny's actions and throws their mutual safety into jeopardy.

The *time of the events* in this picaresque film is created visually by the train moving as well as by the events drawn on the dramatic line. *Timing* helps these events project the chronology of the film. The length of each shot is determined by the action that happens in it, and this action is supported by the objects that help to create it. For example, on the way back home, Johnny Gray and the girl stop for firewood. He tries to throw the wood onto the train, but he throws it too far; the wood teeters on the train, then falls off. He runs to the other side of the train, throws the wood up, mistakenly starts to run to the front of the train, then runs to the wood source again. All this action is enclosed in the larger time line, for they are being chased. The timing of the actions in relation to objects (the wood and the train) creates the gesture that extends the narrative.

Through film history, the use of objects to create action becomes significantly more important. Chaplin's cane, Keaton's pieces of wood—each creates both character and action. The movies use objects uniquely, one reason being that through photography they are easily recognizable.

Stan Laurel and Oliver Hardy were particularly adept at creating comedy from objects. In *Two Tars* (1927), for instance, they play two sailors caught in a traffic jam. As arguments develop between Laurel and Hardy and the other drivers, the comedy is created by the destruction of things: motorcycles, cars, parts of cars, hats, and more.

The silent comedy of the twenties in America showed that character through gesture can uniquely create movie action. By extending the form of the chase and showing action through character involvement with *things,* they helped to increase the dramatic power of the moving image.

Then came sound to complicate all this and, eventually, to make the narrative film even richer.

Josef von Sternberg, *Blonde Venus* (1932). (The Museum of Modern Art/Film Stills Archive. Courtesy of Universal Pictures.)

John Ford, *Stagecoach* (1939). (The Museum of Modern Art/Film Stills Archive.)

Michelangelo Antonioni, *L'Avventura* (1959). (The Museum of Modern Art/Film Stills Archive. Courtesy of Janus Films.)

Alain Resnais, *Last Year at Marienbad* (1961). (The Museum of Modern Art/Film Stills Archive. Courtesy Audio Brandon Films, Inc., the 16mm rental distributor in the U.S.A.)

Akira Kurosawa, *Yojimbo* (1961).
(The Museum of Modern Art/Film
Stills Archive. Courtesy Audio Brandon Films, Inc., the 16mm rental
distributor in the U.S.A.)

Ingmar Bergman, *The Silence* (1963).
(The Museum of Modern Art/Film
Stills Archive. Courtesy of Janus
Films.)

Michelangelo Antonioni, *The Red Desert* (1964). (The Museum of Modern Art/Film Stills Archive. Courtesy Audio Brandon Films, Inc., the 16mm rental distributor in the U.S.A.)

Jean-Luc Godard, *Two or Three Things I Knew about Her* (1966). (The Museum of Modern Art/Film Stills Archive. Courtesy New Yorker Films.)

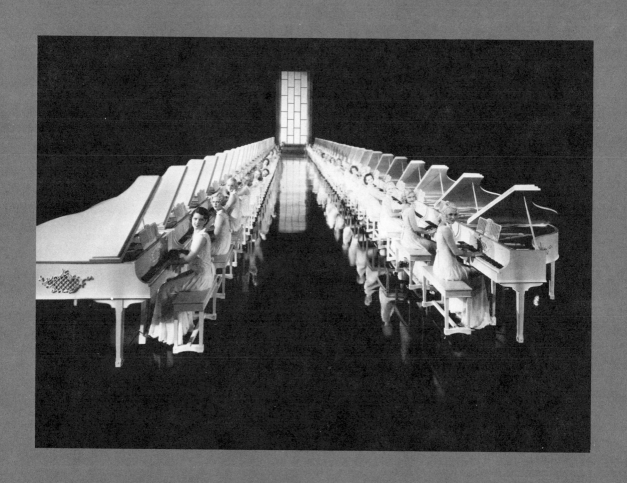

Evolution of the Sound Narrative Film

6

Sound was not new to movie goers, but the use of lip-synchronized dialogue was. In 1927, the sound motion picture was born when Al Jolson, in *The Jazz Singer,* spoke a few lines and sang several songs through the magic of the screen.

Yet, the new freedom that sound provided was not explored immediately. Sound was new, and people had to consider its uses very carefully.

Early Sound Films

The first all-dialogue "talky," *The Lights of New York* (1928), showed that the camera movement of the silent era was being placed second to sound in six ways.

1. Dialogue assumed the burden of the action. The result was an overuse of the audial so that the pictures seemed only to support the words. Movies were thrust back into stage drama.

2. To cover cameras so that the microphones would not pick up their noise, the cameras had to remain more or less stationary. A pan or tilt shot was about all the movement these early sound movies showed.

Opposite page: From *Gold Diggers of 1935.* © First National Pictures Inc. 1935. Copyright renewed 1962. Courtesy United Artists Television. (The Museum of Modern Art/Film Stills Archive.)

3. The spoken word replaced gesture as a defining quality of character.

4. Film's ability to show "real" places through location shooting was severely limited. Movies were placed back into the studio. However, this eventually resulted in some of the most creative uses of studio shooting since the German cinema of the 1920s. Space was limited yet ironically redefined through studio shooting. Controlled lighting, for instance, so importantly extended by the Germans, became a defining quality of many motion pictures. The use of soft focus (or a transparent cloth over the camera lens) combined with back-lighting and soft side-lighting defined "feminine beauty." Among the most expert directors to do this was Josef von Sternberg.

5. The so-called producers' system standardized movies. Every detail of a film—its script, its production, and its editing—was controlled by one individual called a producer. The way films looked and their mass-audience appeal evolved specific standards that industry movies had to meet. For instance, producer Irving Thalberg, who at age twenty-five became a vice-president at MGM, stringently supervised and controlled productions. Under his iron control, writer and director became little more than extensions of the producer's will.

6. Through this period in America, two general types of narratives emerged: the story that incorporated fantasy, and the highly realistic, theatrical story. The fantasy story can be seen in the musical; the realistic story can be seen in the

6.1 Marlene Dietrich in Josef von Sternberg's *Blonde Venus* (1932); here beauty is shown through soft focus and side lighting. (The Museum of Modern Art/Film Stills Archive. Courtesy of Universal Pictures.)

Western and the gangster film. Through these we can observe the expansion of both sound and visual techniques in the thirties and early forties.

Uses of Music

The Jazz Singer, at the beginning of the sound age, showed the dramatic possibilities of music. It was entertaining; it caught audiences' atten-

tion; and, most important, it used lyrics and melodies to organize the narrative.

Two films that experimented with sound in order to create this structure are Norman McLeod's 1932 *Horse Feathers,* starring the Marx Brothers, and René Clair's 1931 *A Nous la Liberté* ("Freedom for Us").

The action in any Marx Brothers film is always chaotic. The dramatic line of *Horse Feathers*

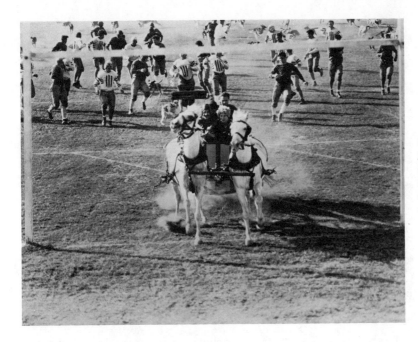

6.2 The Marx Brothers in *Horse Feathers:* Harpo, Groucho, and Zeppo in the garbage can, winning the football game. (The Museum of Modern Art/Film Stills Archive. Courtesy of Universal Pictures.)

holds events together. Groucho is the new president of a small college that needs to beat its rival football team. The College Widow plays the middle between Groucho's son (played by Zeppo) and the opposing college. She tries to get the signals to ensure defeat for Groucho's school. Groucho and Zeppo and the other two Marx Brothers, Harpo and Chico, all interact with one another and frequently cancel out each other's actions by assuming the opposite of what the other states.

Two major ideas control the development of the action: (1) The extension of realism (the settings and the basic thematic idea) into the preposterous, and (2) the use of the song "Everyone Says I Love You" as a motif that eventually combines all the action into one thematic construct.

A recognizable world such as a college demands fairly predictable, structured behavior. Preposterous behavior arises from actions opposite to those the setting indicates. *Horse Feathers* is about this type of nonconformity; it is at once anti-establishment and a satire on college education. In a sociological sense, the film appeals to the anti-intellectualism of American audiences. The Marx Brothers circumvent expected behavior by appearing to act just as they feel. The events that control them are usually of their own making; only secondarily are they thrust upon them.

Each of the Marx Brothers plays off each other in an identifiable way. They form a nucleus of insanity that we can identify with. When near the climax, Harpo and Chico escape from the building they have been locked in by sawing their way through the floor, it seems right that Harpo would hop into an awaiting garbage can attached to two horses and gallop away like a charioteer. Later,

6.3 Scene from René Clair's *A Nous la Liberté,* showing people as automatons. (The Museum of Modern Art/Film Stills Archive. Courtesy Contemporary/McGraw-Hill Films.)

in the chariot, he helps to win the football game. Unexpected actions yield unexpected results, and this removal from reality is called fantasy.

Music helps structure this removal from reality. "Everyone Says I Love You" is sung by Zeppo, is sung and played by Chico on the piano, is sung by Groucho, and is whistled by Harpo (to a horse). This use of music as the *leitmotiv* helps to hold the action together.

In *A Nous la Liberté,* René Clair threads the song ("A Nous la Liberté") through the film. Each time it is sung, however, it takes on a quality peculiar to the theme and the action at the time. The theme of the movie is automated man in the mechanized world in conflict with free man in nature. The story is about two tramps thrown in jail. One escapes and eventually becomes a powerful industrialist, making and selling record players. The other also later escapes and eventually gets an assembly-line job in the record factory, joining the mechanically organized activity

that various shots run as a motif through the picture. Now neither industrialist nor worker has freedom again. Gangsters discover the industrialist's real identity and try to blackmail him. The industrialist escapes, trying to take with him a suitcase full of money, but the suitcase gets lost on the roof of his new completely automated factory. The next day, at the ceremonies to dedicate the factory, a heavy wind blows the suitcase open and the money flies around the courtyard. While an elderly speaker is orating, there is chaos in the audience, with everyone scrambling for the money. Later the industrialist and his friend become tramps again. And the other former factory workers fish and dance as the machines go their own automated ways.

Clair has said, "If you believe that work is the most important thing in your life, don't go to see *A Nous la Liberté* but send your children to see it." He suggests that "if man were not at the service of machines, this film would make no sense."

Clair believed that fantasy might save people chained to the assembly line—that fantasy (though perhaps only a temporary solution) is an important aspect of our lives and that movies could provide us with fantasy for our imaginations to enjoy.

In this movie, sound is used to restructure reality into fantasy. A mechanical bird "sings." A lady's voice becomes the voice on a record player (the phonograph runs down and we see her exit from her house). As the action moves through highs and lows, the music comments by changing tempo, by sadly recalling the free life its lyrics express.

The narrative structure that emerges from the fantasy and music of Clair's film shows how a movie can create a believable atmosphere. By creating sounds that do not exist in the world, a film can make unrealistic images into a believable construct. In life, we operate according to the normal expectations of cause and effect. Films that deal with fantasy surprise us by circumventing normal expectations. (Magicians of course work their tricks this way, and, interestingly, the first fantasy films were created by the magician Georges Méliès, whom Clair studied and admired.) For instance, one scene in *A Nous la Liberté* thwarts normal expectation when a man, instead of hanging himself, finds the force of his body breaks open the prison bars. The same is true when Harpo rides the "chariot" in *Horse Feathers.*

Music acts as a motif to control both films and the lyrics give sense to the action, sometimes by supporting it and sometimes by opposing it. When Groucho sings "Everyone Says I Love You" to the college widow, we know he does not mean it. When Zeppo sings the same song to the widow, we know he means it, yet in an adolescent way. In *A Nous la Liberté*, René Clair creates a "music" from the machinery noise. This stretches the atmosphere beyond the limits of the frame and supports the authenticity of the environment.

Both music and created noise are artificial. They are used in movies to enrich and extend the theme. In more realistic movies, these functions are created by dialogue. But in these two movies, dialogue works in some new and important ways.

The unrealistic nature of the Marx Brothers' speeches is tied to their crazy behavior. For instance, in the classroom scene from *Horse Feathers:*

GROUCHO: Now then, baboons, what is a corpuscle?

CHICO: That's easy. First there's a captain. Then there's a lieutenant. Then there's a corpuscle.

GROUCHO: That's fine. Why don't you bore a hole in yourself and let the sap run out?

The note is struck at the beginning of the film as Groucho addresses the college. He sings, "Whatever it is, I'm against it." Harpo, walking by some cardplayers in a speakeasy, hears one say, "Cut the cards." Harpo pulls out an axe and literally cuts the cards. When words do not make conventional sense, or when they are taken too literally and hence lead to unexpected behavior, they lead to unpredictable actions. The Marx Brothers' dialogue fuses language with image in ways that are outside normal experience.

Dialogue in *A Nous la Liberté,* on the other hand, is minimal. We can watch the film without subtitles and perfectly understand it. The atmospheric noise and the music carry the story. When dialogue is used, it supports the images rather than presents information. This film shows us that sound other than dialogue can be used creatively.

Another move into fantasy was created during the thirties by the American musical. This was the time of the Great Depression. Unable to travel or

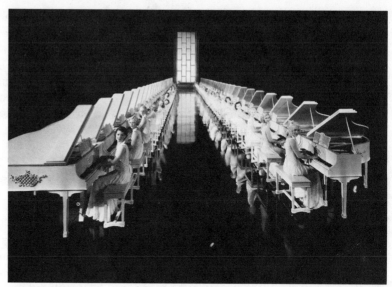

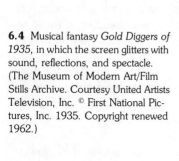

6.4 Musical fantasy *Gold Diggers of 1935,* in which the screen glitters with sound, reflections, and spectacle. (The Museum of Modern Art/Film Stills Archive. Courtesy United Artists Television, Inc. © First National Pictures, Inc. 1935. Copyright renewed 1962.)

even sometimes to eat, people packed the movie houses. Their hopes and fantasies were played out for them by stars "bigger than life" and by spectacles the likes of which they had not seen before.

Working for Warner Brothers, choreographer Busby Berkeley directed some of the most truly fantastical spectacles ever photographed. With cameras craning to create new angles, with moving overhead views looking down at so many shifting dancers in a kaleidoscopic fantasy, new visual experiences were invented. Mirrors reflected people in mirrors reflecting people. Sequins shined against mirrors and against illuminated violins and horns. Dream land existed, and anybody with a dime for a ticket could live there—for a while.

Berkeley drew the musical from the stage and transformed it into cinematic form. He mixed music and light with people and glitter, and structured new spaces along the way. In *Footlight Parade,* and the *Gold Diggers* films of 1933–37,

he followed Méliès's footsteps and made fantasy for us all.

Berkeley's extravaganzas were usually molded into love stories, incorporating dance, song, and melodrama. The major studios, such as MGM, Paramount, and RKO, created their own styles through the producers' system of extended conferences, high pay, carefully organized shooting, and iron control. They insisted on giving stars and directors long-term contracts, which sometimes killed creativity. Buster Keaton, for instance, after signing with MGM and making a couple of films, found himself unable to adjust his talents to the producers' wills.

Fred Astaire and Ginger Rogers projected great skill through the rhythms of their dances, and epitomized the screen love affair. The voices of Nelson Eddy and Jeanette Macdonald became standard attractions in film operettas such as *Rose Marie* (1936).

As MGM showed in its compilation feature, *That's Entertainment* (1974), the American musi-

6.5 John Wayne as the Western hero—strong, potent, handsome, and protective of his woman and his reputation. From John Ford's *Stagecoach* (1939). (The Museum of Modern Art/Film Stills Archive.)

cal provided controlled but frequently beautiful images to eighty million moviegoers a week. The contrived sophistication and sentimentality of many of these films comment as much on the audiences as on the film companies. People needed the release from their own lives that these pictures gave them; they demanded that they be "entertained."

Riding the popularity of bad taste and extravagant style, Hollywood occasionally arranged live spectacles, such as Jean Harlow's funeral in 1937, during which Nelson Eddy and Jeanette Macdonald sang "Ah Sweet Mystery of Life" from *Rose Marie* to the spectacular bronze casket.

Still, the musicals and the Busby Berkeley phantasmagorias showed that movies could be structured around dreams. They proved that the images of the imagination know no bounds.

The Western

Since the Western originated in Edwin S. Porter's *The Great Train Robbery,* the events of the form were conventionally keyed to the outdoors. Though its story lines are few in number, their possibilities appear almost infinite. Here are some of them.

1. Whereas the musical could offer the stuff of dreams, the Western could offer fulfillment. The Western hero became the archetypical American male: strong, potent, handsome, and protective of his woman and his reputation.

2. This hero may have been conventionally bad (as John Wayne's Ringo in John Ford's 1939 *Stagecoach*), but he stands for the forces of good.

3. Action frequently is that of the chase or a modification of it, such as a cattle drive or an attempt to get to Fort Smart before the Apaches do.

4. Westerns are frequently anarchistic. The law is either applied by a local judge or stems from the strongest person.

5. Action is often confined to an isolated location, frequently a prairie town, where the confrontation between good and evil would be resolved, usually through the classic gunfight.

6.6 Monument Valley, called "John Ford Country," as seen in *Stagecoach* (1939). (The Museum of Modern Art/Film Stills Archive.)

6. Open spaces allowed vistas for the camera and gave the film a documentary look.

7. The roles were almost as ritualized as Greek drama. Audiences knew that the heroes were destined to win and the bad guys shot down or run out of town, but this did not stop their interest in seeing how the action would be played out.

Stylistically, *Stagecoach* (1939) by John Ford is one of the most influential films ever made.* By necessity of his topic John Ford liberated film from the studio. Although he still shot interiors there and used Western towns built on the studio's back lot, he settled on Monument Valley in Arizona and Utah for his primary vista location.

Ford also broadened the narrative possibilities of the wide-angle lens. He composed in depth, and in his interiors he was the first person consistently to use ceilings as an important part of the set.

In *Stagecoach* he integrated his images with the myth of the bad man redeeming himself against heavy odds. In doing this, he consolidated a form that was both epic and dramatic. The epic nature of Indian attacks and a long trek in the stagecoach interweave with Johnny Ringo's personal story. The conflict between man and nature (his own inner nature as well as that of the great outdoors) is presented through the confining interiors of houses and of the stagecoach as juxtaposed with the grandeur of Monument Valley.

The Gangster Film

The theme that the bad guy was not all bad was also expressed in the 1930s gangster film. Mervyn

---

*When asked the primary influences on him, Orson Welles said, "John Ford, John Ford, and John Ford." Reportedly, Welles studied *Stagecoach* while preparing to make *Citizen Kane,* viewing the film forty times. Interestingly, Ingmar Bergman also mentioned Ford, as well as Welles, as influences on his style.

Le Roy's *Little Caesar* (1930) expanded narrative form by advancing the use of point of view. This film told its story from the gangster's viewpoint, rather than from the lawman's viewpoint.

As was to occur later in *The Godfather* (1972), *Little Caesar* humanized the gangster. By creating interiors as atmosphere through high and low key lighting and through composition in depth, this film organized its story from Edward G. Robinson's extraordinary performance as Rico. The events of the chase and the human qualities of the gangster structured the clash between good and evil. At the end of the film, when Robinson gets machine-gunned behind a billboard, he says, "Mother of Mercy, is this the end of Rico?" It makes the viewer feel like saying, "No!"

Little Caesar injected the gangster form with empathy and pathos and pointed the way to later pictures that explored the psychological and social reasons for good and evil. Such films showed how viewers could examine themselves through the screen experience.

Like the Western, gangster films penetrated the viewer's consciousness by taking such attributes of the American myth as the assertion of virility and the idea of man being a law unto himself and extending these attributes into American (and eventually European) civilization. The gangster film, then, contributed to the evolution of the narrative film (1) by creating atmosphere through lighting, decor, and acting, and (2) by extending and formulating psychological cinema.

The Individual Against Society

Films that investigate the relationships between institutions and people were as dominant in the 1930s as they are today. For instance, Jean Vigo's 1933 *Zéro de Conduite* ("Zero for Conduct") is

6.7 *Little Caesar,* with Edward G. Robinson, used naturalistic decor and sophisticated lighting to create its atmosphere. (The Museum of Modern Art/Film Stills Archive.)

a highly original look at a boy's school in France. It fuses dream and reality in several ways.

On one level it shows the story of boys returning to school for a new term and revolting against the authorities. Some of the authorities are caricatured: the headmaster is a dwarf; the obese science teacher is a lecher after little boys. A sympathetic new instructor, himself a caricature of the uninitiated teacher, entertains the boys by performing a Charlie Chaplin dance. The food they eat always seems to be beans. The instructors oversee them during sleep and awaken them in the morning.

A revolt in the dormitory becomes a slow-motion ballet of pillow feathers and student power. A cartoon drawn for them by the sym-

6.8 In *Zero for Conduct,* the new instructor performs a Charlie Chaplin dance. (The Museum of Modern Art/Film Stills Archive.)

6.9 The slow motion ballet of pillow feathers and revolt from *Zero for Conduct.* (The Museum of Modern Art/Film Stills Archive.)

pathetic teacher suddenly becomes animated and dances around.

When the boys take to the barricades and attack the school's board of visitors, an anarchistic sort of freedom reigns—one that is unique for each person. Thus, we learn that though revolt against archaic institutional structures creates chaos, it is the job of those who revolt to reorder that chaos ethically. Whether in fact the boys do this is left to the audience to decide.

The film's action combines fantasy (the ways that the boys see the institution) and reality (visuals of urinals and classrooms, of town streets and smoky train compartments). The surreal ways things appear become the way they are. Vigo sensed cinema's potential for wedding the fantastic and the realistic, and he presented both aspects as "true" from the boys' points of view. He organized the film around realistic and sur-

realistic images as well as through symbolic actions and objects (a balloon that bursts; rain that only seems to get people wet yet has the power for rebirth; smoke that hides things as they are; a dwarf as incompetence; feathers as liberty). Thus, the emotion that the film projects becomes its subject. Created through cinematic techniques, this emotion suggests that what is shown is only a part of truth, that what we see is only a part of the whole reality.

Citizen Kane

Citizen Kane is about an attempt to seek truth. When newspaper magnate Charles Foster Kane dies, a news team putting together a newsreel biography of him discovers that although he was one of the world's most wealthy and powerful men, little is known of his private life. Because Kane's dying word was "Rosebud," the newsreel producer assigns a reporter named Thompson to find out what it means, thinking they will thereby discover the "real" Kane. "Rosebud," then, is the object the plot turns on.

To discover the meaning of "Rosebud," Thompson interviews Kane's friends and associates. The film is organized around six points of view, namely, Kane as seen through the eyes of six different people. These points of view move from the most objective—that of Kane's public self as expressed in a newsreel—to a biased, complex report by Kane's second wife, Susan Alexander. Finally, the manager of Xanadu, Kane's grand and unfinished estate, tells about Kane's last days. Thompson also interviews Jed Leland, Kane's college friend from whom he eventually becomes alienated, and Bernstein, who started with Kane when he bought a defunct New York City newspaper and built it into an empire. From these five stories, a dimensionalized view of Kane emerges. Except for the newsreel, each view is a third-person-limited viewpoint; that is, each story is told from what each person remembers. This is also true in the first information source Thompson goes to—the library that keeps the records of Mr. Thatcher, Kane's ex-guardian and a Wall Street tycoon.

Thompson reads Thatcher's reminiscences of Kane and listens to what Susan Alexander, Jed Leland, Bernstein, and the estate manager tell him. As this occurs, the film shows us what is being told, but the audience has to keep in mind that one person may see an event differently from how another sees it. To reinforce this idea, the film constantly keeps bringing us back to the present of Thompson doing his interviewing. From the different sources of information, we see Kane as an egocentric man caught between his desire to do good and his self-righteous revolt against authority.

Citizen Kane is structured cyclically. We begin with the camera penetrating layers of fence, pools, hills, and walls into Xanadu. This action prefigures the film's attempt to penetrate Kane's life. We see Kane dying. He holds a glass ball filled with artificial snow; then he drops it, whispering "Rosebud." Next we cut to the newsreel *News on the March*. The newsreel ends and we find ourselves in a smoke-filled screening room. Thompson is given his assignment. He goes through the Thatcher papers, which tell of Thatcher going to Colorado in winter to pick up Kane as a child, and the four interviews. At the end of the film, we are once again in Xanadu. Thousands of art objects, furnishings, and the like that Kane collected are being inventoried and crated. Some of the least valued pieces are being destroyed. Thompson reports to his boss that he has been unable to discover what Rosebud means. We cut to a huge furnace into which Kane's junk is being thrown. The camera dollies forward into a sled catching fire. We dissolve to a closeup of the sled. On it is written the name *Rosebud*. Then the camera travels back, past the layers of the estate it penetrated during the beginning of the film. The audience remembers: when Thatcher came to pick up Kane, the child had a sled and was playing in the snow. The sled is Rosebud. "Rosebud," then, represents the freedom that Kane forever lost, the lost childhood he could never recover, the innocence he could not keep when he went with Thatcher to New York and on to the life of a wealthy young man. Thus, to all who knew Kane, "Rosebud"—and hence Kane's private dreams—remains hidden. Only the audience is privileged to know all the layers of meaning, as Figure 6-10 shows.

This organization of several points of view to discover truth was one of *Citizen Kane's* contribu-

6.10 The different layers of meaning in Orson Welles's *Citizen Kane*.

tions to the narrative cinema. Welles used film's power to jump back and forth in space and time to project images of memory. He realized, as did Vigo, that a movie can show us the same action more than once, with different or more complete meanings each time. In *Citizen Kane,* as in *Zero for Conduct,* this is structured through point of view. Welles's film, however, is much more complex; it is as complex as Kane's life.

The visual style of *Citizen Kane* is distinguished by the use of the wide-angle lens. Compositions in depth form images that work from within the setting as well as from the sides of the frame. In one scene, for instance, Susan Alexander is seated in the foreground putting together a jigsaw puzzle. Kane enters from the back of the room. He does not come into the frame from the side. This type of entrance is frequent in the movie. It shows the additional dramatic emphasis the wide-angle lens can give. Another example shows Kane walking past double mirrors in a hallway after Susan has left him. His image extends into infinity.

The use of the wide-angle lens, combined with upward camera angles to show the ceiling for interiors, is consistent in this film. This technique, derived from the pictures of John Ford, creates a more total atmosphere for the action. At once in depth and enclosed, the environment becomes a visual envelope for the emotions conveyed in it.

Citizen Kane expressed the dynamic feeling the wide-angle traveling shot can provide. In a famous shot, the camera cranes through a sign advertising Susan Alexander Kane (after her divorce) as the singer in a sleazy night club. The camera appears to move through the sign and then through the club's skylight to an overhead view of Susan Alexander sitting at a table. Such unusual camera angles, created through camera movement, are frequent in the film.

Gregg Toland, Welles's director of photography, deserves much of the credit for the visual style of the film. His creative use of lighting, together with his mastery of the image in depth, supports the qualities Welles desired. Shadows

6.11 In *Citizen Kane,* the ceiling is constantly used to create a more total atmosphere for the action. Here, Jed Leland (left, played by Joseph Cotten) and Bernstein (right, played by Everett Sloan) respond to Kane's idealistic Declaration of Principles, which he is publishing in his newspaper. (The Museum of Modern Art/Film Stills Archive. Courtesy RKO Radio Pictures, a division of RKO General, Inc.)

play an important part in the picture, and frequently scenes are sharply balanced between darkness and light.

Imaginative use of sound helps to extend the story and enrich the plot. At one point, a scene ends with the line, "Merry Christmas . . ." and the next scene, some years later, completes the transition through time with ". . . and a Happy New Year."

Near the end of their marriage, when Kane has Susan Alexander confined in Xanadu, he decides to have a picnic for his innumerable guests. At the picnic, Kane and Susan are isolated in a tent, arguing loudly. Through the argument, which emphasizes their now almost totally ruptured marriage, a woman's voice screams either in sexual ecstasy or in terror, apparently from the tent next door.

6.12 Unusual camera angle in *Citizen Kane*. Kane's first wife, Emily (Ruth Warrick), learns firsthand of her husband's affair with Susan Alexander. (The Museum of Modern Art/Film Stills Archive. Courtesy RKO Radio Pictures, a division of RKO General, Inc.)

In another scene, as Susan Alexander is angrily walking out of Xanadu, a parrot in the foreground bursts a loud squawk at the cut to the scene. This noise both jars the audience and serves to remind us of Susan's harping voice, her ugliness in anger.

These few examples indicate the orchestration of image and sound within the complex narrative framework that makes *Citizen Kane* one of film history's most influential pictures. For one of the few times in his career, Welles was given control over the film. As a result, he became a hero to many later filmmakers, particularly those in France, who saw that the film controlled by one individual had a consistency of style and vision absent in most other films. To avoid the restrictions imposed by Hollywood's producers' system, Welles went on to finance his several later pictures with money he made by acting.

Rossellini, De Sica, and Neorealism

Before World War II, Italian narrative films were notorious for their sentimentality, for their happy endings, and for their glorification of the Italian people. But millions of human tragedies and awful destruction of the war produced widespread disillusionment in Europe, and people began to question the conventional values of morality, God, and individual freedom. In Italy, Mussolini's promise of national splendor had ended with the destruction of Fascism, and Italians began to reevaluate their political system, their role in the war, and the possibilities for their future.

In 1943, Professor Umberto Barbaro coined the phrase *neorealism* to suggest that the Italian cinema show authentic emotions rather than distort reality. Pictures with happy endings, he pointed out, did not relate to life as it was. Historical films of ancient Rome or of Renaissance Florence could not show the harsh life the Italians were presently experiencing. Movies adapted from fiction ignored society as it was. Motion pictures, Barbaro declared, should do away with "naive and mannered clichés" that show everybody happy most of the time; rather, they should be realistic.

Neorealism, as expressed by such directors as Roberto Rossellini and Vittorio De Sica, grew from these ideas. Their films showed the human condition. They were concerned with the usual, rather than the unusual. They examined the personal tragedies of people barely surviving economic chaos. They expressed life's larger difficulties and made them universal. Rossellini spoke of letting film show "a man without faking the unusual." The unusual had to appear true.

Neorealism centered on peasants and workers, and it frequently showed them caught in a bureaucracy they could not control. These concerns can be seen in three different neorealistic films: Rossellini's *Rome: Open City* (1945), and De Sica's *The Bicycle Thief* (1948) and *Miracle in Milan* (1950).

Rome: Open City is both a documentary and a story film. For this picture, Rossellini brought the camera into the streets late in the war while the Germans were fleeing Rome. Some of the action was caught with concealed cameras. The movie was shot with whatever film stock was available. This created a less polished picture, yet it showed that strong content could overcome the graininess, bad lighting, and unrehearsed action. The use of available film stock, together with shooting by available light, gave an honest quality to the picture. It let the actions speak for themselves. Indeed, some historians feel that *Rome: Open City* fathered contemporary cinema. In using realism, it certainly pointed the way for new narrative techniques.

In *The Bicycle Thief*, De Sica further enriched the realistic cinema. As did Rossellini, he used nonactors (actual citizens without training) to star in his films. This story of a man who needs his bicycle to keep his job, and whose bicycle is stolen, is one of cinema's most poignant examinations of personal tragedy. *The Bicycle Thief* mostly shows a father and his son searching the streets of Rome for the bicycle. The simplicity of the film's style again indicates how strong characters can create reaction to human values.

That the father and his son do not find the thief shows how (in Federico Fellini's phrase) "unsatisfied expectation" can cause us to feel the depth of personal tragedy. At the end of the picture, after the father has unsuccessfully tried to steal a bicycle himself, we see the two alone in the midst of the city. With no bicycle, there is only despair. The experience, however, has created a bond of understanding between the father and the son.

6.13 A German soldier tries to calm a hysterical Roman citizen, in Roberto Rossellini's *Rome: Open City* (1945). (The Museum of Modern Art/Film Stills Archive. Courtesy Contemporary/McGraw-Hill Films.)

6.14 In *The Bicycle Thief,* the father, in despair over not finding the thief and over the loss of his job, is comforted by his son, who has joined him in the search for the bicycle. (The Museum of Modern Art/Film Stills Archive.)

6.15 The poor have all been given tophats, thanks to one of the miracles, in Vittorio De Sica's *Miracle in Milan.* (The Museum of Modern Art/Film Stills Archive.)

This understanding shows that there is hope in love for those whose spirits have been destroyed.

The political comment in this film shows that the "system" does not go beyond mere formality to help the individual. The police do not care about the plight of one man caught in a web of circumstances he did not create.

The Bicycle Thief, Richard Griffith says, "is among the great films of all time":

Few films have matched it for its integrity, its profound humanism, its social comment on employment and unemployment, its portrayal of simple human relationships, its use of nonactors, its wholly successful interpretation of real life on the screen with a minimum contrivance and great subtle technical skill.*

The Bicycle Thief and *Rome: Open City* provided techniques for showing a new honesty in

the narrative film. These films are simple, direct, filmed on location, and true to life. They made audiences participate with social reality rather than be distracted from life with melodrama and sentimentality.

De Sica's *Miracle in Milan,* though a fable, also deals with social realities. The story is about the rich against the poor and shows how a miracle helps one of the poor give his friends what they want. The poor people build a tent city and hold off against the rich who want to use their land for industry. The comedy that arises from the interaction between the two groups is reminiscent of René Clair, whom De Sica called his "great master."

The conclusion by De Sica is that we should all live by brotherly love; and at the end of the film, as the poor ride brooms, fairy-tale-like, through the air past the Milan Cathedral toward the heaven that belongs to all, we sense that in

---

*Paul Rotha and Richard Griffith, *The Film Till Now,* rev. ed. (London: Spring Books, 1967), p. 743.

God's eyes they are the inheritors of eternal peace.

This sense of humanity and the tragedy of the underprivileged occurs in other neorealist films. De Sica's *Umberto D* (1952) is about the efforts of an old man with a pension too small to live on. He sells his books to help pay his rent. He pretends he is sick and goes to the hospital for a while to be taken care of by welfare. He trains his dog to hold a hat to beg for coins. After unsuccessfully attempting suicide, he is left again with the dog (that he had tried to give away), facing an indeterminate future.

In Federico Fellini's *Nights of Cabiria* (1957), a street prostitute is shown with humanity and understanding. The woman falls in love, only to learn she has been tricked. She attempts suicide, but this fails. Finally, she dances with a circus band of partying people, happy, but also facing an indeterminate future.

These films, and many more, show that characters in real locations could provide authentic human experiences. Even a fable such as *Miracle in Milan* shows that human respect and individual dignity allow humanity to persist. In a faceless system and an unconcerned world, individuals will assert strengths they did not know they had, and will survive. What neorealism tells us is that survival is based on self-respect. Only in the personal story can this truly be observed.

The French New Wave

The New Wave or *Nouvelle Vague* emerged in French filmmaking in the late 1950s. It is not, strictly speaking, a movement. Rather, it includes many persons who worked from certain basic events and ideas. Writing in the influential film journal *Cahiers du Cinéma,* Alexandre Astruc, François Truffaut, Jean-Luc Godard, and others postulated that a film *auteur* (author) could create a movie much the way a novelist uses words. In the 1948 article *"Le Camera Stylo"* ("The Camera Pen"), for instance, Astruc claimed that the camera was the filmmaker's pen, and that a film could be "written" by its author "just as . . . an essay or a novel." Hence, a film or a series of films could reflect the personal vision and style of the filmmaker.

It was not until the late 1950s, however, when certain technical inventions were perfected, that the *auteur* film began to be defined. These inventions, together with a reconsideration of attitudes toward the cinema (including those of neorealists), showed several new possibilities for the narrative form.

1. Filmmaking equipment became more sophisticated and more portable. The lightweight, hand-held camera, portable sound equipment, and fast film that did not need a lot of lighting all allowed more nonstudio shooting. Thus, scripts became more versatile in terms of locations.

2. Such equipment permitted more informal shooting. Settings could be less stagey. Location shooting allowed the camera to respond more spontaneously to what was discovered.

3. As a consequence, the uses of *mise-en-scène* (the scene's "atmosphere") were extended. The cameraman was forced to respond to the total environment, rather than just to a section of it created in a stage set. This changed acting and directing techniques.

4. Influenced by neorealism, as well as by the philosophical movement of Existentialism, which declared that people form their lives by their own choices, themes in films focused on the problems of human existence.

5. Generally, there was a breakdown of the mass audience. For many viewers, film became "aristocratic" and "intellectual," in the manner of the other arts. This further caused cinema to get caught up in the idea of "individual expression."

In their films, such *auteurs* as Godard and Truffaut used references from other directors' movies—for instance, showing a poster for an American film or using the structure of the gangster film (as in Godard's *Breathless,* 1959). In this way they paid tribute to their heroes, men such as Alfred Hitchcock and Orson Welles. Some critics felt such blatant eclecticism showed a lack of originality, but others believed it provided film with a tradition of "borrowing," much the same as other arts such as literature or music.

They also used documentary techniques such as on-location shooting and improvised acting. Their films frequently used shots that were comparatively long in duration—as long as twelve minutes, for example. They broke from the international style by using jump cuts.

But the New Wave filmmakers did not all make similar films. Their basic idea was to make *personal* films—author films—that contained their original visions. Their main artistic idea was to use *mise-en-scène* rather than the film's story to assert the characters' private worlds. Space became as important as time.

Truffaut's *The 400 Blows* (1959) is about a boy who is rejected by his parents, falsely accused of stealing a typewriter, and sent to a juvenile home. In the final sequence, the boy is placed in an environment (the seaside), which is distinctly opposite that in which his story has taken place (Paris; the city). The *mise-en-scène* creates the story's final meaning. It positions the boy at the end of his attempt to escape (from the city, from his pursuers, from the wrong done him by

the adult world) by a freeze frame, which shows his suspended, unanimated gaze into the camera. The movement ends. Time is suspended.

In his article *"Le Caméra Stylo,"* Astruc had suggested that "The fundamental problem of cinema is how to express thought." The New Wave filmmakers attempted to express thought partly by *poststructuring,* in the editing process, their films from the primary images given by the *mise-en-scène.* This is the opposite of *prestructuring* a film in the script. Thus, in *The 400 Blows,* the boy's story emerges from his actions within his environment, rather than from an imposed symbolic system that would give the story a literary structure.

Perhaps a key to New Wave theories and films is the word *natural.* These filmmakers tried to oppose artificiality by showing experience through the experience itself. In this sense, the New Wave appears close to the ideas of the Italian neorealists. However, the neorealists paid more attention to the story, whereas the New Wave filmmakers paid more attention to personal style.

Godard, Truffaut, and Alain Resnais all play with style. The neorealists generally hid style in content; they were satisfied to show the simplicity of human life and the strength of human spirit. The New Wave filmmakers were self-consciously concerned with how style can create thought. In this sense, they were at times as concerned with philosophy as with inventing new ways to make story films.

Alain Resnais, for instance, deals with the philosophical problem of time and space. His *Hiroshima, Mon Amour* was shown at the 1959 Cannes Film Festival, together with *The 400 Blows.* These two films drew wide attention, and their screening at Cannes is considered the formal beginning of the New Wave.

Critic Bernard Pingaud sees the structure of

6.16 A young boy against an indifferent society, in Truffaut's *The Four Hundred Blows* (1959). (The Museum of Modern Art/Film Stills Archive. Courtesy of Janus Films.)

Hiroshima, Mon Amour to be a triangle.* Two sides of the triangle represent past events—one the heroine's love for a young German soldier during World War II when she was a girl in France, the other the atomic bombing of Hiroshima. The third side is the present which takes place in modern-day Hiroshima and concerns an affair between the heroine and a Japanese architect.

Typical of Resnais, this love story shows that we can never escape from the past. Memory is a part of the present, and past events reoccur in memory to influence present action.

Resnais expresses this idea by juxtaposing shots from the past with shots from the present. This creates a total psychological reality. For instance, when the heroine touches her Japanese lover, this may evoke a memory of her German lover in France during World War II. Resnais explains people's present actions by showing us their memories. The past is unescapable, and is a part of the present.

Resnais's *Last Year at Marienbad* (1961) confuses time by seemingly arbitrary cuts between past and present events, between events remembered differently by various people and shown as fragmented images.

Je t'Aime, Je t'Aime (1968) is about a time experiment that fails. The main character, Claude, is strapped into a couch in a machine shaped like a brain. He is the subject of an experiment in which he is sent back into his memory actually to relive events as if they were happening for the first time. Because of mechanical failures, Claude gets caught between past and present. He constantly tries to get back either into the past or into the present. Finally, he is able to circumvent time and space and return to the machine from the outside.

Resnais's experiments with time extend the use of subjective fantasy that we first saw in Edwin S. Porter's *The Dream of a Rarebit Fiend.*

---

*Bernard Pingaud, "A propos de: *Hiroshima, mon amour*," *Positif*, July-August, 1960, pp. 1–11.

6.17 *Hiroshima, Mon Amour* (1959): In the love affair between the French actress and the Japanese architect, the past is a part of the present. (The Museum of Modern Art/Film Stills Archive. Courtesy Audio Brandon Films, Inc., the 16mm rental distributor in the U.S.A.)

Resnais's personal style visually suggests memory through using very smooth, slow-moving dolly shots. Taking full effect from parallactic motion, these shots frequently accumulate with others to support the theme that the past exists in the present.

In showing ways that cinema can evoke personal vision through style, the New Wave filmmakers suggest that film can be an eclectic medium. They pay tribute to their influences such as gangster movies, as Godard did in *Breathless* or Truffaut in *Shoot the Piano Player* (1960). They pay homage to their heroes by incorporating film posters in the mise-en-scène. For instance, at one point in *Last Year at Marienbad,* the camera shows us a life-size cutout of Alfred Hitchcock standing in the shadows of the Baroque corridors. Resnais's "in" joke also shows his indebtedness

6.18 Movie-making within a movie, in François Truffaut's *Day for Night*. (The Museum of Modern Art/Film Stills Archive. Courtesy Warner Bros.)

to Hitchcock for the form of psychological mystery. In *Day for Night* (1972), Truffaut shows us a memory sequence in which the central character, as a child, steals posters from a theater where *Citizen Kane* is showing. The homage to Welles is clear. They pay honor to the motion-picture medium. *Day for Night,* for example, is about a director trying to make a typical American "B" film (one which uses slick techniques, is action

oriented, and relates superficial values). In these ways, their affection for the movies as well as their indebtedness to other directors is shown.

Contemporary Directions

The New Wave filmmakers were largely responsible for the many changes of the last two decades.

They influenced the tastes of viewers who now go to films because of the director's name as well as the actors'.

The breakdown of the mass audience has led directors into making films to satisfy different audiences rather than to satisfy everybody. If the cinema has become "aristocratic," it has also produced films for distinct audiences whether interested in youth, blacks, sex, or violence. The maxim that industry films had parts that would "satisfy everybody" has now changed.

Television has been partly responsible for this. The former "B" pictures have been replaced by made-for-television features as well as by series shows. Also, with more things to do with extra time, people are more carefully choosing those films they want to see.

Yet, there are still mass-appeal films. The James Bond series did a big box office, as did *The Godfather, The Godfather—Part Two, The Sound of Music, The Sting,* and *The Exorcist.* In the hundreds of films produced every year, most are made with market considerations in mind.

Changes in shooting techniques and a more versatile technology allow many films now to be made more cheaply than before. They do not need to be seen by millions of theater-goers to be economically successful. An audience of only thousands will produce a profit. Also, the market for 16 millimeter reduction prints (reduced from the usual 35 millimeter) has grown considerably. After a film's theater and television life, it can frequently survive for several years off the rates charged by specialized distributors who rent films to colleges and film societies.

This does not mean, however, that movies can be made without large sums of money. Because of recent hard times, the American film industry has had to cut corners. To provide work for some technicians, for instance, the specialized unions have cut their demands for having so many individual technicians on the set. The costs of an additional ten or twenty technicians to do the jobs that others already hired could do might mean the difference between producing a picture or not.

Also, many American filmmakers have picked up the practices of New Wave directors and have gone into the private production film. In this type of production, a group forms its own company, or works independently under the sponsorship of a major studio, to make films at lower cost than if the whole picture were created in the studio. A small, independent company, organized as a limited partnership, can shoot almost entirely on location, with actors and crew members who receive a small salary in addition to signing a contract for a certain percentage of any net profit the film may show.

The change from the traditional studio system has led to themes and styles that can compete with television by providing different types of visual experiences—for instance, the wide screen, CinemaScope, Panavision, and Cinerama, which evolved during the sixties. Anyone who has seen *2001: A Space Odyssey* in Cinerama with multi-track sound knows that the same film projected in 16 millimeter offers a much less complete experience.

Cultural impulses have also helped to form individual styles. Ingmar Bergman, for instance, has used film as a philosophical tool to investigate the human condition. Not categorized in any "movement," his influence is as enormous as his films are unique.

Through striking visual imagery and his frequently mystical subject matter, Bergman's films show the influence of the Scandinavian temper and climate. Sweden's deep, dark nights lead to introspection, to deep shadows and the play of light across memory and physical objects. *The*

6.19 Ingmar Bergman's *The Magician* (1958): The magician and his assistant (who turns out to be his wife) in the coach at the beginning of the film. (The Museum of Modern Art/ Film Stills Archive. Courtesy of Janus Films.)

Magician (1958) begins with riders traveling in a coach through a dark forest through which fingers of light are trying to reach them. The riders then pick up a man who describes his own death to them. *Wild Strawberries* (1957) begins with a series of surrealistic images that represent a dream of the old man whose story the film will show. Later, he observes images from his childhood.

The first scenes of *The Silence* (1963) show us a lady, her ten-year-old son, and her sick sister tightly enclosed in a train compartment. They stop at a town in a foreign country whose language none of them know. This device, together with the film's presenting mostly interiors, shows people's private moments so intensely that the picture is almost embarrassing. Bergman's penetration of individual human beings has given us some of the most remarkable films made.

In Italy, several filmmakers have significantly contributed to extending the narrative form—not only Rossellini and De Sica, but also Federico Fellini, Michelangelo Antonioni, Luchino Visconti, and Bernardo Bertolucci. An overriding impulse in these directors' films is the creation of individual visual styles. These styles are influenced by the long history of the visual arts in Italy—a land of unparalleled visual beauty, where painting, architecture, and sculpture have flourished. Each of these filmmakers draws upon his own resources to examine his uniquely seen world. Antonioni carefully frames and colors his pictures to show us the conflict between mechanized society and individual action. Although his films seem too slow for many Americans, who have been trained to enjoy a faster pace, his idea is to create rhythms close to those in life, where exciting action happens only rarely. He abstracts his images from the patterns and shapes of the world around us.

Fellini, on the other hand, creates a unique combination of fantasy and reality. His images

6.20 The old man observes images from his childhood in Bergman's *Wild Strawberries*. (The Museum of Modern Art/Film Stills Archive. Courtesy of Janus Films.)

are sometimes grotesque, sometimes humorous, but only rarely common. He is strongly influenced by his childhood memories and by his early addiction to the circus, and both become metaphors in many of his pictures. As in *Juliet of the Spirits* (1965), *The Clowns* (1970), or *8½* (1963), he shows us that childhood does not leave us as we become adults. As we lose our innocence to the adult world, we yearn for the naivety, purity, and ignorance of our youth.

Bernardo Bertolucci, in *The Conformist* (1970) and in *Last Tango in Paris* (1973), has shown a vision that is objective in the documentary sense, yet is intensely personal. Like Antonioni, Bertolucci uses color with great sophistication. Whereas Antonioni gives us colors that are frequently more intense than those we see in the world, Bertolucci at times creates an almost diffuse, or impressionistic, world through his use of color.

Yasujiro Ozu and Akira Kurosawa, among other Japanese directors, have shown us some unique rhythms cinema is able to create. Ozu consistently places his camera about three feet off the floor, and shows us action in wide-angle long shot. His camera rarely moves. Kurosawa, on the other hand, has made pictures of violence of mythic proportions, such as *Throne of Blood* (1957), which retells Shakespeare's *Macbeth*, and *Yojimbo* (1961), which casts the tradition of the Japanese Samurai into thematic situations similar to the American Western.*

American films are going in a number of directions. John Cassavetes, influenced by the freer techniques of the New Wave, is producing films that are more spontaneous in style and that use the camera frequently to react to action rather than just report it. His *Faces* (1968) uses hand-

---

*Indeed, *Yojimbo* provides the basic plot structure for Sergio Leone's *A Fistful of Dollars* (1966). Kurosawa's *Seven Samurai* did the same thing for John Sturges's *The Magnificent Seven* (1960); and *Rashomon* (1950) became Martin Ritt's *The Outrage* (1964).

6.21 The sisters and the ten-year-old child in the train compartment at the beginning of Bergman's *The Silence*. (The Museum of Modern Art/Film Stills Archive. Courtesy of Janus Films.)

held shots and close-ups to emphasize the psychological problems of the stress and strain of success in business and the difficulties it can create in marriage. *A Woman Under the Influence* (1974) examines the problem of female identity with a technique that emphasizes acting as a part of cinema's creative language rather than simply as raw material that cinema can use.

Stanley Kubrick, in *2001: A Space Odyssey*, has shown what careful control can create in terms of imagery and special effects. Franklin J. Schaffner's *Patton—Lust for Glory* (1969) gives new dimensions to the epic war picture by humanizing its subject within the context of spectacular action and panoramic vistas. Robert Altman expresses a personal vision through innovative techniques in *Nashville* (1975), a picture that interweaves passion, personal characteristics of people, and general cultural commonness (country music) through unique style.

6.22 The showdown, in *Yojimbo* by Akira Kurosawa. (The Museum of Modern Art/Film Stills Archive. Courtesy Audio Brandon Films, Inc., the 16mm rental distributor in the U.S.A.)

Directors used to work their way up in the industry. Now, people such as Francis Ford Coppola (of *The Godfather*) and George Lucas (of *American Graffiti*) are showing us that bright young people coming out of university film-study programs can make pictures of quality.

Experimentation is flourishing today in the narrative film. Although Hollywood is again creating its big studio spectaculars, the movies have also become a medium for personal expression. Many people who once might have gone into painting, literature, or drama now are making films to express themselves. Cinematic possibilities are being studied anew. Everything from use of video techniques to ways of dealing with formerly taboo subjects are being investigated.

It may be too early to categorize movements of the last twenty years, but we can see that the traditional narrative form, derived from theater and from literature, is again being changed into forms that are unique to the nature of film. Here are some of them.

1. The documentary style of *cinéma-vérité* (which includes the use of the hand-held camera and improvised acting styles) is being investigated by such filmmakers as John Cassavetes and Paul Morrissey/Andy Warhol (*Trash,* 1970, and *Heat,* 1972).

2. By combining *cinéma-vérité* techniques with subject matter that does not appeal to the mass audience, filmmakers are investigating, in very personal ways, such topics as political philosophy, sex, and religion, as in Haskel Wexler's *Medium Cool* (1968), Paul Mazursky's *Bob and Carol and Ted and Alice* (1969), and *The Exorcist.*

3. Directors are frequently using their own personal experiences to build original stories rather than to adapt already successful novels

and plays, as in Paul Mazursky's *Alex in Wonderland* (1970) or Federico Fellini's *Amarcord* (1974).

4. In dealing with problems of human freedom, the contemporary cinema is more and more using the dream mode. Through flashbacks and flashforwards, pictures such as George Roy Hill's *Slaughterhouse 5* (1972) or Sidney Lumet's *The Pawnbroker* (1964) use techniques earlier experimented with by Alain Resnais.

5. The increased use of the mind's images form structures that result from free associations among images. These associations combine illogical connections with the logical happenings of the everyday world. Parts of Dennis Hopper's *Easy Rider* show that image qualities (such as color, object movement, camera movement, and composition) can create emotional relationships different from the meaning that physical action can give. A well-structured example of this occurs in the "Star Gate Corridor" sequence of *2001: A Space Odyssey*.

6. Location shooting explores the possibilities that *mise-en-scène* can help form a story by the way characters respond to their environment. Examples are Godard's use of the French countryside in *Weekend* (1968) or the way the streets and subways of New York City create a distinctive atmosphere in William Friedkin's *The French Connection* (1971).

7. Experiments with sound, as in Robert Altman's *McCabe and Mrs. Miller* (1971), suggest new ways to bring objects outside the frame into the action being seen. With the invention of directional microphones, which can be pointed at a source to select one sound from many, a more controlled "mix" of sounds can be created. In a much more sophisticated way than ever before, this lets sound complement the image, rather than just support it.

8. Less restriction on filmmaking in relation to story and style helps directors create more personal films.

9. Because cinema is an art form that uses machines, it is being used to study the effects of our machine culture. Antonioni, Kubrick, and others change the visual forms of the industrialized world into narrative forms.

10. Cinema's capability to reorganize reality can totally reconstruct the world we know, and and today's filmmakers understand that this has ethical implications, that happy endings and stereotyped housewives deprive audiences of an accurate examination of life. Films, then, are becoming more honest.

11. This honesty is reflected in the ways central characters are presented. The *anti-heroes* permeate today's films, persons just like most of us, with unrealized dreams, trying to find meaning in the chaos around them. Many films today investigate human behavior, then, rather than just show human action.

12. Animation is moving into new territory. Ralph Bakshi's *Fritz the Cat* (1972) testifies to the ways an underground hero can influence the cartoon form stylistically and thematically. *200 Motels* shows the possibilities of using solarization and video techniques, together with live action, in a feature picture.

The form of the traditional Hollywood film was tightly controlled by a producer who dictated both style and content to directors and film editors. The companies invested heavily in stars, and they exploited their images with all the resources of public relations. This idea of providing us with an escape from reality is still with us today, for it has saturated television and can be seen in studio pictures such as those of Walt

Disney Productions and such mass-appeal films as *The Way We Were* (1973), *The Towering Inferno* (1974), and *Earthquake* (1974).

Emotions expressed this way are stereotyped. They emerge from superficial expression, from clichéd actions, and from the myths of feminine beauty, of male dominance, and of all Americans living well. But some filmmakers today see that an important contribution of the cinema is to investigate the truth of these myths. Many of the films of the last twenty years, rather than imposing values on us, give us values to question. Sam Peckinpah does this with violence and male virility; Stanley Kubrick does it with violence and war (*Dr. Strangelove,* 1963) and violence and love (*Lolita,* 1962). Even the musical, which glorified these themes at one time, has changed. In *Cabaret* (1972), the songs are separate from the rest of the picture and are enclosed by the cabaret scenes.

An old theme in the narrative arts is that lives lived too formally at the expense of feeling are hollow and meaningless, a type of death. The forms we live in may structure our actions and thinking, but they do not kill our feelings. Unless we are so passive that we never act, only react, we try to make self-discoveries. More than ever before, narrative filmmakers today are giving us films that do not answer all the questions they pose. They force us to participate rather than simply watch. Movies more and more today are structuring themselves around feeling and thought.

Still, cinema is deceptive. Because it is so believable, it has to be used wisely. Narrative films can structure our actions for us. They can create our beliefs. They can impose ideas on us almost subliminally.

From early experiments with sound, to the freeing of the camera from the studios, to the strong influence of neorealism and the New Wave on today's filmmakers, the form, style, structure, and content of the narrative film continue to evolve.

Censorship and Obscenity

7

An important problem in America is the relationship between the media and the law, particularly on matters of censorship. In movies censorship mainly refers to the display or suggestion of sexual activity. Religious matters and violence, however, have also been subject to censorship.

The Problem of Censorship

Because movies are a popular representational medium, it was seen very early that they had the power to affect people's beliefs as well as their instinctual feelings. It is not surprising that society —or a significant group in it—would issue their moral attitudes as criteria to restrict the content of a medium that was open to everybody.

Attempts to censor movies have been a search for two types of definitions. The first is the attempt of the courts to determine what obscenity is. Moral standards change, yet they ironically remain the same for a powerful middle group in our society. That is, although behavior and attitudes change, they are set against the moral stance of the puritan influence. A majority seems to feel that public display of sexual activity is degrading and destructive to morality. Yet others claim traditional morality has never worked universally, it leads to hypocrisy, and that one group should not impose its own morality on another.

The second search is for a definition of the film medium—whether it is an art form subject to free expression, a public medium that is protected by the First Amendment to the U.S. Constitution, or a business subject to legal constraint.

Attempts to make these two types of definitions concrete arise again and again in the censorship battles in this country.

The Beginnings of Film Censorship

"Congress shall make no law" states the First Amendment, ". . . abridging the freedom of speech, or of the press. . . ." This Amendment appears at first to apply to the national government only ("Congress shall make no law . . ."), implying that individual states could make such laws. However, the U.S. Supreme Court has ruled that the Fourteenth Amendment extends this protection to state laws, too. The conflict of the rights and powers of the state or community versus those of the national government relates directly to the history of film censorship.

Motion pictures had come in quickly—first in nickelodeons, then in movie houses—and

Opposite page: From Hiroshi Teshigahara's *Woman in the Dunes.* Courtesy Contemporary/McGraw-Hill Films. (The Museum of Modern Art/Film Stills Archive.)

their seductive powers were quickly noticed by exhibitors, filmmakers, and the public. People such as Thomas Edison attempted to explain the educational value of the movies. Many who agreed with him also saw the need to control that content which could "educate."

Before 1910, some films had dealt with sexual matters, but they mainly emphasized violence and crime. Moralists began to feel that antireligious values, sexual innuendo, and crime and violence could corrupt the young and the morally weak. This concern arose, of course, during a time when the strong, rural-based, church-centered values of parental love, self-sacrifice, devotion to family, and contentment with one's lot dominated America's thinking.

In 1907, Chicago formed a film censorship board composed of members of the city police department. In 1909 New York City created much the same type of board, and other major cities quickly set up similar panels.

In 1911, Pennsylvania organized the first statewide board of censorship. This started a trend, and in 1913 Ohio and Kansas followed suit.

The first censorship case to reach the United States Supreme Court was in 1915, in *Mutual Film Corp. v. Ohio*. Ohio authorities had invoked the censorship law to prevent the transport of films into the state from the Michigan-based company. The Mutual Film Corporation asserted that this action was unlawful in light of both the Ohio constitution and the First Amendment to the U.S. Constitution.*

The Supreme Court ruled that "motion pictures is a business pure and simple," not "a part of the press of the country or an organ of public opinion." This decision denied freedom of expression to the movies, so that, unlike the press, they

could henceforth be censored. Legally, under this ruling, movies could be denied the protection of the First Amendment.

As more pictures evolved dealing with controversial subjects, censorship boards grew. D. W. Griffith's *The Birth of a Nation* (1915) ran into trouble in the North. The NAACP rightly objected to the film's treatment of blacks as well as to the thematic support it gave the Ku Klux Klan. Riots erupted in St. Louis and the picture was banned there. Riots also erupted in Boston, and the scene of a black man chasing a white woman was cut out of the print. Pressured by the NAACP and other groups, San Francisco authorities insisted on minor changes in the film. Thus, censorship, good and bad, was in progress. Whether censorship might destroy a film's artistic integrity seemed a less important question than the fact that citizen groups had to be pacified.

The Hays Office and the Production Code

As the years went on, criticism of stars worsened, due in part to the conduct of some of the stars themselves. Comedian Fatty Arbuckle made headlines with his drinking and sex with an underaged girl. William Desmond Taylor's many love affairs were brought to light after his mysterious murder. Wallace Reid died by an overdose of morphine.

Harassment of motion pictures reached a high point about 1930. During that year, American film producers, to protect themselves, formed the Motion Picture Producers and Distributors of America (MPPDA). This organization (later known as the Motion Picture Association of America) was designed to let the film industry censor and govern itself. Its president was Will H. Hays, a former U.S. Postmaster with almost unparal-

---

*See Richard S. Randall, *Censorship of the Movies* (Madison, Wis.: University of Wisconsin Press, 1968) for a more complete discussion on these and other cases.

7.1 The Ku Klux Klan rides to the rescue in D. W. Griffith's *The Birth of a Nation* (1915). (The Museum of Modern Art/Film Stills Archive.)

leled political clout, who was responsible for killing virtually every censorship bill in the state legislatures. The MPPDA became known, of course, as "the Hays Office." On March 31, 1930, the MPPDA ratified its Production Code, whose general principles stated:

1. No picture shall be produced which will lower the moral standards of those who see it. Hence the sympathy of the audience shall never be thrown to the side of crime, wrongdoing, evil, or sin.

2. Correct standards of life, subject only to the requirements of drama and entertainment, shall be presented.

3. Law—divine, natural, or human—shall not be ridiculed, nor shall sympathy be created for its violation.

Under "Particular Applications" were listed the following headings: Crime, Brutality, Sex, Vulgarity, Obscenity, Blasphemy and Profanity, Costumes, Religion, Special Subjects (e.g., "the use of liquor should never be excessively pre-

7.2 The young girl being seduced by the hobo in Roberto Rossellini's *The Miracle* (1947). (The Museum of Modern Art/Film Stills Archive.)

sented"), National Feelings, Titles, and Cruelty to Animals.

The code was generally effective for some years, but its main drawback was that only those producers and distributors belonging to the MPPDA were required to abide by it. As always, the unscrupulous found ways around the code or just did not join the organization.

In 1934, to assure adherence to the MPPDA Code, the Catholic Church organized the Legion of Decency, with the idea of directing Catholics to or away from films. The Legion devised four ratings* for motion pictures, and Catholics throughout the country were required yearly to promise compliance.

Once the Legion of Decency was established, other church groups, such as the National Council of Churches, felt it necessary to offer their own censorship programs. This nationwide movement toward censorship, combined with the despair of the Depression, led to different kinds of movies for the mass of people, who wanted escape entertainment rather than titillation or intellectualization. The result was that the industry, pressured by both public demand and organized religion, cleaned up its movies anyway. By the 1950s, however, the Legion of Decency had lost much of its influence.

The Miracle Decision and Movie Ratings

On May 26, 1952, the Supreme Court reversed itself and declared that motion pictures should *not* be "disqualified from First Amendment protection." "Expression by means of motion pictures," it ruled, "is included within the free speech and free press guaranty of the First and Fourteenth Amendments." This decision is known as the *"Miracle* decision," because it emerged from attempts by New York City officials and the Catholic Church to ban Roberto Rossellini's 1948 picture by that title (*The Miracle* was Part II of *Amore*). The film is about the seduction of a young girl by a hobo whom she takes to be a saint. The Supreme Court finally declared that "We hold under the First and Fourteenth Amend-

ments a state may not ban a film on the basis of the censor's conclusion that it is 'sacrilegious.' " The *Miracle* decision returned to movies the protections granted the other arts. It meant someone or some group could no longer censor or ban a film because of taste or bias.

In 1966 the movie business once more tried to regulate itself. Because of the honesty with which movies were dealing with controversial or personal attitudes and themes, a new code was formed. The President of the Motion Picture Association of America, Jack Valenti, suggested that this new code challenged the filmmaker "to examine the world as it is, and to tell his story honestly, skillfully, and responsibly." Two years later the MPAA declared its "responsibility to make good pictures and classify them honestly," and it issued a system of ratings with four classifications. The original classification system, and its rationale, has been modified since the issuance of the original G, M (then GP), R and X ratings. The most recent rating system is G, PG, R and X (*see inset, next page*).

Because only about 80 percent of exhibitors, producers, and distributors belong to the MPAA, strict application of the new code is impossible. Moreover, within the industry, the classifying board's ratings for movies can be appealed. And though some ratings are indeed changed, any movie can advertise itself at a more severe rating than that which it was given. Some exhibitors feel that more people will attend an *R* picture than a *PG* picture.

Any rating or censorship system is bound to offend somebody, of course. No system of classification can work unless people believe it and subscribe to it—impossible in a diverse culture. Still, the 1968 code, as revised, does allow for individual expression, for the filming of all sorts of subject matter, and for commercial (as opposed to artistic) restraint.

*A-I, morally unobjectionable for all ages; A-II, morally unobjectionable for adults; B, in part, morally objectionable; C, thoroughly objectionable.

A major objection to the code is that it suggests that *only* people under seventeen years of age are capable of being affected by bold subject matter. To some this implies a patronizing society, one in which the adult is always right in imposing standards on the young. What it suggests is that adults, affected by violence or explicit sexual imagery, automatically conclude that their children will be similarly affected. But some of the young say that though the material may not be harmful to them, it could be dangerous for certain maladjusted or psychotic adults.

Obscenity and the Supreme Court

The First Amendment implies that each individual is his or her own censor. A modified view of this idea appeared in the 1973 U.S. Supreme Court case of *Marvin Miller* v. *State of California.* Earlier, in 1957, in *Roth* v. *United States,* the Court had declared that "Obscenity is not within the area of constitutionally protected freedom of speech or press" and that "implicit in the history of the First Amendment is the rejection of obscenity as utterly without redeeming social importance." The ticklish problem on the 1957 decision was to define obscenity. The Court declared that the test of obscenity is "whether to the average person, applying contemporary community standards, the dominant theme of the material as a whole appeals to the prurient interests." In the 1973 *Miller* case, the Court then reaffirmed the *Roth* decision that "obscene material is not protected by the First Amendment."

The *Miller* defendant had been convicted of mailing unsolicited sexually explicit material in violation of a California law, and the Supreme Court upheld this. "A work may be subject to state regulation," the Court declared, "where that work, taken as a whole, appeals to the prurient interest in sex: portrays, in a patently offensive way, sexual conduct specifically defined by the applicable state law: and taken as a whole, does not have serious literary, artistic, political, or scientific value." But, the Court went on, "The jury may measure the essentially factual issues of prurient appeal and patent offensiveness by the standard that prevails in the forum commu-

The Motion Picture Rating System

G

General audiences. All ages admitted. This is a film which, in the judgment of the Rating Board, contains no material which would be objectionable or embarrassing for audiences of any age. A G-rated motion picture is *not* by definition a "children's" film, but it is a film which is considered generally acceptable for the entire family.

PG

Parental guidance suggested. All ages admitted. This film contains some material which some parents might consider too mature for pre-teenagers. The rating alerts parents to the need for inquiry before allowing children to attend.

nity, and need not employ a 'national standard.' "
Thus, the problem of censorship came back to
the community. In a way, censorship had gone
full circle since 1907.

Now that "community standards" are the
criteria for censorship, the movie industry and
private filmmakers are uncertain about the economic viability of any picture. Standards are different for different communities (and different
groups in them), and a filmmaker cannot be sure
that even a serious film that must of necessity
show explicit material will succeed. Hollywood
has scrapped several projects because of the
uncertainty caused by the 1973 decision.

Implicit in the problem of defining obscenity,
from a legal and ethical standpoint, is whether
in fact obscenity—whatever it is—is bad. In his
vigorous dissent in the *Miller* case, Supreme
Court Associate Justice William O. Douglas
declared: "Obscenity—which even we cannot
define with precision—is a hodge-podge. To
send men to jail for violating standards they cannot understand, construe, and apply is a mon-
strous thing to do in a nation dedicated to fair
trials and due process." Later in his dissent he
asserted:

. . . The idea that the First Amendment permits pun-
ishment for ideas that are "offensive" to the particular
judge or jury sitting in judgment is astounding. No
greater leveler of speech or literature has ever been
designed. To give the power to the censor, as we do
today, is to make a sharp and radical break with the
traditions of a free society. The First Amendment was
not fashioned as a vehicle for dispensing tranquilizers
to the people. Its prime function was to keep debate
open to "offensive" as well as to "staid" people.
The tendency throughout history has been to subdue
the individual and to exalt the power of government.
The use of the standard "offensive" gives authority
to government that cuts the very vitals out of the
First Amendment. As is intimated by the Court's
opinion, the materials before us may be garbage.
But so is much of what is said in political campaigns,
in the daily press, on TV or over the radio. By reason
of the First Amendment—and solely because of it—
speakers and publishers have not been threatened or
subdued because their thoughts and ideas may be
"offensive" to some.

And so the debate goes on. X-rated pictures
with explicitly sexual materials are again playing
the drive-ins and downtown theaters. In the
meantime, big-budget "serious" pictures, which

R

Restricted. Those under 17 must be accompanied to
the theater by a parent or adult guardian. The R rating
indicates a film which is adult in theme and treatment.
Parents may wish to view the picture with their children
so they may together discuss it. A school teacher would
qualify as an adult guardian.

X

Restricted. The rating program provides that no one
under 17 may attend. This is exclusively a film adult in
theme and treatment and this is why no one under 17
may be admitted to the theater. The age limit may be
higher in certain areas of the country.*

---

*From a bulletin by the Motion Picture Association of
America (October 1974).

need a large paying audience in order to be profitable, are dealing more and more with material rated no more "offensive" than PG and sometimes R. Twenty seconds were cut out of Stanley Kubrick's *A Clockwork Orange* in order to make it acceptable as an R-rated picture and hence make some money. At the opening of *Last Tango in Paris* at a small rural theater in upstate New York, the local board of aldermen and the sheriff attended the first night, so that they could make a determination. At the end they declared the picture "not offensive" to community standards and let it run. Mike Nichols' *Carnal Knowledge* was for a time banned in the State of Georgia, though the U.S. Supreme Court later overruled the conviction of the theater's manager who ran it, declaring that a "community" is not a hypothetical "state-wide community."

All in all, the Production Code and the courts serve to put a modicum of restraint on subject matter in movies and to let the public know the general appeal a movie might have for them. The X and R rating system and publicity for an explicit film not only turn people away from seeing it but also, of course, turn people *toward* seeing it.

During the last several years, many sexually explicit films have filled the market. With the 1973 decision, they still play the "open" areas quite successfully. Although some people can never seem to get their fill of pornography, most viewers seem to become saturated rather quickly. Violence is also frequently a film's defining quality, and more and more, the MPAA is rating R or X films with severe violence.

The problem of sex and censorship is perhaps best summed up in the 1970 report of the U.S. Commission on Obscenity and Pornography. Noting that attempts to legislate obscenity for adults and laws prohibiting its sale had not been satisfactory, the commission observed:

The Constitution permits material to be deemed "obscene" for adults only if, as a whole, it appeals to the "prurient" interest of the average person, is "patently offensive" in light of "community standards," and lacks "redeeming social value." These vague and highly subjective aesthetic, psychological, and moral tests do not provide meaningful guidance for law enforcement officials, juries, or courts. As a result, law is inconsistently and sometimes erroneously applied and the distinctions made by courts between prohibited and permissible materials often appear indefensible.

The controversy will continue. Whether the real purpose of censorship is, as Justice Douglas has said, "to make the public live up to the censor's code of morality" or to protect people from getting ideas that could adversely affect their behavior in society, censorship of the movies persists. As society's standards continue to change, so too will the value and definition of obscenity.

Part Three

The Documentary Film

"Truth" and Types of Documentary Films

8

The documentary film tries to interpret or record the real world. "Documentary"—derived from the French *documentaire* ("travelogue")—first came into use in a 1926 *New York Sun* review by John Grierson of *Moana,* a film by Robert Flaherty of primitive life in the South Pacific. Grierson used the word to identify movies that show relationships between people and their environment.

In recent years, additional defining terms have come into currency: the nonfiction film, the film of fact (or factual film), specialized films. The term *nonfiction films* is adequate, but it does not exclude experimental films, and the word "nonfiction" is too literary to use in a nonliterary medium. The term *film of fact* is fairly accurate, but some propaganda films (e.g., Leni Riefenstahl's film about Hitler, *Triumph of the Will,* 1934) distort fact so completely that the name only loosely applies. The term *specialized films* implies films that are made only for specific audiences, although documentaries can be made for a mass audience. So documentary, then, is acceptable to describe materials that have their origins in fact.

Opposite page: From Leni Riefenstahl's *Triumph of the Will.* (The Museum of Modern Art/Film Stills Archive.)

The Problem of Truth

Film is the result of manipulation. There is no such thing as an unstructured film. Even if we were to let the camera run by itself, we would get only what occurs in the frame. If we add a cameraman, then that person selects what the camera shoots. In either case, total objectivity is lost. Thus, "truth" in documentary film must rest on something other than attempts to simply record events.

Grierson suggested documentary films represent "contact with life." A reasonable connection between actual events and their projection on the screen may result in giving us an *emotion* similar to that in the actions themselves.

The distinction between "objective" films and films that *editorialize* identify two major kinds of documentary films: noninvolved and polemic. In the *noninvolved film,* filmmakers do not assert their values. Obviously, this noninvolvement depends on how much or how little the materials are allowed to speak for themselves. In the *polemic film,* the filmmaker has a point of view that controls the process. Polemic films can be deceiving, because they may be so carefully formed that they appear objective. At their best (as in Dziga Vertov's 1928 *Man with a Movie Camera*) the validity of events is created by "camera truth" rather than by the actual events.

As we shall see, the documentary film has tried to make the camera second to physical reality.

Still, in film, as in life, truth is relative to the observer.

Ten types of documentary films are explained in this chapter, and they are not each unique, for conventional styles and attitudes mix to produce new styles and ideas. Sometimes a film's purpose identifies what type it is; at other times how the medium is handled or the equipment used describe it. But each type deals with the problem of truth as it tends toward being either noninvolved or polemic.

The Theatrical Documentary

This first type of documentary is close to the narrative film. It has a dramatic structure and it usually focuses on a central character we can generally identify with. Although nonactors are used in this type of film, events are frequently staged.

The theatrical documentary tells a story. As in Lionel Rogosin's *On the Bowery* (1954), real locations are used. This film shows the story of New York's skid row as seen through one of its inhabitants. Rogosin hired an ex-alcoholic to portray the central character. The director also went into bars and set up lights and filmed action that frequently had prepared dialogue. Although the film shows some spontaneity, especially because of the concealed camera, the events filmed are fairly typical Bowery activities, not unique occurrences grabbed by the camera.

Filmmaker Robert Flaherty also did this. His *Man of Aran* (1934) portrays the struggle between Ireland's Aran Islanders and nature (the sea and the rock-filled farm land). Flaherty frequently filmed several shots of the same activity with different size lenses in order to have a variety to choose from for editing. This shooting method helped him structure the romantic style of the film.

The theatrical documentary often centers on one individual or on a family. It gives us information by dramatizing events rather than by showing them. However, thematic conflict is imposed upon and controls the picture. In *On the Bowery,* the conflict is that of a "normal" existence versus an alcoholic's existence. In *Man of Aran* the conflict is the struggle of man against nature.

These documentaries are carefully controlled by lighting, composition, and dramatic progression. They are generally prestructured. They usually show noninvolvement in their visual style (the camera just observes) but their dramatic line makes them tend toward the polemic.

The Unstaged Documentary

In the unstaged documentary, the events are influenced by technique rather than by staging. The unstaged documentary may be either dramatic or totally unstructured. Examples are such British "Free Cinema" as *Nice Time* (Alain Tanner and Claude Goretta, 1956) and *Momma Don't Allow* (Karel Reisz and Tony Richardson, 1956). These films light the interiors of found locations, such as a jazz club in *Momma Don't Allow,* yet the action appears spontaneous. The candid-camera approach, indeed, is one of the defining qualities of the unstaged documentary. The style is not so free as in *cinéma-vérité* (which developed later). Because these films show social behavior, their dramatic line is imposed by the time of the actual events. In *Nice Time,* for instance, which is an impressionistic film of a weekend night's fun at Picadilly Circus in London, the movie is controlled by the progress of human events from dusk to dawn.

Another example of this type of film is *The Maple Sugar Farmer* (Craig Hinde and Robert Davis, 1974). Showing how an old Southern

Illinois man who has spent his life making maple sugar relates to his craft, the film is at once informational and biographical. Carefully structured through voice-over, dubbed sounds, lighting and composition, the film is the portrayal of a farmer who has performed naturally in front of a tape recorder and camera. Thus, it is unstaged in the traditional sense, yet it is carefully constructed.

The Lyrical Documentary

Lyrical documentaries (also called poetic or experimental documentaries) have imaginative editing, sound, and camera techniques. Style usually is more assertive than in other documentaries.

Alain Resnais's 1955 *Night and Fog (Nuit et Brouillard),* for instance, describes the evolution of the Nazi concentration and extermination camps. It uses compilation footage as well as footage shot for the film. Scenes of the present are in a muted, postcard-like color; scenes of the past are compilation material in tinted black and white. Resnais, all of whose films deal with time, shows that our memory makes the present important, that we never escape the past. In the present Resnais often uses the color green, as in grass and shrubbery growing through once barren areas, and the distinction between life and death is shown by the green grass growing now in areas once occupied by the dying. The fluidity of the traveling camera in the color scenes slows down natural rhythms and supports the distancing effect of the color.

Through color and camera movement, this polemic film shows that the past is contained in the present. This past is fully documented, showing Nazi film of deportees being rounded up and jammed into boxcars as well as cuts from Leni Riefenstahl's Nazi spectacular, *Triumph of the Will.* The extermination is strictly documented by shots of Nazi ledger books, showing the names of the dead lined out in red, by the Stars of David on the people's clothing, by the numbers tattooed on their arms, by archival film showing the deportation process, and by "N.N."—*Nacht und Nebel* ("night and fog")—sewed on the clothes of the deportees arriving at the death camps in night and fog. The music, eerie and nostalgic, frequently acts as a bridge between the narration and the images. At times it counterpoints the color to imply that memory affects the present.

The narration tries to give some meaning to death and life and the past and the present. The narrator's voice provides information; it catalogues procedures; it questions—sometimes haltingly, as if the reality were too much to speak—the "logic" of the events; it forces our participation by directly addressing us ("But you have to know"). It occasionally cannot maintain the objectivity a documentary requires and ironically comments on what is being seen (for instance, the "architecture" of camp watchtowers). It places the blame on those of us and of World War II Germany who would not allow themselves to look, because to look is to know and to know is to be responsible.

From the first shot, which moves from the peaceful countryside to the camp within it, to the evolution of the extermination process, and finally to a traveling shot along the fence—passing then pausing and panning to look back at the carrier that fed corpses into the furnaces, the device now rusty in the green of the grass—*Night and Fog* unrelentingly forces us to look.

The Propaganda Film

This type of totally polemic documentary manipulates cinematic materials to present a particular attitude toward a subject. It either editorializes, in the sense of arguing for a position, or it creates a "new" truth from the events photographed.

A good example of this is Leni Riefenstahl's *Triumph of the Will,* a theatrical documentary of the 1934 Nazi rally at Nuremberg. The events were staged for Riefenstahl's cameras, and the action was choreographed to produce the most visually powerful scenes that could be created. At times, the director had as many as ninety-six cameramen—all the cream of Germany's cinematographers—shooting the thousands of troops assembled to pay homage to their *Führer.*

The opening shows an airplane soaring through the clouds. The impression is very mystical, as if a god were descending to earth. These shots are cut with views of Nuremberg from inside the plane as it circles to land. We see the "god's-eye view" of a city preparing for celebration. The plane lands and Hitler emerges to the accompaniment of powerful romantic music. As the celebration continues into the night, we see the troops preparing for the next day's activities. Speeches are made, and we see all the stars of the Nazi high command.

The next day comes and we see the early morning preparations. The colosseum (for that is what it suggests) is full of thousands of troops— Wehrmacht ("armed services") soldiers, the German youth, the high brass, the agricultural corps, and more—all in powerful array. Their sheer numbers allow Riefenstahl to present a picture of a Germany unified behind the power of the *Führer.*

The propaganda film creates a new "truth" from actual events and directs that truth to a particular audience. *Triumph of the Will,* for instance, was made to show the German people the united purpose of the Nazi Party, and to instill in them a feeling of national pride. Since Germany was just emerging from the depths of a horrendous depression, the film gave Germans a sense

of prestige and a strong argument for national survival. Hope was not lost. Here was the savior!

The propaganda film can also promote a rationale for the benefits of technological civilization in an underdeveloped society. For instance, Basil Wright's *Song of Ceylon* (1935) subtly shows the interactions between a highly religious rural culture (Ceylon) and a modern industry-based culture (Great Britain). The film implies that underdeveloped societies can become modern without losing their spiritual basis.

A propaganda documentary will frequently promote an unpopular product or agency. Some films about the programs of the National Aeronautics and Space Administration (NASA) have done this. Propaganda documentaries may be made to oppose or support such ideas as the need for military spending or the moral basis for a war. During World War II, for instance, the government sponsored a *Why We Fight* series, directed by Hollywood director Frank Capra.

Knowing that film can present information as if it were actually happening, and hence make it appear spontaneous and "real," should make us want to look at documentaries more carefully. Once we see how events and the ideas they express can be created by cinema, we are better able to separate apparent authenticity from true factuality.

Cinéma-Vérité

Cinéma-vérité is a term many filmmakers and critics do not like to use, or use reluctantly. Great Britain uses the phrase "direct cinema," but America has retained the French name. Translated as "cinema truth," the term defines at once an attitude toward filmmaking and the use of particular types of equipment. For our purposes,

8.1 Hitler (in the middle) reviews the troops at the 1934 Nazi Party rally at Nuremberg, in *Triumph of the Will*. (The Museum of Modern Art/ Film Stills Archive.)

let us define *cinéma-vérité* as a documentary approach that attempts to show completely spontaneous actions. Although there are difficulties with this ideal, the definition is valid, especially as it applies both to the content of shots as well as to the informal style of the films themselves.

As its name implies, *cinéma-vérité* tries to be as noninvolved as possible with the events it shows. The ideal is to let visual action structure the film's editing, rather than to force statement, drama, or chronology from events. For this reason, many people find much of *cinéma-vérité* boring. In order to get at a more complete truth of an event, the camera will occasionally stay on an action until it is completed. For instance, by remaining on the faces of people talking, the camera supposedly penetrates the surfaces shown and suggests motivations for the conduct. Words

theoretically take on a significance beyond that of mere dialogue; speech becomes an extension of one's personality.

According to this theory, *cinéma-vérité* is thus able to overcome the ways that speech can modify actuality. The telling of an action, it is held, is not the same as that action, any more than the showing of it may be. Because we tend to believe what we see more than what we hear, words in the documentary film have frequently been used to enrich, to embellish, or to add information to the images they accompany. The idea here is like the criticism of psychoanalysis that the analyst is really interpreting the *words* that describe a dream rather than the dream itself.

To overcome this difficulty, *cinéma-vérité* frequently lets people's speech meander on, dominating the fairly uninteresting images of the

8.2 In the animated film *World Population,* white dots, each representing a million persons, show breadth of population explosion. (Courtesy of Frank Paine.)

faces doing the talking. In this way, language takes on a sense of truthfulness rare in motion pictures.

In making *cinéma-vérité* documentaries, sound will occasionally be gathered first (sometimes with a hidden microphone), and the visuals that are to go with them are shot only after the sound tapes have been edited. Again, this gives primacy to the word and audial interest. It is directly opposite the usual method of editing in terms of visual interest. (But this is not always true; if the visual action is informative and dramatic enough, it will dominate.)

The informal style of these films frequently stresses the subject rather than manipulating the drama inherent in it. In this sense, the *cinéma-vérité* documentary can usually provide more subjective truth than can other types of documentary films.

The Informational Film

This category includes educational and instructional films of many different types. *Educational films* are produced to teach a limited topic to a usually preselected audience—for example, students of all levels, persons working in a particular field, or persons working for a particular company or government agency.

A short animated film made by the Film Production Unit at Southern Illinois University at Carbondale, *World Population* (1974), condenses time and space to show the breadth of the population explosion. Centuries are shown flashing by on the screen, while a few white dots, each representing one million persons apiece, appear on a world map as civilization expands. Then, as the film reaches the twentieth century, the dots go wild.

The military makes films that cover all kinds of information, from current events to military history. Among the academic fields, Encyclopaedia Britannica produces films about many different subjects of history, mathematics, the sciences, and literature. The Shell Oil Company has a large list of films, and they are not designed to sell the company's products so much as to educate the viewer on many subjects, including the scientific uses of cinematography.

Instructional films show processes. For instance, there are films for doctors showing everything from step-by-step procedures for open-heart surgery to the latest methods of diagnosing a particular disease. These films use whatever methods are appropriate for clearly showing a process. Animation is frequently used to get under the surfaces of things to show inner workings. Slow motion and accelerated motion are used to study locomotion and physical growth. Voice-over narration explains what it is we are seeing.

Most documentary films are informational. The intended audience and the primary purpose of the film suggest whether it is instructional or educational. These films are usually made in a conventional fashion in order to minimize technique and maximize information.

The Compilation Film

Compilation films (the term was coined in 1964 by scholar Jay Leyda) are films edited originally from already existing footage. Two different types of films that show the possibilities of compilation technique are Bruce Conner's lyrical documentary *A Movie* (1958) and Carol Reed's *The True Glory* (1945).

A Movie uses old newsreel footage, as well as universal leader (which counts down "8, 7, 6, 5, 4, 3, 2, 1''), to compile a film that shows the comedy and tragedy of human experience. The film begins with its title trying to assert itself through the universal leader; heavy pauses make us uneasy, serving to let us know that we are looking at a movie. Finally the title (from some old movie) comes on: "The End." Then the movie starts. As it goes on, it appears to end several times. Only at its conclusion do we realize that "The End" is the real title. The movie takes us through human foibles to the doom and escape implicit in the last shot of a skin diver swimming underwater into a cave-like mouth of a sunken ship. There is no narration, only music—light at first, then somber. The visuals take us along through human frailties into a view of our own universal destruction.

The True Glory shows the Allies' European victory in World War II. Allied combat footage is combined with narration ostensibly provided by enlisted men's voices. This material is edited with shots of maps in relief, with excerpts from *Triumph of the Will,* and with captured German combat footage. The rhythms of the movie, created from thousands of feet of film, emphasize the slow and fast movements of the armies through Europe. The script serves as the basic structuring device.

In the compilation film, the original shots are combined to create something not contained in any one of them. Because these pictures frequently use newsreel footage, they seem true. This, of course, may not necessarily be the case. In *A Movie,* for instance, the juxtapositions of the materials give us the filmmaker's personal view of the human condition. *The True Glory,* on the other hand, attempts to be objective but from the viewpoint of the winning side.

The compilation documentary film can seduce us into believing what we see. If we analyze the purpose of the compiled scenes, we might better understand the filmmaking process.

The Film Biography

Many documentaries show the ideas, activities, and practices of a particular person. Television in particular has given us many films about political leaders and famous people. Ken Russell's television documentary on dancer Isadora Duncan, for instance, brought him to attention; and Satyajit Ray's documentary on Hindu poet Tagore explored the life and ideas of this international figure. Film biographies have been made of Charles De Gaulle, Martin Luther King, Jr., John F. Kennedy, Igor Stravinsky, Queen Elizabeth II, and many, many others. Sometimes these films sketch an aspect of a person's life; at other times, they deeply analyze a person's beliefs.

The film biography is by no means limited to the famous. Newsman Charles Kuralt has done many five-minute mini-biographies of the less than well known in his "On the Road" interviews, seen on the *CBS Evening News*. Biographies may be more extended, as in W. Craig Hinde's *The Birch Canoe Builder* (1970), which is about an old man in Minnesota who makes birch bark canoes in the manner of the American Indian.

Biographical films may emerge from unique occupations as well as from a person's fame. There are films about people who make violins, about drag queens, and about sports super-stars. Although television is the main outlet for biographical films, they frequently find their way into government and university film libraries.

Film biography technique usually includes the subject's narration as he or she has talked at random into the microphone. This sound helps the filmmaker select and structure shots that emphasize or extend the spoken information. For instance, on the sound track of *The Maple Sugar Farmer,* the old man at one point reminisces about his childhood in a one-room school. Over the voice, we pan and zoom still photographs of the schoolroom and substantiate through their editing the pacing of a good story well told. The old man's voice tells us about a mouse that used to sneak out of a hole in the floor while school was on. As he describes the mouse's habits, the camera zooms in to a floor board in a one-room schoolhouse. In the present, as we observe the old man tapping his maple-sugar trees, his voice explains the process to us. At the same time, we hear the syrup drip into the pails, the birds chirp, and the wind blow. Country music from his youth is heard, and we see montages of still photographs move to these musical rhythms.

The filmmaker of the film biography, then, can creatively round out information about people by artistically showing their activities.

The Film Autobiography

Autobiographical films have been made for some time, particularly by experimental filmmakers. Recently, Federico Fellini has developed the form in very personal ways.

Three of his autobiographical films are *Fellini: A Director's Notebook* (1968), *The Clowns* (1970), and *Roma* (1972). *Amarcord* (1974) effectively combines autobiographical and narrative techniques.

Fellini: A Director's Notebook shows some of the preproduction problems of *Fellini-Satyricon* (1969), as well as his attempts to make a never-produced movie called *The Voyage of Mastorna.* Made for television, the picture takes us on an excursion through dead sets, rooms of dead props, and piles of drawings and diagrams. The film explores the director's creative difficulties. We experience his attempts to find a film form different from that of his previous pictures. Just as his 1963 narrative film *8½* explored the influences of memory, illusion, and reality on a famous film director (who was both Fellini as he is and Fellini as he might be), so in the autobiographical documentary Fellini probed his unconscious and his creative urges.

Many of Fellini's past movies referred to the circus and to clowns. The music of his regular composer, Nino Rota, and the faces and costumes of his many characters testify to this. In *The Clowns,* Fellini himself searched for movies, photographs, and information about clowns. With a cameraman, sound man, and script clerk with him as actors in the film, he was able to use the medium to explore his own feelings about this influence on him. In *The Clowns* we move from Fellini's memories into the actuality of his staging a circus. Thus, clowns, the circus, life, and creativity all merge into a show simultaneously being filmed and viewed.

In *Roma,* the camera as metaphor is even more apparent. Fellini explores the city he loves to try to understand it. He brings his camera into Rome through severe rain. He travels underneath the city and finds the perfectly preserved ruins of an ancient Roman villa. Fellini attempts here to document his city by using cinema to explore relationships between himself and the raw materials that he uses to give life to his creations. In this sense, *Roma,* like *The Clowns* and *Fellini: A Director's Notebook,* is as much about the director as about his subject.

A feeling of direct and immediate experience occurs only rarely in documentary films. Some of the best *cinéma-vérité* makes this happen. In Fellini's autobiographical documentaries, as focused and as restrained as they are, such feelings do come about.

The Newsreel and the Archival Film

Before television, of course, newsreels were an important part of the movie experience. They would be distributed weekly to theaters to inform the public about recent events. Such compilations as *Fox Movietone News* served much the same purpose as news clips do now on television. And, at fairly regular intervals, there were such longer pieces as those prepared by *The March of Time,* which would cover in some detail an event or personality of importance. Television today is the primary means of delivering newsreel information. News clips, with correspondents' voices explaining them, carry the evening news shows, with an anchor man or woman briefly introducing the clips.

News film is, of course, shot on the spot. Sometimes it is shot with elaborate preparations, with much attention to placement of lights and microphones; sometimes the news event has to be "grabbed" spontaneously. News film is fairly predictable. For example, we can usually depend on the interview to explain what visuals show; sometimes we see only the person interviewed. The commentator sums up what we have seen, then the image usually takes over for a moment, with the camera panning a scene, zooming out from it, or resting for emphasis on the object of discussion.

News film can provide a visual record that may be useful to historians, political scientists, and students. In addition, motion pictures may be deliberately shot only for archival purposes. A conversation with a visiting distinguished person at a university, the demolition of a building, the hitting style of a baseball player, a military parade, the funeral of an important person, or the reminiscences of an elderly person—all are materials for films that can be shot for archives, to be viewed later by scholars and other interested people.

Stylistically, archival films are undistinguished. Their main purpose is to record events as conservatively as possible, without using the medium to add comment to it. For example, films of basketball games shot for the use of coaches and players do not need fancy zooms, cutaways to cheerleaders, and close-ups of the coach's face. Showing the players execute the strategy is what is important if the film is to be valuable to future strategy through analysis of plays.

Thus, newsreel and archival films are important records of human activity. They allow us to see and analyze significant events and are invaluable aids to research.

The various types of documentaries indicate that style and technique are important for us to consider in testing the reliability of the events films show us. The degree of truth in a picture frequently is directly related to the purpose of the film and the skill of the filmmaker.

Evolution of the Documentary Film

9

The history of the documentary film can be studied in three ways: (1) the development of a fascination with a medium that could so accurately show the world, (2) the evolution of ideas about how to use that medium to show reality, and (3) the growth of film technology. This chapter is about these three ideas.

Early Attempts at Recording Reality

By the late 1800s, the whole world was subject to view. Through kinetoscopes in nickelodeons, and at special projection houses, audiences thrilled to scenes of New York City, to panoramas of Buffalo's International Exhibition of 1898, and to views of Chicago at night. Films showed immigrants arriving at Ellis Island and authenticated the Inauguration of President McKinley.

By 1910, hundreds of films showing unusual places and practices were available. A 336-page *Catalogue of Educational Motion Picture Films,* put out in that year by George Kleine of the Kleine

Opposite page: From Robert Flaherty's *Man of Aran.* Courtesy Contemporary/McGraw-Hill Films. (The Museum of Modern Art/Film Stills Archive.)

Optical Company, lists titles, content, length, and prices of scores of films under twenty-nine headings from Agriculture to Zoology, varying in subject matter from Kindergarten Studies to Railroad to Religion. The catalogue shows that some of the ideas of what we now call the documentary film were used and considered in early films. As an introduction points out about the title, "The word 'Educational' is here used in a wide sense, and does not indicate that these films are intended for school or college use exclusively. They are intended rather for the education of the adult as well as the youth, for exhibition before miscellaneous audiences, as well as for more restricted use." An introductory essay, "The World Before Your Eyes," by University of Chicago professor Frederick K. Starr, makes a rationale for the documentary film that contains basic ideas about film's ability to show the world *(see inset,* page 178).

The range of films available is enormous, and the catalogue not only lists films but also describes them, sometimes with scene-by-scene notation *(see inset,* page 179). The catalogue makes fascinating reading, especially as it reminds us of the interest filmmakers have had from the beginning in unusual practices and exotic places. The fascination of the "travelogue" impelled people to use film for documentary purposes through the entire early history of motion pictures.

Views of an Eminent Educator: "The World Before Your Eyes"

I have seen Niagara thunder over her gorge in the noblest frenzy ever beheld by man; I have watched a Queensland river under the white light of an Australasian moon go whirling and swirling through strange islands lurking with bandicoot and kangaroo; I have watched an English railroad train draw into a station, take on its passengers, and then chug away with its stubby little engine through the Yorkshire Dells, past old Norman Abbeys silhouetted against the skyline, while a cluster of century-aged cottages loomed up in the valley below, through which a yokel drove his flocks of Southdowns [sheep]; I have beheld fat old Rajahs with the price of a thousand lives bejeweled in their monster turbans, and the price of a thousand deaths sewn in their royal nightshirts as they indolently swayed in golden howdahs, borne upon the backs of grunting elephants; I saw a runaway horse play battledoor and shuttlecock with the citizens and traffic of a little Italian village, whose streets had not known so much commotion since the sailing of Columbus; I know how the Chinaman lives and I have been through the homes of the Japanese; I have marveled at the daring of Alpine tobogganists and admired the wonderful skill of Norwegian ski jumpers; I have seen armies upon the battlefield and their return in triumph; I have looked upon weird dances and outlandish frolics in every quarter of the globe, and I didn't have to leave Chicago for a moment.

No books have taught me all these wonderful things; no lecturer has pictured them; I simply dropped into a moving picture theatre at various moments of leisure; and, at the total cost for all the visits of perhaps two performances of a foolish musical show, I have learned more than a traveler could see at the cost of thousands of dollars and years of journey.

Neither you nor I fully realize what the moving picture has meant to us, and what it is going to mean. We're living at a mile-a-second gait in the swiftest epoch of the world's progress—in the age of incredibilities come true. We fly through the air, chat with our friends in Paris by squirting a little spark from a pole on one shore of the Atlantic to another pole on the other side, and so we take as a matter of course that which our great grandfathers would have declared a miracle.

The talking machine has canned the great voices and master melodies of our time, but the moving picture machine has done more—it is making for us volumes of history and action; it is not only the greatest impulse of entertainment but the mightiest force of instruction. . . .

The moving picture machine is an advantage—a tremendous, vital force of culture as well as amusement. It affords a clean entertainment, lecture, and amusement all rolled in one. In its highest effort it stands above the literature, in its less ambitious phase it ranks above the tawdry show house. . . .

The moving picture is not a makeshift, but the highest type of entertainment in the history of the world. . . . Its value cannot be measured now, but another generation will benefit more largely through its influence than we of today can possibly realize.

Two Examples from the 1910 Catalogue of Educational Motion Picture Films

Mecca Pilgrims

Approximate Length 440 feet. Code "Mecca."

This annual pilgrimage to Mecca of devout Mohammedans from all parts of the Eastern World is one of the most remarkable sights to be witnessed, and our operator was fortunate in securing passage on a steamer crowded with pilgrims from Port Said to Jeddah, the port of debarkation for Mecca. His difficulties were numerous, for the Moslem objects strenuously to the camera as an unholy device. Only by looking in another direction—after focusing the groups—could he take his pictures. The subjects innocently thought that he was photographing something within the circle of his own gaze, but in reality the eye of the camera was on them, while his own were casually fixed on the distant scene.

Order of Pictures:

1. Panorama of Port Said, the Pilgrim Harbor. Crowded boats.

2. A marine barber; shaving the pilgrims by primitive and painful methods.

3. The mouth of the Suez Canal.

4. Progress along the Canal, with views of passing traffic, desolation of its banks, with an occasional palm grove oasis.

5. The Red Sea. Views from the turtle deck. Beautiful spray and wave effects.

6. Sunset in the Red Sea. Cloud and moonlight effects wonderful. The dark background and the scintillating water adding peculiar charm to the scenes.

7. The Asiatic Coast. Towns on the banks. Smooth waters, indented land scenery.

8. Outside Jeddah Harbor. Pilgrims preparing to land. A motley crowd with few clothes, but many umbrellas.

9. Transferring passengers from the ship to the surf boats. Interesting scenes of native shows and other craft.

10. The Quarantine Harbor. Boats sailing hither and thither. Steamer lying off.

11. Jeddah. Panoramic distant and close views. A most interesting picture.

The Acrobatic Fly

Approximate Length, 200 feet.

Here is the greatest and most interesting novelty in a motion picture that has ever been produced.

It has been written about by most of the leading daily newspapers and by all the trade papers in the country. It is a splendid example of Micro-Kinematography, that is to say, the photographing of minute objects by means of a microscopic attachment to the camera. Thus, we see a common house-fly, seemingly as large as a fox-terrier, while lying on its back, perform a number of acrobatic feats which would do credit to the most skillful Japanese juggler.

First, we see it balance a beam on its feet, then twirl a bar-bell and spin a monster ball on its feet, upon which another fly cleverly keeps its balance. Lastly, the fly actually sits in an arm-chair of a size proportionate to itself, and in that position rolls a big ball, held at "arm's length," in its feet. The fly's tongue is frequently thrust out, looking like an elephant's trunk. The hairs all over its body resemble porcupine's quills more than anything else. Don't miss the "Acrobatic Fly."

Robert Flaherty

Robert Flaherty was an American explorer with an interest in anthropological field work. During the 1910s he traveled to the Arctic Circle to accumulate "visual notes" on Eskimo life. After several years, he returned to Toronto and tried to put his material into some dramatic form. In those days, nitrate film stock was standard—and it also was very flammable, and Flaherty accidentally ignited about 30,000 feet of film. Although the film represented a lot of work, Flaherty was not unduly distressed, for he realized the footage was quite bad. He decided, therefore, to go about it again.

Sponsored by Réveillon Frères, a Paris fur company, Flaherty spent two months in Port Harrison on Hudson Bay with two new Akley motion picture cameras, which he had tested for the cold, and processing and printing equipment. For this second attempt, Flaherty wisely decided to show Eskimo life as exemplified by one person, and he chose an Eskimo named Nanook. In the film, Nanook's innocent smile and interest are genuine and beguiling. Moreover, Nanook proved to have an innate dramatic sense, and he helped Flaherty by thinking up new scenes typical of Eskimo life for the picture. (Not all were successful. When Nanook thought that one good scene would be to show him hunting and killing a polar bear, the bear proved large and uncooperative, and Nanook and Flaherty had to run for their lives.) One powerful scene, which shows the battle for survival against the elements—the basis for conflict in Flaherty's many films—shows Nanook, his family, and his sled dogs rushing for safety in the midst of a howling windstorm. (About two years after Flaherty left Port Harrison, Nanook died in a similar storm.)

Released in 1922, *Nanook of the North* was the first full-length documentary film. Many people date the evolution of the form from this picture, and though this is not accurate, *Nanook* does represent one of the first documentaries with a style and theme beyond simple observation. In this as in Flaherty's later films, we see the camera used to give us a feeling for place and situation, rather than merely to present the subject. Flaherty not only had a descriptive and dramatic eye; but by his own humanity and interest, he was able to pull natural performances out of the people he filmed. His famous use of the pan shot, which some say seems to "caress" what it sees, testifies to this. His romanticism, as evidenced by his beautiful compositions and the use of motion within shots, underscored his primary theme—that of man against nature.

One biography of Flaherty is entitled *The Innocent Eye,* * and Flaherty's cinematography and his editing do indeed give his films a quality of innocence. Although critics rarely discredit his images, they sometimes fault his vision, saying, for instance, that his man-against-nature theme does not apply to the industrial twentieth century. Yet this theme deals with ideas, and *Nanook of the North* represents a breakthrough in the documentary form, for this film is in part a documentary of ideas. Flaherty believed the camera was a tool for exploration. It not only observed but it penetrated the mysteries of humankind's interconnection with the natural world. By letting us see for ourselves rather than being told what to see, the image became the primary tool for exploration, presenting material for interpretation.

As Flaherty continued to perfect his style, he created images of incredible beauty. He main-

---

*Arthur Calder-Marshall, *The Innocent Eye: The Life of Robert J. Flaherty* (New York: Harcourt Brace Jovanovich, 1966; Baltimore, Md.: Penguin Books, 1970).

9.1 A will to survive is shown in *Man of Aran* by Robert Flaherty. (The Museum of Modern Art/Film Stills Archive. Courtesy Contemporary/ McGraw-Hill Films.)

tained his noninvolved approach to show human behavior through the atmosphere suggested by the images. To get exactly what he wanted, he shot a great deal of film, with a high ratio of footage shot to footage used. For instance, in *Louisiana Story* (1948), he shot 200,000 feet of film, but the final print was only 8,000 feet. This sacrifice of spontaneity results in a highly disciplined "nonstyle," in which the atmosphere relates emotions similar to those the subjects of the films express.

Movies became for Flaherty the perfect medium for expressing his romanticism. A basic idea of romanticism is that content and feeling predominate over traditional structures. Because film has no traditional structure (although it borrowed dramatic structure from theater and literature and used imagistic structures from painting and still photography), Flaherty saw the opportunity to explore the limits of the medium in relation to his own views of the world.

This can particularly be seen in his third documentary feature, *Man of Aran* (1934), which shows the harshness of life in the Aran Islands, off the west coast of Ireland. The sea is a stormy and unpredictable enemy that the islanders have to confront to survive. The land is without soil and so they must dig seaweed from rock crevices to form beds of earth in which potatoes can grow. In order to show the cruelty and the beauty of this harsh existence, Flaherty spent several months living with the people and shooting film. As in *Nanook,* he concentrated on one particular family. To get the visual atmosphere his theme required, he used the telephoto lens. By shooting men in their small boats from as much as half a mile away, he was able to create an impressionistic sea. In *Man of Aran,* the striking final shots of

Man of Aran (continued). Another example of man against nature. (The Museum of Modern Art/Film Stills Archive. Courtesy Contemporary/McGraw-Hill Films.)

the sea crashing against tall cliffs and sweeping over rocks was shot from two miles away. The shimmering textures testify to how cinematography can express the world through its own unique ways of seeing. Flaherty also used the telephoto lens to catch the light and shadows of the sun baking the Aran Islands, showing that if anything can sustain people in the harsh battle for survival, it is that beauty of shadow and sun that patterns rock, wood, the people, and the sea. Flaherty's almost physical textures, created from light reflected against rough surfaces, illustrate a will to survive that transcends the mere physical.

Louisiana Story, shot fourteen years later (he made two other pictures before it), shows the life of a boy in the Louisiana swamps and examines the imposition of technology, in the form of oil wells, on nature. Flaherty's sense of awe controls the first sequence. The camera, which is continually moving, tracks the boy, who is in a boat with his pet racoon. He travels almost dreamily through the swamp, observing birds, alligators, and other wild life. A feeling for the sublime is projected to us by seeing the innocence of uncorrupted man (the boy) confronted with the beauty and mystery of nature. As the boy and the camera —both floating in boats—rhythmically penetrate the primeval world the images suggest, Flaherty contrasts the feeling of looking at the swamp with being in it.

As in *Man of Aran,* Flaherty shot simultaneously with more than one camera, frequently with a different lens on each. This gave him variety of materials to select from in the editing room so that he could exploit the internal rhythms of these shots to emphasize the feeling for mystery and awe.

Flaherty has said that the "camera is like a horse with blinkers on"; that is, it sees only what it is directly looking at. But the parts of a scene the camera sees become a metaphor for the whole. At the same time, the images themselves contain power. Through the composition of the images as well as through their rhythms, the documentary filmmaker, according to Flaherty, can "discover and reveal" to us the world. This is what exploration is all about, and this is, finally, what the "innocent eye" can reveal: a world truly seen.

Dziga Vertov and the Kino-Eye

The polemic documentary appeared during the 1920s. The theories and films of Dziga Vertov (real name Denis Kaufman), a Ukrainian, show the possibilities of the documentary that creates reality through cinematic contrivance. After the 1917 Russian Revolution, Vertov assumed the job of editing all newsreels for the whole Soviet Union. Lenin had declared that film was to be a primary propaganda tool for the revolution, and Vertov set out to create a documentary form that could express this notion.

His idea of the *Kino-Eye* ("camera eye") was that the camera could become a person's eyes. He believed that the camera lens was more perfectable than the human eye, and that if it were manipulated, it could achieve a higher truth than could the human eye. In 1919, he issued a "Manifesto" (revised and published in 1922), in which he described the possibilities of a new cinema, one that would give audiences news rather than dramatic entertainment. By 1924, he and his co-workers, known as the *Kino-Eye Group,* had put out newsreels to the Soviet public. One series was known as *Kino-Pravda* or "movie truth" (which translates into French as *cinéma-vérité*—Vertov influenced recent *cinéma-vérité* filmmakers). By 1925,

Vertov and his Kino-Eye Group headed all Soviet documentary filmmaking.

To get Soviet cinema "to enter the arena of life itself," as Vertov put it, and to create a cinematography of facts, he theorized and experimented with all sorts of camera manipulations. Armed with the idea that the camera is as portable as one's person and could go anyplace, he set out to find the "truth" in as much of Russian life as he could. His basic idea was that the camera could be manipulated to achieve the truth of an action.

He also experimented with frame-rate speed, declaring that in any shot there is a particular rate of cranking that will capture the essential nature of the action. In addition, he believed that camera angle could show an action's point of most reality, that an object could be studied by means of the freeze frame, and that the camera could track or otherwise move with a moving object to achieve the sense of motion that most described the essence of the action.

These and other ideas were used in his 1928 feature documentary, *The Man with a Movie Camera,* made with his cinematographer brother, Mikhail. This film uses split-screen images, the freeze frame, stop motion, slow motion, accelerated motion, animation (single-frame shooting), superimposition, montage, associational editing, the moving camera, the concealed camera, the hand-held camera, and just about every other manipulative device known at the time. The result is a virtuoso performance of the *Kino-Eye.*

The picture was shot in Moscow, Kiev, and Odessa, and it attempts to recreate the rhythms of a large Soviet city from morning till evening. But it does more than this. The film repeatedly shows us the cameraman taking the picture we are seeing.

This second level of reality is set up in the beginning sequence, which shows us an empty theater being made ready for the audience. The seats of the auditorium chairs fold down like row after row of identically strung puppets. The audience crowds into the theater, we among them. The carbon arcs, the light sources of the projectors, are fired. In the orchestra pit, the leader raises his baton, and presumably the orchestra in our movie house begins to play as the conductor gives his cue.

The curtain opens, and the film begins on the screen in front of us in the movie. Then that screen becomes the screen in our own auditorium. We see an apartment house in early morning. A man comes out of it with his camera and tripod on his shoulder. During the movie, this man seems to go everyplace and shoot everything. We are privileged to see a young lady waking up, washing, and getting dressed. We observe deserted, early morning streets. As the morning wears on, the streets become more crowded.

Through it all, Vertov shows us that the *Kino-Eye* is everywhere and that what we see being filmed can be life itself. Signs and billboard posters show us Lenin and give us slogans. Machinery starts up in factories. Street trolleys leave their garages and enter the streets. An aristocratic-looking lady and her friends ride in a horse-drawn carriage. We see the cameraman tracking them from a moving automobile, and we see the shots of her that he takes. Some people respond to the camera; they wave at it, grimace at it, try to hide from it. Other people are unaware of the camera or do not care about it.

The cameraman shoots from the dangerous heights of a tall industrial chimney and from an open cable car precariously riding over a huge waterfall and reservoir. He shoots a train coming at him (us) from the angle of the tracks themselves, and he squeezes between trolley tracks to show

9.2 Classification of shots for the movie we are seeing, from *Man With a Movie Camera*. (The Museum of Modern Art/Film Stills Archive.)

us vehicles simultaneously coming and going, their images occasionally split on the screen. We see the cameraman at the beach, after the work day, shooting swimmers and sunbathers. We are given the rhythms of life through the camera's eye.

We see the editing room where the picture we are watching is being assembled. We see the editor cut a shot of a close-up of a young boy's face, then we are shown the shot we have just seen cut. At the end of the film, we are brought back into the theater. The camera, personified through animation, takes several bows, presumably to the applause of the audience.

The techniques of the *Kino-Eye* provide a life for events we know are photographed. There is no attempt here to "hide" the camera in the action, as Flaherty did. Morover, whereas in Flaherty's films, space takes over time—that is,

the events and actions play themselves; the objects filmed create the reality—in Vertov's film time takes over space. The rhythms created by sometimes astonishing camera manipulations and by editing, rather than the actual events themselves, create what we see.

Sound in the Documentary Film

The popularity of the documentary film continued into the 1930s. The coming of sound offered the form new possibilities, for now the sounds of people's voices and activities would further verify their patterns of life.

The newsreel was one of the first types of documentaries to do this. In 1927 George Bernard Shaw talked for Fox Movietone News. In the film he ambled up a garden path, saw the camera, greeted the audience, and—stopping right on cue, under the fixed microphone—began to chat. Perhaps because of the playwright's reputation for volubility, the audience was apparently not affronted by this monologue.

Newsreels, with a narrator's voice and appropriately dubbed-in sounds, came to be expected by weekly movie goers. Soon short features such as travelogues, animated cartoons, and humorous monologues, also became regular fare. Satirist Robert Benchley starred in a series of monologues in the role of a speaker of sorts at a public meeting. His *The Sex Life of the Polyp* (1928), supposedly delivered to a lady's group, discussed with total ignorance the mating habits of this miniscule animal.

It did not take long for documentary filmmakers to see uses for sound outside the straight one-to-one relationship between what is heard and what is viewed. Voice-over narration, music, and sound effects came to be used regularly. Before 1934, they were mostly used in parallel sound situations, in which the narration gave the viewers information about what they were seeing, the music supported the emotion of the images, and the sound effects either arose from action or created an environment. Dialogue and actual sounds were seldom used, and such subjective sounds as reminiscences in the mind of a character were even rarer. Artifact sounds were mostly dubbed-in sound effects.

In 1934, Basil Wright's *Song of Ceylon* showed the possible uses for sound/image counterpoint. Produced by John Grierson for the Ceylon Tea Propaganda Board, this film juxtaposed rural Ceylonese life with the imposition of Western industrial life. The theme of the film was that the two cultures could live side by side, each deriving cultural benefits from the other. The film is divided into four major sequences: (1) "The Buddha," (2) "The Virgin Island," (3) "The Voices of Commerce," and (4) "The Apparel of God."

The first two sequences show us the fusion between Buddhism and the Singhalese way of life. We see primitive methods of planting and harvesting and get a picture of a peaceful life involved with nature. We see the jungles, the villages, the huge statues of Buddha. We observe the tranquility of the people through their actions and the contentment on their faces. Up till this point, the film seems like a well-made travelogue. Strong rhythms are created by the beating of drums and the chanting of young boys taking dancing lessons. This rhythm builds to "The Voices of Commerce."

This third sequence immediately suggests the imposition of the industrial West on this Eden. The rhythm of the chanting from "The Virgin Island" gives way to the chugging of a train. It whistles, as if to announce an intrusion into Singhalese life. The train noise continues, counterpointing shots of lush jungle, taken from the train. Western technology enters Ceylon in this way, visually and audially penetrating the interior of both the island and its ritual culture. We see a shot of an elephant and his master pushing over a tree, presumably to make room for more railroad tracks. The train's chugging slows down and seems to strain in concert with the elephant at work. As the tree is uprooted and falls, a loud gong is heard.

Enter the "voices of commerce." As detached voices quote the commodities market, we hear radio messages and the signal of Morse code. Typewriter chatter comes in. We see telephone operators busily plugging calls into their boards. The busy life of modern Western civilization, given to us primarily through sound, counter-

9.3 The Acropolis and statues of perfect form, from the opening of Leni Riefenstahl's *Olympia, Part One.* (The Museum of Modern Art/ Film Stills Archive.)

points the images of elephants, of a boy climbing a tree for coconuts, of the religious life. The film becomes a "song" in counterpoint. The rhythms of native life are juxtaposed with the rhythms of industry, with the idea that they can merge for the mutual benefit of both.

The fourth sequence, "The Apparel of a God," tends to contradict this idea. We see ritual dances of the steps toward achieving *Nirvana.* We see a lone man bring a bowl of rice to a huge sleeping Buddha, say a prayer, then go on his way. The film seems to be saying that, despite the modern intrusion, the ancient way of life will endure.

However flawed the film may seem today, forty years later, we must be aware that it was intended to be shown to British audiences still sympathetic to the notion of colonialism. That it successfully expresses the values and rituals of the Singhalese people speaks well for the objective stance of Wright and Grierson. The use of sound to indicate the intrusion of "progress" into Singhalese life perhaps supported the audience's view that the British Empire (and the Ceylon Tea people) were trading civilization for tea. Yet the difficulty with the innovative use of sound in the film is that most people are struck by and believe images. Sound can embellish, explain, and contradict the images, but the picture still remains primary.

Harry Watt and Basil Wright's *Night Mail* (1936) further advances the use of sound in the documentary film. This film shows us the British

postal system's procedures in moving night mail by train from London to Glasgow. The rhythms the procedure creates are emphasized by montage accompanied by actual sound (the chugging train), by music, and by a rhythmically read poem of W. H. Auden (written especially for this film).

In Pare Lorentz's 1936 *The Plow that Broke the Plains,* shots of American farmers at work in their fields during World War I are rhythmically edited with sounds of the military marching and fighting. Virgil Thomson's music adds an idiom of place and historical time to the film by using folk tunes as basic melodies and World War I songs such as *"Inky Dinky Parlez-vous."*

In *The River,* Lorentz shows the lyrical uses of voice-over narration. Thomson's music also

works well here, as it flows through this picture about the misuses of the Mississippi River, accompanied by poetic, though propagandistic, narration.

Two Polemic Styles

Two polemic documentary styles were developed in the 1930s: (1) the documentary of classic structure that attempts to create myth and (2) the subjective social documentary. We can see these expressed in Leni Riefenstahl's *Olympia* (1936–1938), in Jean Vigo's *A Propos de Nice* (1930), and in Ralph Steiner and Willard Van Dyke's *The City* (1939).

Riefenstahl's Olympia

The 1936 Olympic games in Berlin provided the raw material for Leni Riefenstahl's two-part film, *Olympia*. The opening sequence of Part I is one of the finest beginnings in film history. Designed to trace the Olympic games from their origins in Greece to the modern games in Berlin, this sequence is at once a romantic overture and a masterpiece of propaganda. Heavily romantic music accompanies a view of barren land, seen through clouds. The camera is constantly moving, and we see the land give way to a slow, rhythmic pan shot of ancient figures preparing for games or battle, sculptured in relief against stone. The music crescendos as we discover that we are on Mount Olympus. Close-ups of statues with perfect features seem to move through space. We see the Parthenon, then enter it to observe its architectural perfection. Movement dissolves into movement and we eventually see the famous statue of the discus thrower. With a thrust of music, the statue dissolves to a naked man, of the same build and in the same posture. We see naked women rhythmically exercising. Finally, a modern 1936 athlete lights a torch at Mount Olympus. He runs with it and passes it to another athlete. As the runners bring the torch closer and closer to Berlin, maps in relief dissolve and superimpose with them. At last, torch and runner arrive at Berlin, and in a low-angle shot, designed to equate the *Führer* with the gods at Olympus, the camera looks up at Hitler in his majestic box, making him seem a Roman emperor for whose purposes the people gather and before whom the Olympic teams parade.

This opening sequence suggests not only affinities between the gods and Hitler, it also stresses a direct link between perfect form and the purity of the German race. It honors the human body by showing its rhythms and textures, and it links Teutonic mythology with Naziism. Germany, personified by Hitler, is seen in mythic proportions, drawn by the controlled composition of this sequence. Shadow and light play off against strong linear composition; perfect bodies glisten in heroic poses.

The rest of the film shows highlights of the various track and field events. Occasionally, there is a shot of Hitler reacting to the action, looking through binoculars, or discussing matters with the Nazi high command. We see very little of Jessie Owens, the American black track star and world record holder who won the hundred meter dash, the two hundred meter dash, and the running broad jump. The film shows him in action only once, and the scenes of his being awarded the laurel wreath and of Hitler refusing to shake his hand are left out altogether.

Vigo's A Propos de Nice

Jean Vigo's 1930 *A Propos de Nice* ("About Nice") is very montage-like, with quick cuts and unusual juxtapositions. It is not surprising that the cameraman was Dziga Vertov's brother, Boris Kaufman, who evidently had a distinct editing style in mind.

The film covers the streets and shops of the French Riviera city of Nice. It shows us tourists' faces, people preparing for Carnival, dances, and gaiety, all under the protective roofs and chimneys of the old city. It shows us the beaches and the promenades of the very rich and contrasts this activity with the faces and actions of the poor, the neglected people who are the city's real proprietors.

This silent film takes a strong social stance and at times caricatures the tourists—all in visual terms, without titles. In one scene, for instance, similar physical attributes and positions equate figures in a cemetery with figures of the rich on the Promenade. This lyrical documentary shows the power of associating conflicting images to provide social comment based on the premise that most people are fools.

Steiner and Van Dyke's The City

The City was made by Ralph Steiner and Willard Van Dyke for the 1939 New York World's Fair, where it was shown daily to large audiences. Sponsored by the American Institute of Planners, the film strikes out against pollution and inadequate living standards in the big cities.

The first sequence suggests that the simple, rural-based New England life made us in tune with ourselves and with nature. The second sequence contrasts this ideal bucolic existence with images of mud streets, tenements, and factory workers' shacks enveloped in dirt and smoke. "Smoke makes prosperity," the narrator intones over these despairing images, "even if you choke on it."

The third sequence is about humans as automatons. Through montage, city dwellers are shown as crowds rather than individuals. Pedestrians try to cross streets thronged with cars. Trucks, cars, and taxicabs create traffic jams. Always in a hurry, people walk faster than they can ride. One famous scene shows people at a lunch counter eating as automatically as the toasters and pancake-making machines that prepare the food. The editing rhythm finally increases to show two ladies seated at the counter; in synchronized movements, they finish their coffee, pick up their tabs, and leave.

The fourth sequence shows the weekend mad escape from the city. We see jammed-up highways with people eating picnic lunches beside the road, still suffering the agitation of the city. There seems to be no escape from the technological, mechanistic monster humankind has created; it

seems bent on destroying us. The final sequence, however, suggests a possible solution—new cooperatives where nature and industry can complement each other. Based on the idea of the New England community, such towns would give workers a better way of life by making them interdependent with each other and with nature. An "American Dream" could be achieved, the film suggests, in which workers serve the community and retain their family life.

The City structures narration, music, and natural sounds (cars, horns, factories, birds) to influence its progression. The hectic rhythms of the middle section and the slow rhythms of the second section are juxtaposed with the idealism of the first and fourth sections, which frame modern life. Although dated, *The City* is still an exciting film, and Americans certainly have not yet taken its message to heart.

From 1930 to 1950

Great Britain during the 1930s and 1940s gave direction and definition to the evolving documentary form. As theoretician, writer, and movie producer, John Grierson was largely responsible for giving freedom to experimental documentary filmmakers; he also influenced the social responsibility of the documentary film. He realized that the documentary film, by the very fact that it deals with social institutions, has to take into account ethical and social values. He encouraged government agencies and private industry to sponsor films.

As film producer for the Empire Marketing Board, and later head of the GPO (General Post Office) Film Unit, he produced scores of films, many of them using techniques new to the documentary. The Empire Marketing Board, through Grierson, was responsible for getting the sponsor for the *Song of Ceylon* and other films. The GPO Film Unit supported the work of such important British filmmakers and critics as Len Lye, Paul Rotha, Basil Wright, Harry Watt, and Alberto Cavalcanti. Through all this activity, documentary filmmakers continued to explore techniques that could both show and comment on people's relationships to institutions.

The War Documentary

The growing sophistication of technique helped the rapid evolution of the British war film. When Britain stood alone against Germany and the people rallied around Prime Minister Winston Churchill, the documentary film became, from 1939 on, a device to support the war effort and to instill pride and fortitude in the British people. One such film was Humphrey Jennings's *Listen to Britain* (1941), which uses the actual sounds of the country to present an aural and visual record of the war effort in the British Isles. Sound, then, is the predominant structural device. Designed as a symphony, the picture uses compilation techniques to give a sense of place and to provide a historic structure.

The Royal Air Force Film Production Unit also continued the tradition of the British documentary. *Desert Victory* (1943), directed by David McDonald, covered the famous battle between German Field Marshal Rommel and British Field Marshal Montgomery in Africa. Informative and compelling, this film showed that the war documentary could derive a narrative line from the events of a battle and, through the use of battle footage, could translate them into a powerful drama, authentic at its core.

In the United States, Hollywood director Frank Capra assumed the job of producing and directing wartime propaganda films for the Army. As producer of the *Why We Fight* series, he produced such films as *Prelude to War* (1942), *The Battle of Britain* (1941), and *The Battle of Russia* (1942–45).

The war helped bring the documentary film to a large audience. The newsreels of the war, the *Why We Fight* series, and such compilations as *The True Glory,* advanced the form's structure while at the same time it made it more intimate, for the hand-held camera created informal images, thus providing material that was compiled rather than prearranged. These war documentaries brought the battlefields into local theaters, and were precursors of the battlefield cinematography of the Vietnam war, which through television brought the battlefield into the home.

The British Free Cinema

Following World War II, social consciousness permeated the communication arts. "What did it all mean?" "What can we do now?" "Where are we going?" were questions asked with the hope of building a better, more peaceful world. The war was fought by civilians, not generals, and the war documentaries brought real people, caught unawares, onto the movie screens.

After the war, the British Film Institute set up a so-called Experimental Production Committee, which supported filmmakers involved in making noncommercial movies with uncommon subject matters and styles. This "free cinema" idea not only underscored the importance the British had been giving the cinema for two decades, but it also emphasized their interest in advancing documentary techniques through experimentation. British Free Cinema became an important turning point in the evolution of the documentary film in England and in documentary history generally.

Free Cinema applied new, freer structures to

the traditional documentary concerns of showing institutional processes and illustrating social issues. The forms of many of these films focused on the difficulties of people who were lost in the maze of their own culture.

For instance, *Every Day Except Christmas* (1957), by Lindsay Anderson and others, shows the delivery process for Covent Garden, London's once-famous produce and flower market. The picture, however, does more than explain procedures; it shows the story of workers whose lives are formed by the institution and their commitment to it. The film suggests their motivations by sympathetically viewing people at their jobs, by recording their dialogue, and by concentrating the camera on their physical characteristics. In other words, Covent Garden works, the film suggests, because of the people's personal commitment to it.

Free Cinema used some of the ideas and techniques created by the Italian neorealists, such as the concentration on individuals searching for meaning in society's attitudes and institutions. Lorenza Mazzetti and Denis Horne's *Together* (1956) is about two deaf mutes isolated from society and connected to each other by their common disability. The camera observes them among streets as desolate as their lives. We see them at work as longshoremen and we feel the jibes ignorant children throw at them. The film also has a fantasy sequence that interweaves their objective problem and their subjective feelings around the need to be loved by a woman. Seeing them both cold and detached as well as through their emotional needs, we are impelled to examine society's personal attitudes.

In *Nice Time* (Alain Tanner and Claude Goretta, 1956) and in *Momma Don't Allow* (Karel Reisz and Tony Richardson, 1955), the camera is almost totally objective. The first film shows Piccadilly Circus on a weekend night; the second film describes a typical evening at a jazz nightclub. In each case, an underlying theme is that people, faced with the necessity to "have fun," try to overcome their loneliness by participating in social institutions designed for a "good time." The search for a good time—at once pathetic and dehumanizing—results from attitudes society has bred in us.

These films imply that a person's search for individuality itself becomes structured. They suggest that the lives of ordinary people are hollow and predetermined, and that their patterns of behavior are strongly influenced by society.

The move toward examining behavior within institutions—rather than the procedures of the institutions themselves—was an important factor in moving the narrative film toward more realism, particularly in Great Britain. Several of the Free Cinema filmmakers (among them Tony Richardson and Lindsay Anderson) went on to incorporate their ideas into significant narrative films.

The Rise of Cinéma-Vérité

Cinéma-vérité represents a revival of ideas expressed by Robert Flaherty and Dziga Vertov. Flaherty believed the documentary should be as objective as possible and that film structure should not get in the way of content. Dziga Vertov believed that the cameraman should go to where things were happening and shoot them spontaneously and that the camera could—and possibly should—be a part of the information shown.

In its attempt to show "truth," *cinéma-vérité* ideally lets people speak for themselves as they react both to their lives and to the camera. *Cinéma-vérité* filmmakers try not to interfere with the events they film. The difference between people being aware of the camera and hence not acting natural and people unaware of the camera and thus being themselves is an important problem for these filmmakers. For *cinéma-vérité* is basically an attitude toward one's subject as well as toward the film medium itself. *Cinéma-vérité* is neither a movement nor a style, but rather an attempt to accurately show the world through cinema's technology.

Although some people call any film in which the shots jump and zoom and the camera appears to be hand-held *"cinéma-vérité,"* the basic idea, as we saw in the last chapter, emerged in the late 1950s and early 1960s with the development of new kinds of equipment and technology: light-weight, portable cameras that could be hand-held; light-weight, portable sound equipment; directional microphones, which could be "aimed" at a subject in order to select speech from a distance; and faster film stock, which did away with the need for extensive lighting.

These developments were accompanied by a general move in filmmaking toward examining people's motivations rather than just describing their actions. *Cinéma-vérité* filmmakers discovered that if they let their subjects talk long enough in front of their cameras, they would continue to reveal more and more about themselves. This idea of revelation can become almost anthropological in the attitude a filmmaker takes toward a subject. In studying the behavior patterns of individuals to determine the growth of cultural institutions and attitudes, many *cinéma-vérité* filmmakers have an almost scientific detachment toward their work.

It is not surprising, then, that the first full-length *cinéma-vérité* documentary, *Chronicle of a Summer—Paris 1960,* was made by an anthropologist, Jean Rouch, and a sociologist, Edgar Morin. This film is structured on the activities of several people in Paris during the summer of 1960. The filmmakers in no way try to shape the film from preconceived ideas or organize it around a "message." The camera, informal and mostly hand-held, observes people talking to it and to each other. The people in the film are a Jewish woman who was an inmate in a Nazi concentration camp, a factory worker at the Renault automobile company, a young African man, a young Italian woman who has come to Paris to live more freely, and those with whom they interact. We see people's awareness of the camera by their talking to it, or to the cameraman, or by responding to it with a gesture. At other times, knowing the camera is there, the people ignore it. The film shows us that the camera's presence can help create the reality the camera records.

All the people in the film had a part in creating it. A most telling scene occurs near the end, in a screening room, where the participants all view the film taken to that point, then sit around and talk about it. This discussion reveals even more about them. Another trenchant moment occurs when the Jewish woman is seen in long shot as she wanders around the Place de la Concorde. Rouch and Morin had wired a microphone to her and given her a tape recorder to carry. As she walks around and thinks out loud, we discover to an almost embarrassing degree her emotional makeup and her private thoughts. The fact that this action was "set up" does not detract from the honesty the scene projects.

A problem that extends from *Chronicle of a Summer* through many recent documentary films is the ethical justification of a filmmaker's penetrating a person's privacy, then showing it publicly. The automobile worker loses his job because his boss discovers he is in a movie. What is the position the filmmakers should take to their

9.4 Anthropologist Jean Rouch and sociologist Edgar Morin's full-length *cinéma-vérité* documentary *Chronicle of a Summer. Top:* Marceline, the Jewish woman. *Bottom:* Rouch and Morin discussing their film. (The Museum of Modern Art/Film Stills Archive. Courtesy Contemporary/ McGraw-Hill Films.)

subject? Should they help the person and hence interfere with objectivity? Should they use whatever materials they need, no matter how private, that are most revealing of character and circumstance?

Many people believe that because *cinéma-vérité* is directly involved or *engaged* in the action being filmed, no material should be surrendered to personal need. Once any part of a film is edited to avoid embarrassing a subject, they maintain, the film becomes polemic. Rather than telling the "whole truth" available, they say, it would manipulate that truth, however slightly. Not being willing to do this, Rouch and Morin take us into the Italian woman's neurotic and self-pitying frustrations, as she explores her fears of loneliness and growing old. The African, when asked about the meaning of the Jewish woman's concentration camp tattoo, cannot understand what the concentration camps were. The automobile worker berates the factory he works for and the class system of society.

By being "engaged," *cinéma-vérité* forces us into sympathetic relationships with the characters. *Chronicle of a Summer* lets us see that actions show only half a person, that the other half is feeling and thought. The *cinéma-vérité* film, when successful, does not just penetrate the surfaces of reality; it shows us how those surfaces are built—from the inside out.

Since 1961, many filmmakers have used some of the techniques of *cinéma-vérité* not only to show behavior but also to help us arrive at more informed generalizations about people and society. The informal style of these films has also been borrowed, modified, and used in narrative films, and the hand-held camera and on-location shooting both characterize much of modern cinema.

An increasingly sophisticated technology has produced such feature documentaries as *Wood-stock* (Michael Wadleigh, 1970) and *Gimme Shelter* (Maysles brothers, 1972), films that use large-screen presentation and quality sound to give us a spectacle of apparently spontaneous activity. *Woodstock,* for instance, presents a large rock-music festival by means of multitrack sound and the camera observing, zooming in to see something, panning, and generally showing us images that seem similar to the actual experience. *Gimme Shelter* shows the Rolling Stones rock group in private and in public moments, as they tour America. The film's crucial point reveals a murder at the Stones' rock concert in Altamont, California, which we see in slow motion through a screen on an editing machine. This incident almost surrealistically plays back to us through the medium that in a sense caused it to happen, for the Altamont festival was in part staged for the documentary cameras.

The line between privacy and public exposure becomes hazy when the camera penetrates people's most personal actions. Allan King's *A Married Couple* (1970) takes us into the home of a young Canadian couple. Any camera awareness they may have had gives way to the couple's play, arguments, and conversations. In the television documentary *An American Family,* the Loud family of California exposes itself in ways sometimes embarrassing for the viewer. And John Marshall and Frederick Wiseman's *The Titicut Follies* (1967), which takes us into an institution for the criminally insane in Bridgewater, Massachusetts, shows us actions so removed from common concepts of decency that we are forced to question the nature of so-called civilized institutions.

The flexibility of the hand-held camera, which can react immediately to an action, helps to establish the spontaneity of events. But, though it records things "on the spot," the camera's images result from the cameraman's decision about what to shoot and the editor's decisions about how and what to cut. Thus, total objectivity is impossible. And the camera—whether concealed or simply not noticed by the subjects—nevertheless is involved in the action being filmed by the fact that it occupies the same place. Especially when the camera is in a closed area, such as a home, it both forms the environment and participates in it.

The zoom lens has helped the problem of objectivity by allowing cameramen to stay in one position, away from the events they are shooting, and zoom in and out without interference. Yet, this probing from a distance of people engaged in private activity suggests a use of the camera as *voyeur*. No longer do we simply sit back and observe the action; we penetrate privacy with the help of the camera as Peeping Tom. Such public viewing of private moments can make dilettante sociologists or clinical psychologists of us all, but it can also invite us to introspection and social action. *The Titicut Follies,* for instance, shows men naked in isolation cells, the officious interest of a psychologist listening to a paranoic trying to explain he is not crazy, a patient being force-fed by a doctor whose cigarette ash appears ready to drop on him. The camera penetrates the world of the mad, and we see that their world differs from ours only by degrees, by place, by context.

Cinéma-vérité documentaries can also make actions more believable by giving them predominance over image quality. Perfect visuals can give a slick and hence less authentic look to filmed reality. The more polished a film is in lighting, editing, and composition, the less spontaneous it appears and the more it will be accepted as fiction. When actions control the camera's response to them, the more informal results lead to a stronger sense of actuality.

In this sense, *cinéma-vérité* can liberate content from the artistic demands of the medium. When a person acts for the situation (of which the camera may be one part), then that situation seems more truthful. *Cinéma-vérité* does not, however, use the raw materials (the action filmed) as elements of montage to create rhythms and to discover reality through the medium. Rather, the truth is to be found in the playing out of the events themselves.

The Contemporary Documentary

More and more, independent filmmakers are making pictures about interesting people and local situations. Such biographical pictures may incorporate *cinéma-vérité* or they may be carefully controlled and more formally structured.

An example of the former is Brian Patrick's *Testimony* (1969), a quarter-hour picture shot in and near Athens, Ohio, the filmmaker's home. This film is about an evangelical group belonging to a church called the "Apostolic Lighthouse." Interviews with several of the parishioners and hand-held shots of members giving public testimony in downtown Athens counter shots of the dancing, preaching, and singing in the church to provide an authentic picture of these people.

A more formally structured biographical documentary is W. Craig Hinde's *The Birch Canoe Builder* (1970), about an old man in Minnesota who is one of the few people left who knows how to make birch-bark canoes as the Indians did. Hinde taped his subject as he rambled on about his life, his youth, and his work, then edited the tapes into a form that could support and create a dramatic line. Well-organized shots were constructed around the man's narration—shots showing him finding a birch tree, peeling off the bark, treating it, building the frame of the canoe, and so on. As the man tells of his past and of his youth, appropriate pictures create a sense of nostalgia and give us the old man's feeling for nature. Whereas in *Testimony* the only sound used is that taken at the time of shooting, in *The Birch Canoe Builder* voice-over narration is used frequently—usually that of the voice of the subject—and the sound track is created through a mix of various sound effects. Almost inadvertently, the film teaches us how to make a birchbark canoe.

Today, as in the past, the documentary film has no thematic bounds. Its subjects are as varied as society itself. News items that receive wide public attention, such as inflation, recession, pollution, political scandals, and foreign affairs, often provide topics for more lengthy, broad-based documentary investigation. Public relations firms make documentaries on cities for chambers of commerce. Political consulting firms make documentaries on people running for office. News-oriented documentaries are made for television digest programs, such as CBS's *60 Minutes.* Local television stations, fulfilling their obligation to air programs of regional interest, regularly make documentaries.

The contemporary documentary is exhibited in three ways: television; commercial theaters; and special group showings, particularly at universities and colleges.

Television has been the primary outlet for the films of Frederick Wiseman and Arthur Barron. Wiseman's full-length studies of American institutions, such as *Law and Order* (1972), which studies the Kansas City police force, or *Essene* (1973), which takes us into the life of a monastery, were shown originally on the PBS network. Later they were distributed to smaller theaters and rented to school film clubs and classes. Arthur Barron's three half-hour films in the series *The Great American Novel* were originally shown on CBS in 1968. Barron tried to see if the attitudes and sentiments expressed in these classic novels still existed in America. One film, *The Grapes of Wrath,* showed a family from Tennessee, no longer able to live off the land, and their trek to and survival in Chicago. *Babbitt* was about men who belong to the Lions Club, and other fraternal organizations, in Duluth, Minnesota, and their attitudes toward politics and typical Midwestern values. *Moby Dick* was about a fishing fleet captain and his crew off Alaska. After their run, these films also became available for sale or rental. Television has also served as the primary outlet for documentaries made by big-name narrative film directors such as Roberto Rossellini and Federico Fellini.

Feature-length documentaries, such as *Woodstock* or *Gimme Shelter,* are made for exhibition at commercial theaters. Sarah Kernochan and Howard Smith's *Marjoe* (1972) examines the life of an evangelistic showman, playing upon the flamboyance of a profession that sells its product as deliberately as does the Bible salesman in the Maysles brothers' *The Salesman* (1969).

All the above films use the *cinéma-vérité* method, striving for objectivity through noninterference in order to achieve the "truth" of what is being filmed. During Barron's filming of *The Grapes of Wrath,* for instance, the Tennessee family's second-hand car needed repairs en route to Chicago. The family found at a thruway service station that the work would cost the father almost all his money, leaving him almost nothing to support the family on when they got to Chicago. The problem for Barron was, should he let the man borrow the money from him? If he did, he would have interfered with the "truth" of the story he was filming. He would have changed events so that the "reality" being shown would have changed. He decided not to loan the money

—and from ethical standpoints, he did not ease the man's personal problems—but the resulting film is no doubt richer for this decision.

Today the documentary film is investigating cultural institutions not only in terms of the people in them, but also in relation to the filmmakers themselves. As we saw in the previous chapter, Federico Fellini, in *Fellini: A Director's Notebook, The Clowns, Roma,* and *Amarcord,* counters *cinéma-vérité's* objective rendering of information by making highly subjective films. His autobiographical documentaries search institutions (movie-making, the circus, a great city) through the substitute eye of the camera. Highly stylized, as are all of Fellini's films, these pictures interweave fantasy, memory, and reality, sometimes examining the never-never land where they merge, to give us a fusion of the narrative and documentary forms.

Other films also do this. Paul Morrissey and Andy Warhol's *Trash* (1970) uses real locations, improvised dialogue, and actors who seem to play themselves to improvise a movie out of their experience. In films such as John Cassavetes's *Faces* (1968) and Haskel Wexler's *Medium Cool* (1969) *cinéma-vérité* techniques give an appearance of spontaneity visually similar to that achieved by more factual films.

The public's current strong interest in nonfiction literature bodes well for the continuing acceptance of the documentary. Moreover, people's increased reliance on visual means for receiving information has given increased vigor to educational, informational, and news films. And although videotape may sooner or later be used to record much of the material now shot on film, the documentary will continue its examinations of our institutions and values.

When Professor Starr wrote in 1909 that film's "value cannot be measured now, but another generation will benefit more largely through its influence than we of today can possibly realize," he was making an extremely accurate prediction. And, if the past is a guide, the influence of the documentary form will continue and will convey to us even more complex information.

Part
Four

The Experimental
Film

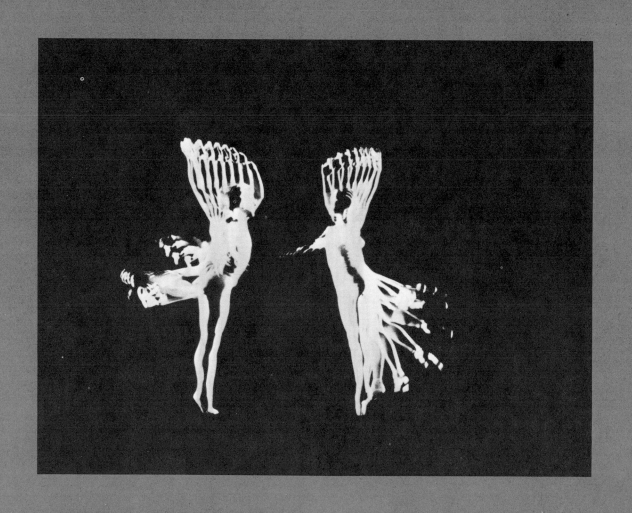

Types of Experimental Films

10

Any film that tries new techniques could be considered an experimental film, but here we mean it as a category of personal filmmaking that tries out ideas—much as a painter or a composer might—and is concerned with film's potential as an art form. Primarily imagist manifest, the experimental film usually does not show a story (like the narrative film) and does not try to verify reality (like the documentary film). On the contrary, the experimental film is a *nonreality* film, especially when the filmmaker is trying to find equivalents for mental states. The experimental film—also called the *avant-garde* and the *underground* film—explores topics and techniques outside the main line of narrative and documentary films. It is usually made outside the organized film industry and has little concern for financial gain.

Subject Matter

Although experimental films defy specific definition, they have certain characteristics that we can look at to try to understand them. Frequently they use unconventional or controversial subject matter: homosexuality, child molestation, heroin

Opposite page: From *Pas de Deux.* Courtesy National Film Board of Canada. (The Museum of Modern Art/Films Stills Archive.)

addiction, corrupt nuns, lecherous priests, adolescent prostitutes, alcoholism, political corruption, paranoia, among other themes. Of course, with today's audiences being more selective about what they see, and with violence and catastrophe being screened close-up in color, unusual subject matter may be fast running out for the experimental filmmakers.

On the other hand, in the experimental film technique has become content. The *ways* the subject matter is shown convey information. For instance, in the 1929 film *Un Chien Andalou* ("Andalusian Dog") by Luis Buñuel and Salvador Dali, the unpredictable editing is a metaphor for the arbitrary nature of the mind. Like mental images, the picture illogically jumps from one event to another. Satirizing the conventional structure of narrative films and the audience's expectations of a "story," *Un Chien Andalou* points out the unreliability of human experience. In one scene, a man's mouth disappears from his face; only skin covers where his mouth used to be. He looks at a young lady. She raises her arm, and reacts to the disappearance of her underarm hair. Next we see the man again, with the underarm hair instantly grown on his face. Purposely repulsive and humorous, this scene forces a fusion of fantasy and reality into something that combines both and is neither. The very device of cutting one shot with another combines editing technique with the mind's ability to "cut" illogically; hence, images can be created that reflect a person's subconscious.

A more recent picture, Stan Brakhage's 1955 *The Wonder Ring,* takes us on a four-minute ride on New York's Third Avenue elevated train. The trip is a series of colors and objects seen out the window of the El. The colors blend with the objects and the train's movement to show us not just things but moving patterns. The camera's free movements form a film that gives us a view of a ring (perhaps a finger ring) as seen from inside it. The content—the subject—of the film is movement itself. At the end of the film, we sense having intimately experienced a circle as tangible as a finger ring. Directly visual and nonliterary, *The Wonder Ring* allows us to construct a thing out of the ephemera of motion and images. The ways subject is treated, then, frequently help define an experimental film.

Style

The technique that frequently becomes the content of an experimental film arises from the personal vision of the filmmaker. The unique ways a filmmaker orders and handles materials creates identifiable characteristics.

In the experimental film, nonstyle can become a defining aspect of the picture's comment. For example, in *Empire* (1964) Andy Warhol used a static camera to record the Empire State Building for eight solid hours. For anyone patient enough to sit through this film, the noninvolved manner of shooting can in itself create involvement, for viewing such a film bores one into distraction and self-evaluation. The shape of the Empire State Building suggests other forms to our minds, and we become aware of frustrations, anxieties, attitudes, imaginings. We daydream, become bored, walk out, return. On one of these returns to the film—as it continues to show us

something we think we have seen in all its respects—we might then think of the building, conjecture about its activities, and consider its place against the changing sky and the influence of its form on the surrounding New York City skyline. The experience of such a film can antagonize us to the point, perhaps, of disgust and noninterest. It comments on our nervous system itself.

The style of the film—noninvolved and unoriginal—suddenly begins to make sense. As in Warhol's famous pop art paintings, common objects take on significance by their presence —by their imposition on us away from the visual environment created by other things surrounding them. A nonstyle becomes a style, and the artist's vision of the world is presented for our consideration. A prolonged examination of a common object can call up both its uncommon nature and our own most private feelings and imaginings.

Some people, of course, are not willing to try to understand the style of some of these films. Negative criticism is frequently caused by lack of interest, and lack of interest can be a rationalization for a lack of imagination or a device to protect one's own beliefs. The experimental film often antagonizes people who feel threatened by styles, contents, and themes that might tear down ideas of self built up over a lifetime.

On the other side of the coin are people who too easily embrace every new device and unusual nuance. But one cannot create a serious style by fluttering with the winds from any direction. Although to keep an open mind is commendable, never to close it so that what has entered can be examined is to surrender taste for mental indigestion.

These observations are particularly important in assessing style in the experimental film. Experimental filmmakers freely play with ideas in order to discover new patterns of sense, which create style. An informed and open-minded observer can enter into the creative process with filmmakers by viewing and "experiencing" their films. But to do justice to ourselves, we as viewers have an obligation to analyze and interpret the material presented to us.

Experimental filmmakers, through style, influence the subject as well as ideas about the subject. A part of their subject can be the viewer, who is brought into the flow of the film equally as a participant and observer. Because of the highly personal nature of so many experimental films, we do not usually identify (as in the narrative film) with particular characters and their problems so much as with emotional and psychological expressions, which become subject matter. The style of an experimental film not only relates the filmmaker's personal vision of the world, but it draws us into that vision. We as well as the filmmaker influence the work by our complex reaction to it.

The Subjective Film

Whether its apparent style is objective or totally involved, the experimental film usually contains some subjectivity. Historically, avant-garde filmmakers have been concerned with specific and personal examinations of subjective states—fantasy, the dream world, private emotions, images of ideas, personal fears, loves and frustrations. Through visual technique they attempt to get inside things or people to examine their workings. The experimental film has therefore developed visual contrivances—many later adopted as standard techniques in narrative films—to show subjective occurrences. For instance, in the 1920s experimental filmmakers put grease on the camera lens to distort the world and to suggest the mental state of the person whose eyes the camera became. In the late 1800s, Georges Méliès used superimposition to show fantasy, a technique still used today. The use of flashbacks and flashforwards to show jumps through time in a person's mind have become standard. Progressive visual distortion through fade-outs and fade-ins to initiate a transition to a dream or memory were used in the 1930s, and for awhile became standard techniques in narrative pictures. The use of gauze over the lens to soften a view and make it dreamlike and the use of fog filters to create much the same impression were used by avant-garde filmmakers in the 1920s and 1930s.

Soft-focus and out-of-focus shots have long been used to indicate mental states, as have strong, low-key lighting and shots of images reflected in mirrors. Dollying or zooming into a close-up of a person's eyes, then cutting directly to a scene of action that person is remembering or fantasizing has become a standard technique. Frequently, the use of slow motion to show the action of a dream has been used, as have distinct changes in film contrast and the use of makeup and decor. Alternating between black and white and color to key scenes as dream or reality is becoming more popular. The use of distorting lenses and unusual angles in dream sequences differentiates the situation for the viewer, as does exaggerated acting, fantastic costumes, and certain editing techniques such as using longer takes for dream sequences. The rhythm and fluidity of traveling shots can indicate scenes as "memory," especially when contrasted with shots that are more static, which use montage, or are otherwise different in style.

Thus, the use of cinema for expressing feelings and dream states is now standard. And it was through the experimental film that the techniques were developed.

Playing with Images

Abstract films play with images only. They are different from representational films, which show things clearly and accurately, and from distorted films, which show things as recognizable but misshaped. Abstract films show pure images in motion.

Abstract cinema developed along with abstract painting. Many of the same ideas lie behind both, including the investigation of forms, shapes, and contours totally removed from the solid forms that give them sense. Abstract cinema also investigates the qualities and properties of motion.

Advocates of so-called *pure cinema,* conceived in the 1920s to give abstract films some rationale, believe that discrete forms in motion are the definitive area for cinematic investigation. Without reference to any outside system—such as the visuals representing mental images, or extreme close-up shapes being light reflecting off water—pure cinema shows related patterns of image and form. Frequently there is no preconceived structure and there certainly is no preconceived story idea. Such films, experiments in the true sense of the word, try out techniques and explore the possibilities of the medium.

An example of one of the first abstract films is Viking Eggeling's *Symphonie Diagonale* (1921–24), which uses geometric forms to try to determine the intervals, or time relationships, in motion pictures. Just as intervals in music represent the difference between two pitches of the same note, Eggeling tried to discover the differences between two or more "pitches" of the same image in motion.

In computer films, such as John Whitney's *Matrix* (1971), pure forms mingle to create rhythms, meters, and patterns that can be experienced visually as music can aurally. In fact, many abstract films have at least implicitly used music as a metaphor for the images created. Others, such as Douglass Crockwell's *The Long Bodies* (1947), investigate the "four dimensions" that cinema can create: length, breadth, width, and time.

Although the techniques of making abstract films are varied, they are essentially of two kinds: in-camera techniques and noncamera techniques.

In-Camera Techniques

In-camera techniques are the most standard. Most people think of motion picture images resulting from the use of a camera. One technique is *animation,* in which the form is shot one frame or a few frames at a time. To get abstract images, the forms are created prior to shooting, then filmmakers consider possible relationships as they shoot them one at a time. Sometimes they guess and go for surprise.

There are several ways to create animated experimental films. Slips of paper of prescribed shapes and colors may be cut out, arranged, and shot. Shapes may be drawn with charcoal, crayon, or paint on a nonporous surface and then photographed. One may paint on glass or plastic (or on several pieces of glass or plastic) and photograph each application through the glass. Parts of objects may be photographed with distorted lenses. One may photograph (as did Crockwell in *The Long Bodies*) the ends of clumps of colored waxes all mixed and melted one with another, constantly chipping off pieces for each shot.

Other ways to get abstract images are to shoot video screens, which offer numerous possibilities for achieving abstract forms. Abstract films have

10.1 *Symphonie Diagonale,* an attempt to determine intervals in moving abstract images. (The Museum of Modern Art/Film Stills Archive.)

been created by programming computers and shooting directly off the screens on which the image is produced. Finally, shooting extremely undercranked shots, with or without camera movement, can result in highly vibrating, textural images, when the film is projected at normal speed.

Noncamera Techniques

Many experimental filmmakers have created images directly on film, not using a camera. Film images have been created from objects placed on raw stock, which is then exposed to light. Drawing both images and sound directly on film has produced pictures that are varied and exciting. (Film sound is received by optical patterns on the optical track. Hence, sound can be created by drawing it.) The National Film Board of Can-

ada's Norman McLaren has been in the forefront of making films in which both image and sound are created by pen and clear film stock. Images taken originally by camera photography can be manipulated in various ways by using an optical printer, a machine that is both a camera and a projector, which can create a variety of distortions by printing effects for a film one frame at a time. Scratching the emulsion side of raw film stock with a sharp instrument, especially on color film, can create interesting abstract images.

Abstract filmmakers help relate experience through recognizable forms. Circles, tubes, and squiggles shape action that is not narrative and certainly not documentary yet that implies human behavior. One reason for this is that the human mind tends to relate whatever it can to experience — it apparently needs to order meaning from meaninglessness.

Ernest Pintoff and Mel Brooks's *The Critic* (1962) is based around this human impulse. *The Critic* shows a series of abstract forms—squiggles, semicircles, twisting colors—accompanied by the voice of a man in his seventies, trying to make sense out of the film he is viewing. He gives the abstractions animate qualities. As two squiggles seem to "get together," he comments on it being a "dirty movie." Lamenting the price he has paid to see the film, he attempts to translate the forms into visual symbols that can suggest action and content from his experience.

As members of the same audience as we, his satire expresses the common notion that if a film does not in some way show us the known world, then it is useless. That the film he is criticizing is bad adds substance to this. Not that we are always right or wrong—and not that critics are always right or wrong either. As Brooks's voice suggests in the film, "I know what I like." What we like, of course, can change as our minds grow.

Animation

Animation—which can produce abstract, distorted, and representational-like forms on the screen—is used for narratives and documentaries as well as for experimental films. As we mentioned, animation creates its images by shooting forms one frame at a time. In representational animation—such as Walt Disney's *Snow White and the Seven Dwarfs* (1938)—standard backgrounds are used for individual scenes, while celluloid cutouts (called *cels*) of the characters in different postures are placed over them. Because each second of film requires twenty-four separate shots, and hence twenty-four different cels, much time, energy, and expertise are required to make even a short animated film.

Different animated figures have distinct qualities of shape and movement. Walt Disney's figures seem to flow lightly, as if they were moving in partial gravity. Others, such as the coyote and bird in the Roadrunner cartoons, move rapidly, sometimes jerkily. Such characteristics are associated with the visual styles of the figures themselves. Disney's characters, for instance, seem sometimes like balloons, with floating tubular parts.

Single-frame filming of puppets is another widely-used animation technique. Puppets' facial expressions as well as their bodily movements can be changed through each shot, and various backgrounds can be used, including "real" backgrounds created by projecting still photographs or movies through a rear screen.

A problem Disney solved in the late 1930s was how to show parallactic motion, which can give a better illusion of reality with moving camera shots. The Disney filmmakers developed a multiplane animation stand. The camera shot down through several layers of foreground and background objects, some of which would be moved between takes to give the effect of different planes moving against each other. Such dynamic motion gives more authenticity and visual interest to animation.

Oskar Fischinger, Len Lye, and Norman McLaren all devised ways of showing abstract forms moving to music. Fischinger choreographed geometric forms (using charcoal on white paper) to music as diversified as Brahms and Mozart. Lye used the negative image and color film stock to create solarization (which inverts some of the tones of an image); he also painted directly on film. McLaren created several films with hand-drawn images, hand-drawn sound, and stroboscopic effects created by multiple printing.

Some interesting films have been created using single frames or a few frames by *pixillation,* which shows movement through jump cuts of shots that at times are undercranked. J. L. Anderson's *Football As It Is Played Today* (1962) is a humorous five-minute film about a football Saturday at Ohio State University. The film's pixillation photography shows the spectators arriving, the cheerleaders, the marching band, the football game, the half-time activities, the rest of the game, and the crowd leaving—all in staccato-fast time. Frank Paine's *Motion Picture* (1962) takes us on a funny stop-motion automobile trip from Illinois to New York City. In both films, the pacing comments on the subject, as scenes are shown quickly or leisurely. For instance, in Paine's film, shot from inside a car, the trip progresses rather rapidly, then there is a long scene of a slow-moving truck in front of us. In another shot, the camera is static while a rest stop is enjoyed. Animation techniques allow filmmakers to take advantage of evolving technology. At the same time—because of their closeness to the graphic arts—such films can be seen as adjuncts to the history of modern art.

Minimal Films and Structural Films

Minimal films are about as totally removed from the events they show as films can be. Some experimental filmmakers use a static camera and just let it observe whatever happens in front of it. David Rimmer's *Real Italian Pizza* (1971), for instance, is a ten-minute film that simply observes a New York pizza stand from time to time during a nine months' period. Totally objective, the camera does not aim at anything other than what its fixed position dictates. As life passes by, a statement is made of people's presence in the world and the automatic behavior of daily life.

Standish Lawder's *Necrology* (1970) also uses a static camera. The first half of the film is a single shot of about ten minutes, showing people ascending an escalator after work in New York's Pan Am Building. The fatigue and despair, the anxiety and hopelessness of these people clearly comments on modern urban living. The faces and the constant upward movement suggest a type of death only the living can endure; they show a society of automatons appearing as so many collected spirits, empty of purpose and devoid of feeling. After this long shot ends, the "credits" come on, adding a humorous yet tragic dimension, for the credits identify each person —Menstruating Secretary, Pederast, Man Picking His Nose, the filmmaker himself. This further detracts from their individuality.

Structural films are like minimal films, but with an important difference: they specifically examine one or more attributes of the cinematic medium. For example, Michael Snow's *Wavelength* (1967) studies the possibilities of the zoom lens. The film is a forty-five-minute zoom shot from one end of a room to another. Parts of the room are seen, then disappear forever as the zoom—sometimes smoothly and sometimes spasmodically—moves forward into a close-up of a picture showing sea waves. The new pictures continually given us show how movement can create space; they also show the narrative possibilities of the zoom lens. Action happens, and continues to happen, as the zoom passes it by. Through the picture, the electronic sound track increases in decibels, until a very high pitch ends the zoom (which becomes both aural and pictorial). In *Wavelength,* time, space, and sound combine to shape themselves into purely cinematic form.

Structural films examine the possible uses of different lenses, as well as different framings. In *All My Life* (1966), Bruce Baillie explores the possibilities of the pan shot by showing a full 360-degree pan.

Structural films offer material for the careful and scientific study of particular limited aspects

10.2 Midway through the forty-five minute zoom shot across a room in Michael Snow's *Wavelength*. (The Museum of Modern Art/Film Stills Archive.)

of the film medium. They are true experiments— laboratory exercises that provide material for observation and interpretation.

The "Home Movie" Aesthetic

There is a fine line between motion pictures taken only to preserve events and those so informal they are deceiving. The "home movie" aesthetic in experimental films is a real direction. The controlling idea for such films is that spontaneous reaction of the camera to events within one's own world can be direct equivalents for those experiences. The home movie aesthetic is given this term for two reasons: (1) it uses subject matter from the filmmaker's direct experience and (2) it is highly informal in style (and "informal" does not mean "chaotic").

One filmmaker who, consciously or not, has developed this aesthetic is Stan Brakhage, who

is frequently accused of making films so personal that they have no sense to others. Filming his home, his children, his wife, and himself, he has produced some beautiful movies.

His method in many of them is to associate images through seemingly arbitrary connections among pattern, color, and motion. At their best, these images have a feeling about them in which not only our eyes but our bodies become extensions of the camera. In his *The Weir Falcon Saga* (about 1970), for instance, the camera at one point is in a tree, looking up at the sky through the branches. Hand-held, it moves almost spastically at times; at others, there are controlled pans showing patterns of limbs and leaves in textural relief against clouds, sky, and sun. We feel as if we are experiencing the climb up the tree and the communion with the mystical. This perception destroys conventional time and space and creates a view that removes us from our common experiences by giving us new ways to see.

Some people criticize this aesthetic by saying that anybody can do it, a comment also directed against many abstract paintings. The obvious answer is: "Try it." The combination of experience, imagination, control, and structural sense that allows the filmmaker to take artistic advantage of spontaneous shooting belies this superficial criticism. It takes a lot of practice and concentration for a painter to get to the point where he can draw a line with skill and originality; similarly, it takes much the same type of training before a person can "paint with motion."

How an Experimental Film Conveys Meaning

How can one interpret an experimental film? The main source of information is the images themselves, which are perceptual in nature and frequently convey no message that can be expressed in words. In the experimental film, *how* the images are formed is frequently more important than *what* they show.

Using abstract images more than do other types of films, experimental films express feeling through rhythm, image, and sound. More personal both in design and in rationale, good experimental films require us to join in the experiment. In these terms, the experimental film intelligently plays with ideas and filmic structures in order to expand our knowledge.

If we can work from emotions rather than from ideas, we can reenter a film's experience by examining the structures that made that experience. Because so many experimental films deal with abstract notions presented in unconventional ways, we must question our own responses to see why we were affected, bored, or uninvolved.

The experimental film does not usually try to achieve financial or artistic success. Experiments can be failures and can still show us something new. Many filmmakers feel that the most important thing about their work is that it expresses a *possibility* about feeling, human behavior, or an abstract idea (such as motion, beauty, hate, love). They feel no obligation to entertain or explain, but simply to explore their usually limited areas of interest. Because it is image-manifest, the experimental cinema accepts vision as our primary sense. It offers not words, but shapes, contours, forms, and colors for interpretation. Unlike fiction films and documentaries, experimental films do not generalize about human behavior, even when they deal with it. Often illogical and "nonreal," they enrich experience by showing us other possibilities for our lives. They accept fantasy as equally an important part of human experience as the physical.

Unlike most narrative and documentary directors, experimental filmmakers expect their pictures to be shown more than once to the same audience; they expect them to be analyzed, rerun, run in reverse, run without sound, and otherwise critically examined. Experimental films are the most purely conceived motion pictures; hence, they are often among the most limited and complex. Like good lyric poetry, they can be carefully scanned and interpreted on different levels. Dealing with the unusual, they demand of us unusual sorts of responses.

Evolution of the Experimental Film

11

Early experiments with cinema were nonstructured. There was no history and no body of criticism to give filmmakers ideas to try out. Film was looked upon both with wonder and with annoyance. It was rightly seen by many to be a popular form catering to the illiterate. Others looked on motion pictures as a fad, a toy of the growing technological world. The medium had hardly a past and only a future.

The Formative Years

Almost every film made from the late 1800s up through the 1910s could be called experimental. As early as 1889, Thomas Edison used a cylinder phonograph record synchronized with motion picture images presented through a kinetoscope. Various people intermittently experimented with sound and film during ensuing years.

The use of color in motion pictures was conceived of very early, and Georges Méliès, Edwin S. Porter, and others had prints of their films hand-painted. Also, the use of colored, or tinted, stock eventually came into use to indicate the emotional qualities of scenes: red for passion, blue for tranquility, amber to give a sense of relief and three-dimensionality to the pictures.

Opposite page: From Robert Wiene's *The Cabinet of Dr. Caligari.* (The Museum of Modern Art/Film Stills Archive.)

In some of the early motion devices such as the praxinoscope, animation was used to convey stories. Two techniques of animation were also experimented with in film. Winsor McKay's *Gertie the Dinosaur* (1909) put drawn characters into motion. Ladislas Starewicz in 1912 used stop-action photography of puppets in his *The Revenge of a Kinematograph Cameraman,* a comic tale of bugs and movies.

Early in the evolution of cinema, before film directions were categorized as narrative, documentary, and experimental, some people saw that motion pictures could express fantasy as well as create their own reality by manipulating and distorting images of the actual world. Just as the magician could find an unpredictable logic to create surprise, so the filmmakers, almost from the beginning, were able to use film the same way. They found that space (what we see) and time (the flow of actions) could be used in film to reorder the world, so that if they showed a man standing in a room and then suddenly made him disappear, it changed the viewer's sense of space and time.

Georges Méliès, the French magician whose "artificially arranged scenes," as he called them, were important in the development of film continuity, also helped demonstrate that film could express fantasy. The thousands of fragmentary films and the longer story films (such as *Journey to the Moon,* 1902) were frequently used as part of his magic act. In addition, many of his films found their way into kinetoscope parlors and

11.1 *This page:* Pablo Picasso's Cubist painting, *Les Demoiselles d'Avignon* (1907), which shows the rearrangement of space and form through the arrangement of shapes and contours of the figures. (Oil on canvas, 8′ × 7′8″. Collection, The Museum of Modern Art, New York. Acquired through the Lillie P. Bliss Bequest.) *Opposite page:* Marcel Duchamp's influential painting, *Nude Descending a Staircase, No. 2* (1912), which shows one figure in multiple forms created by the motion of going down the stairs. (Oil on canvas, 58″ × 35″. Philadelphia Museum of Art: The Louise and Walter Arensberg Collection. Photograph by A. J. Wyatt, Staff Photographer.)

movies houses and became popular in their own right.

Méliès used cinematic contrivance to make space unstable and time unpredictable. He showed that reality could be distorted through such manipulations as stop motion, dissolves, superimposition, masking, fade-ins, fade-outs, animation, and reverse motion. Using these tricks together with elaborate settings and stage devices (mirrors, trap doors, smoke), Méliès gave audi-

ences fantasy before their very eyes. Recreating new spaces out of existing ones by tampering with our innate sense of time, he showed that the world is not only what it looks like but is also what it appears to be.

This distinction between reality and appearance has a time-honored tradition in literature and painting. Part of the idea of interpretation —that is, of finding levels of meaning under the first meaning—is to discover the real reasons

for things. Often these reasons can be found by examining a work of art to see how its structure expresses its content.

Méliès—like every other magician—sensed that illusion is not different from reality; rather, it is a different reality. Although the obstinate among us will continue to disbelieve something after we have seen it, most of us will suspend that disbelief in order to become part of the experience. We will believe an experience in the con-text of the fantasy we are given; yet, only rarely will we trust it as being the way that the world really is. Méliès's films presented the unbelievable as events occurring before our eyes; he showed that cinema could uniquely create illusion. While some filmmakers went on to explore the medium's potential for showing the world realistically, others experimented with its ability to create illusion by manipulating time and space.

Edwin S. Porter, known primarily for *The Great Train Robbery* (1903), also experimented with film's potential for illusion. In *The Life of an American Fireman* (1902), he used a dream balloon to show a fireman using what can only be called ESP to view a lady in a house on fire. In *The Dream of a Rarebit Fiend* (1906), Porter showed that film could express subjective fantasy, or what goes on in a person's head.

Other filmmakers were experimenting with the medium's space and time possibilities. French-man Ferdinand Zecca followed Méliès's lead with many trick films, and Émile Cohl expanded the art of animation. Jean Durand saw that film could express the illogicality of time. His 1910 *Onésyme Horloger,* about a man who plays with time, showed that cinema could project psycho-logical time, with events seeming to happen faster or slower according to how we perceive them. These and other cinematic pioneers, by demon-strating film's capacity to project dream and reality simultaneously, paved the way for broadened film experimentation.

Early Avant-Garde Films

In the 1910s, the two art movements of Futurism and Cubism began to question traditional ways of seeing the world. The Futurists, mainly Italian artists concerned with showing the influence of technology on life, advocated a life style in tune

11.2 In this Futurist painting, *Dynamism of a Dog on a Leash* (1912), by Giacomo Balla, space is created through motion, giving energy and dynamism to the subject. (Oil on canvas, 35⅝″ × 42¼″. Albright-Knox Art Gallery, Buffalo, New York. Courtesy of George F. Goodyear and The Buffalo Fine Arts Academy.)

11.3 In Umberto Boccioni's Futurist painting *The City Rises* (1910), the energies of movement create the city. (Oil on canvas, 6′ 6½″ × 9′ 10½″. Collection, The Museum of Modern Art, New York. Mrs. Simon Guggenheim Fund.)

with the industrial rather than natural world, and they used the idea of motion as a device to explore the meaning of the modern world. The Cubists, mainly artists such as Pablo Picasso and Georges Braque, attempted to restructure how people saw things, using various visual aspects of objects in space to show how space is recreated by things placed in it.

Two important paintings that represent different experimental directions are Picasso's *Les Demoiselles d'Avignon* (1907) and Marcel Duchamp's series *Nude Descending a Staircase* (1912). The Picasso painting virtually started the Cubist movement. Looking at it, artists began to examine objects from more than one viewpoint in order to see their involvement in space rather than simply their location in the environment. *Nude Descending a Staircase* demonstrates the influence of Futurism in showing the motion of objects through space. It also suggests the influence of photography on painting and on ways of seeing. The Cubist-like shapes combine with the movement of the figure as it moves itself through space. This lets us see motion, while it gives the environment dynamic qualities.

Let us examine the influences of Futurism and Cubism in more detail.

The Futurists

The Futurists frequently tried to show action through motion. The energies or "dynamism" (one of their favorite words) of movement changes the spaces or environments in which that movement occurs. Thus, in Giacomo Balla's 1912 painting *Dynamism of a Dog on a Leash* movement defines the dog. The animal's energies stretch to include the leash and the owner. In Umberto Boccioni's *The City Rises* (1910–12), the forces of the city express the dynamism of the new century. The city is continually created by its accumulated energies as these are collected by the spaces through which movement has occurred.

The Futurists were involved in all sorts of artistic activities. They created sculptures that twisted space and made motion appear in prosaic subjects such as bottles. They designed clothes and wrote manifestos stating that traditional drama and poetry were no longer viable. It is no surprise, then, that within all this activity the Futurists saw film as a contemporary form of expression suited to their ideas. Excerpts from the Futurist manifesto on film (*see inset*, page 218) show the excitement of their ideas, ideas still considered fresh years later. At the same time, it expresses the highly nationalistic character of their movement.

Among the Futurist films were Antonio Bragaglia's *Perfido Incanto* (1916) and three other films of about the same period. Today some of the films are in various stages of decomposition, and none of them is readily available for screening. The films featured a modernistic use of decor, distortions of reality through superimposition, visual puns, and visual tricks played through optical illusion and the use of contemporary *trompe-l'oeil* designs. Still, Futurists extended motion pictures into subjective realms. Their identification of motion as a defining quality of the modern world was expressed in images that are more akin to feelings than to the normal shapes and forms of objects.

The Cubists

The major Cubist artists were only indirectly involved in film. Although they were concerned with space more than with motion, they did influence the cinematic treatment of objects. And one of their number, Fernand Leger, made *Le Ballet Mécanique* ("The Mechanical Ballet," 1924–25), a film that uses shots of parts of machines

1916 Futurist Manifesto on Cinema

The Futurist cinema we are preparing—a cheerful distortion of the universe, an alogical and elusive synthesis of world life—. . . will sharpen and develop the sensibility, will quicken creative imagination, will give a marvelous sense of simultaneity and ubiquity to the mind. Futurist film will thus contribute to the general renewal, replacing magazines (so pedantic), drama (so predictable in advance), and killing books (so tedious and oppressive). The necessities of publicity may compel us to publish a book from time to time, but we prefer to express ourselves by means of film . . . and moving luminous posters.

Cinema, newly born, may appear at first already Futuristic—that is, without a past and free of traditions. Actually, born as Theater Without Words, it has inherited all of the most traditional rubbish of the literary theatre. . . . Cinema up to now has been, and tends to remain, deeply attached to the traditions of the past, while we, on the contrary, see in it the possibility of an eminently Futuristic art and the most suitable means of expression for the multisensitiveness of a Futurist artist. . . .

Cinema is an art in itself. Cinema must therefore never copy the stage. Being essentially visual, cinema must first of all fulfill the evolution of painting: to detach itself from reality, from photography, from all that is pretty or solemn. It must become antipretty, distorting, impressionistic, synthetic, dynamic, free from words.

It is necessary to liberate film as a means of expression in order to make it the ideal instrument of a *new art*, vastly wider and more agile than all of those yet in existence. . . . It will be painting, architecture, sculpture, words in freedom, music of colors, lines and forms, a melange of objects and chaotic reality. . . .

Our films will be:

1. *Filmed analogies,* making direct use of reality as one of the two elements of the analogy. . . .

2. *Filmed poems, speeches, and poetry.* We will show on the screen all of the images that are their elements.

3. *Filmed simultaneity and penetration* of different times and places. We will show, in the same frame, two or three different images, one next to the other.

4. *Filmed musical research* (dissonance, arrangements, symphonies of gestures, actions, colors, lines, etc.).

5. *Filmed states of mind, arranged into scenes.*

6. *Filmed daily exercises to free oneself from logic.*

7. *Filmed dramas of objects.*

8. *Filmed showcases of ideas, events, characters, objects, etc.*

9. *Filmed conventions, flirts, brawls, and marriages of grimaces and mimickings, etc.* For example, a big nose imposing silence on a thousand fingers of legislators, ringing an ear like a bell, while two policemen's moustaches arrest a tooth.

10. *Filmed unreal reconstructions of the human body.*

11. *Filmed dramas of disproportion* (a thirsty man pulls out a tiny drinking straw, which, like an umbilical cord, stretches as far as a lake, and drains it all at once).

12. *Filmed potential dramas and strategic levels of feelings.*

13. *Filmed linear, plastic, chromatic, equivalences,* etc., of men, women, events, thoughts, music, feelings, weights, odors, noises (by means of white lines on a black background, we will show the internal rhythm and the physical rhythm of a man discovering his wife in adultery and chasing the lover—the rhythm of his soul and the rhythm of his legs).

14. *Filmed Words in Freedom in movement* . . .

*   *   *

Painting, plus sculpture, plus plastic dynamism, plus Words in Freedom

*   *   *

plus tune-noises, plus architecture, plus synthetic theater = Futurist cinematography*

---

*Translated by Barry Katz and used with permission.

11.4 *Ballet Mécanique.* Part of the loop of the woman endlessly mounting the stairs. (The Museum of Modern Art/Film Stills Archive.)

11.5 *Rhythmus 21* shows pure forms related to each other in time. (The Museum of Modern Art/Film Stills Archive.)

together with drawings and paintings to explore the symbolic and metaphorical qualities of the mechanical world. This film explicitly suggests sexual associations between machines and people, as well as the self-contained nature of space, as expressed, for example, in a famous loop showing a woman continuously climbing stairs. The Cubists' attention to geometrical forms is evidenced in Hans Richter's *Rhythmus 21* (1921), one of the first of the abstract films. By presenting pure geometric forms related to each other in time, *Rhythmus 21* influenced later experimentation in the 1920s. The forms of Viking Eggeling's *Symphonie Diagonale (1921*–24) also strongly suggest the Cubists' influence.

Like Futurism, Cubism moved away from the strict representation of both story and form. By discovering the aesthetic qualities of forms in space, as Futurism did with motion, it strongly influenced the early direction of the experimental film.

Popular Science and the Avant-Garde

The 1920s in France were a time of artistic freedom, great invention, and rich production. The controversial theories of Sigmund Freud, father of psychoanalysis, about the subconscious and the symbolic nature of dreams were widely discussed. Albert Einstein's theories of relativity were also widely debated. Although his ideas were fully understood by only a handful of people, the superficial sense of his theories—that the world really was not organized in time and space as people had always thought—led to artistic experimentation.

Freud's insistence that our unconscious expresses information about us through dream symbols led artists of all sorts into new areas of exploration. Filmmakers and painters in particular attempted to find underlying explanations for

life by discovering symbols that referred to our hidden instincts.

Freud suggested that the repression of basic urges—particularly the sexual urge—led to neurosis, and that people frequently so suppress these urges that they do not even know they have them. Psychoanalysis, he believed, was a way to discover these repressed urges; a person's dreams could be interpreted to uncover reasons for anxieties, fears, and frustrations.

Freud introduced new words into the language (*psyche, ego, id, libido),* and they were immediately picked up and popularized. The idea that people could be broken down into segments identifying their connection with the real world (*ego),* with the unconscious world (*superego),* and with basic urges (*id)* was fascinating.

The challenge for many artists was to peel off the surfaces—much as a psychoanalyst would—to see what a person was really like. The fact that it was believed that people's "true nature" was tied to their repressed sexual urges only further fascinated the *avant-garde.*

Regarding relativity, Albert Einstein wrote:

The nonmathematician is seized by a mysterious shuddering when he hears of "four-dimensional" things, by a feeling not unlike that awakened by thoughts of the occult. And yet there is no more commonplace statement than that the world in which we live is a four-dimensional space-time continuum.*

Suddenly people in the 1920s were being told that the world was unstable, that the convenient rules of traditional geometry and the predictable organization of the clock were no longer reliable. Space and time now had new meanings, and they fused into a monster with which the mind grappled: space-time.

---

*Albert Einstein, *Relativity,* trans. Robert W. Lawson (New York: Crown Publishers, 1961), p. 55.

The general influence of these ideas on art and the experimental cinema was considerable, especially when combined with psychoanalytic ideas. The observation that objects could be known only through their relative positions in space led painters and filmmakers to explore "what space really is." They picked up on the idea that time and space systems were created from the speeds at which objects moved and that space and time equally were influenced by each other. Motion was studied and played with through editing, camera movement, and framerate speed; space was explored through composition, perspective, three-dimensionality, and, eventually, color (examples are the films of Douglass Crockwell—especially *The Long Bodies,* 1947—and later the films of Scott Bartlett and Ed Emshwiller). Most of these films were either so abstract that they dealt with "pure forms" alone or so personal that they conveyed only private symbolic systems of the subconscious.

Dadaism

Dadaism, centered in France, sprang up around 1916 to deride traditional art forms. The word *dada* is baby talk for a child's rocking horse; it was found by a Dadaist sticking a letter opener into a French dictionary to discover at random a word to name this activity. Such an impetuous act identifies the Dadaists' intent: to rely heavily on intuition and spontaneous action in order to oppose the notions of stability and tradition in art.

By the very nature of their ideas, the Dadaists were not a formal movement. Dealing with irrationality, striking out against everything sacred in art, they freely poked fun at the sanctity of people's experiences and vested interests.

The revolt against traditional art called for the uses of untraditional techniques. In 1923, Man Ray made a film in a few hours by placing nails, tacks, and other small objects on a raw stock, which he then exposed to light. Created purposely to antagonize the viewer, this film was premiered at one of the last Dada parties, "The Evening of the Bearded Heart." Ironically entitled *Retour à la Raison* ("Return to Reason"), the title itself shows the use of antilogic to provide a "logic" most people could not accept. This important little film was mostly made without a camera, and it began a tradition of such films that is still followed today.

Marcel Duchamp's famous *Anemic Cinema* (1926) gets its title from rearranging the letters of the word "cinema" to describe both this particular film and traditional motion pictures generally. Revolving abstract patterns and words play with the viewer's perception of forms and language, creating optical illusions and puns that make no immediate sense.

One of the most exciting of the Dada films is René Clair's *Entr'acte* ("Between Acts," 1924), made to be shown at the intermission of the Dada ballet *Relâche* ("Cancelled Performance"). Erik Satie's music for the film no longer exists, but the picture clearly works on the visual level alone. The film is divided into two parts: (1) a montage of various visual puns and camera and editing effects, starring some of the famous artists of the period; and (2) a chase sequence, which creates rhythms of great power and inventiveness.

In the first part, Clair plays with film's physical properties, as well as with the audience's trained reaction to sequential events. Like Méliès, he exposes the camera's power to see things uniquely. For example, a motif in the first several minutes shows us parts of a female ballet dancer. Since the film was made to be shown at a ballet, the audience assumes that this motif suggests no more than that. After some other scenes, the film returns to the dancer and shows her from below, then her arms gracefully moving, then her feet,

11.6 Revolving circles from Marcel Duchamp's *Anemic Cinema* (1926). (The Museum of Modern Art/Film Stills Archive.)

then her arms—and then the camera slowly tilts down from her arms to show us a bearded man.

Slow motion is used throughout the film. There are multiple exposures of a target a man is shooting at with a gun, and the audience is drawn into his confusion at what to aim at when the target splits into several targets. Checkerboards fly through the air; a bird roosts on a man's hat; events move unpredictably but still with the thread of a story. The first part ends with a man falling from a rooftop.

In the second part, people are following a hearse wagon harnessed to a camel. The camel becomes unharnessed, and the hearse takes off on its own for a hair-raising ride. A montage sequence of the chase begins. People run after the hearse, one fellow apparently without legs pushing himself along in a box. From the viewpoint of the hearse, we see streets, approaching walls and fences, and dangerous curves; roller coaster shots are cut into the movement. The man with no legs arises from his box and starts running; the chase becomes frenzied. Finally, the hearse bumps to a halt and the coffin rolls out. A magician steps out of the coffin and with his magic wand makes each person disappear, then points the wand at himself and he too disappears. The word "Fin" comes on, but it is not the end yet. The magician crashes through the paper of the title. The orchestra conductor enters the frame, looks at him, and kicks him. Through reverse motion, the man reenters the title, and it closes whole again as the movie finally ends.

The film not only satirizes the audience's expectations about traditional narratives, it also pokes fun at life's rituals, particularly funerals. That the visual rhythms of the chase still thrill audiences shows the power of the forward rush of movement created by Clair. Finally, the film is a revolt against our ordinary experiences with time and space. What the camera sees is not necessarily what our *eyes* see, and the movement of the chase is not normally experienced movement. The film's ending tells us our experience was all illusion, tricks conjured by a magician.

At the time of this film, Dadaism was nearing its end. *Entr'acte* suggests that cinema, through its form, could attack tradition in both life and art.

Surrealism

Surrealism grew out of Dadaism, and gave it order. One of the founders of Surrealism, André Breton, had visited Freud, and was particularly taken with the idea that unconscious reality and conscious life could combine to form something new—a super reality.

A basic idea of Breton's was to free the unconscious (a subjective entity) to let it connect with the world (an objective entity) in order to show total experience. Surrealism was a movement of protest—as was Dada—against middle-class values, against society's rituals, against the pre-

dictability of human behavior, and against known science. Revolting also against the growing inhibitions of mechanization, Surrealism attempted to free people's imaginations from the restraints imposed by their bodies.

Dadaism and Surrealism did not directly influence all the films of the period. Yet, there prevailed at this time a feeling for revolt, a recognition of a world different from the one people had always known, and a tendency to put more trust in intuition and imagination. All artists except those utterly isolated could not help but feel the power of these ideas. And whether they rejected them or accepted them, these ideas influenced most of the works of the time. In fact, Surrealism still influences contemporary narrative and experimental motion pictures.*

Perhaps the most famous of the Surrealistic films was Salvador Dali and Luis Buñuel's *Un Chien Andalou* (1929), which stated Dada ideas of revolt and attack. This film revolted against traditional narrative forms and attacked audiences' basic values and emotions. For instance, there is the scene of the cutting of a woman's eye with a razor. This scene is preceded by a shot of a man testing a razor for sharpness, then another shot showing him approaching the seated lady with the razor, then a cutaway showing fake clouds, thin and knife-like, passing a fake moon. The audience is led to think: "He is letting this symbolically suggest the act," and is thus taken off guard. Then the film cuts directly to the razor slicing an eye.

According to one of the filmmakers, this film derives from the recesses of the mind. Contradicting expected behavior with unexpected action, it shows lust, death, and violence as being close to

---

*Indeed, Luis Buñuel is still quite active, making such Surrealistic features as *Belle de Jour* (1967), *The Discreet Charm of the Bourgeoisie* (1972), and *The Phantom of Liberté* (1974).

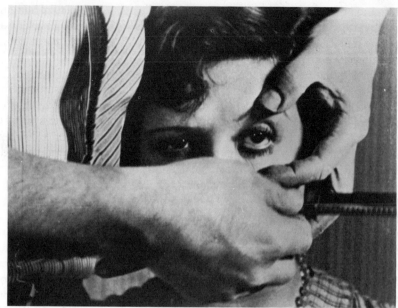

11.7 *Un Chien Andalou.* (The Museum of Modern Art/Film Stills Archive.)

each other in the human being. In combining physical reality with the subconscious to provide a reality different from either, *Un Chien Andalou* attacks and shocks the audience.

The *avant-garde* during this time revolted not only against traditional art forms but also against the narrative cinema specifically. The use of nonconventional subject matter, the distortion of expected behavior, the search of the subconscious for symbol and metaphor, the abstraction of reality in order to play with pure abstract forms, the discontinuity of experience—all emerged in the films of 1920s. Dadaism and Surrealism permeate most of them.

Germaine Dulac's *The Seashell and the Clergyman (La Coquille et le Clergyman,* 1928) virtually bursts with Freudian language. The story of a priest who is frustrated at his own sexual fantasies, the film uses distorting lenses, unusual juxtapositions, and cuts between dream and

reality to show these frustrations. It also attacks the Catholic Church, especially for the ways it restrains free behavior. The film suggests that physical and ritualistic restraints do not prevent the mind from asserting the body's physical needs. It embellishes this idea by suggesting that fantasies—derived even from limited experience—distort ideas of sexual conduct. In other words, it states: if people do not know what sex is all about, yet have the urges, their fantasies will form unrealistic pictures to satisfy them.

Some films of the 1920s sought relationships with literature and music. There are films structured around poems (such as Man Ray's *L'Etoile de Mer,* 1928, formed around a poem by Robert Desnos), and there are many films that used original music by well-known composers (such as Hans Richter's *Ghosts Before Breakfast,* 1926, with a score—now lost—by Paul Hindemith).

Surrealism and Dadaism were responsible for

11.8 Costumes, makeup, the distortion of space through actor placement and set design all suggest the foreboding spaces of the mind in Robert Wiene's Expressionist film, *The Cabinet of Dr. Caligari.* (The Museum of Modern Art/Film Stills Archive.)

advances in themes and techniques picked up years later by narrative filmmakers. Some of these are (1) "memory" and "fantasy" shots to intertwine with present events; (2) distorting lenses to indicate subjective views; (3) animation to show the impact and beauty of simple forms; (4) unconventional or controversial subject matter; (5) the direct showing of violent acts; (6) the expression of erotic acts and sexual problems; (7) nudity; (8) satirical themes; (9) unusual imagery to show the different sides of usual experiences; (10) the influence of other arts on cinema; (11) experimentation with cinema that creates experience through purely abstract images.

Expressionism

In Expressionism, which was centered in Germany, style is especially important, more so than in Dadaism or Surrealism. In Expressionist paintings, for instance, broad, heavy strokes are used; the way the paint is used is a part of the content. In Expressionism, style asserts, rather than explores, the artist's feelings.

The earliest and most important Expressionist film was Robert Wiene's *The Cabinet of Dr. Caligari* (1919), scripted by Carl Mayer and Hans Janowitz. This feature-length film takes us inside the mind of a paranoic as he tells about the evil Dr. Caligari and his murderous use of Cesare, a somnambulist. This movie was probably not only the first horror film, offering movies a direction different from realism, it was also influential in its design.

The sets reflect distortions of reality—a mood the images create to show us that we are in a madman's mind. In addition, the costumes, the makeup, the distortion of space through the placement of actors, and the use of shadows all suggest the foreboding spaces of the mind. The film seems to state that through the unconscious we view a world of anxieties, fears, loves, hidden desires, and primitive motivations. It presents these qualities through the character of the paranoic Francis as he and the story he tells interact with the Expressionistic decor.

For example, Francis's anxieties about his own madness—anxieties that in classical paranoia influence the subject's belief that he is absolutely sane and that the rest of the world is mad—is shown in the opening scene. This is "actuality." Francis, seated on a bench in the woods, is telling a friend (and through him the audience) about the mad Dr. Caligari. He seems totally in control of himself. A young lady ethereally passes by, suggesting the mood of the tale Francis tells, which occupies the main part of the film. As we move into the visual representation of the story, the appearance is that we are entering the insane world of Dr. Caligari. Only at the end of the film, when we are brought back to actuality and see that Francis is an inmate in an asylum that Caligari heads, do we understand that he has transferred his own madness to the doctor.

Francis's fears of the impulses that lead him to distrust others is expressed by the film's dark and distorted lighting. His love for a woman, actually a fellow inmate, is transferred to Caligari's attempts to force the somnambulist, Cesare, to murder her. Francis's sexual frustrations are asserted in the film by such symbols as phallic lines on the set designs, implications of the girl's potential rape by the somnambulist, and a series of gestures and facial expressions. Pervading it all is Francis's desire to protect himself from his own fears by transferring his emotions to Caligari. Internal motion, the use of irises, and the clearly logical progress of the story form rhythms that reflect the intensity of Francis's feelings.

Much of the action takes place at a town fair in the fictitious city of Hostenwall. The establishing shots that begin some sequences show a tight iris, around the revolving hand of an organ grinder. The iris widens to show a carousel moving in the rear. Between the foreground and the background is an area of platforms, with people walking on them. This use of internal motion gives depth to the images, while at the same time it creates a sense of disorder trying to achieve order. It becomes a visual expression of Francis's mind.

As the Cubist painters examined the subsurface shapes of objects in space, so the Expressionists used film to show the interior of the mind. Even in Expressionistic theater, a play such as Walter Hasenclever's *Humanity* used pantomime and set design to show feeling through motion and to show the limited use of words to express emotions. Hasenclever suggested that Expressionism was the human spirit rebelling against reality. This revolt influenced the use of visuals, for feelings can usually be only inadequately expressed in words. Following German poet Goethe's declaration that "Feeling is all," the Expressionists attempted to find visual equivalents for feeling.

The motion picture medium seems well suited to this, for not only can it project expressionistically designed images, but it also can use motion to show feeling. Associating the images with the character of other Expressionist work in stage design, painting, and architecture, *The Cabinet of Dr. Caligari* created a style that showed a world distorted and awry—one that reflected the disquietude of frustrations and anxieties.

Expressionism left its mark on world cinema. American mood pieces, including horror films, used and extended techniques suggested in *Caligari* and similar German narrative films.

The techniques and ideas of Expressionism,

Surrealism, and Dadaism merged into new experiments—not only in film but also in painting, sculpture, architecture, music, and theater. Some scholars believe that the common denominator in this merging was the influence of psychoanalysis. Others believe it represented a consolidation of the many ideas that were reactions against a stable, understandable world.

The Abstract and Animated Film

From the late 1920s on till today, several experimental filmmakers have investigated relationships among image, motion, and musical structures. Among the most important were Oskar Fischinger, Hector Hoppin and Anthony Gross, Len Lye, and Norman McLaren.

Oskar Fischinger

Oskar Fischinger was one of those who made the abstract film a significant part of cinema. From the late 1920s into the 1930s, Fischinger made many short films—"studies," as he first called them—that associated visual and audial forms. Setting his films to musical pieces by such composers as Brahms and Mozart, he painstakingly synchronized the movement of abstract forms to music. Shooting white forms reversed out against the black, he evolved dancing abstract figures that—when they worked best—almost gained personalities of their own.

In the 1930s, Fischinger moved into color, which, along with shapes and music, became a third means of expression. He carefully constructed films such as *Composition in Blue* (1933), in which music by Nicolai commented on moving patterns keyed to blue. In *Circles*

(1933), he used single-frame photography and graphic animation to produce a stirring film to the music of Wagner. In 1939, after he came to America from Germany, he made *An American March* (music by Sousa), in which he showed the increased sophistication with which he was able to pattern shape, color, and sound.

The idea of "pure" cinema influenced much of his work. He created films that usually used no representational forms. The mood and theme of each piece was gathered through its visual rhythms, color associations, and musical qualities. While working briefly at Walt Disney studios, he contributed to the concept that later became *Fantasia* (1940).

Continuing his search for new ways to express feeling through visual and audial patterns, Fischinger made *Motion Painting No. 1* (1949). Synchronized to the music of Bach's *Brandenburg Concerto No. 3,* this film shows the emergence, disappearance, and formation of the colors and shapes of a painting created on glass.

Fischinger advanced animation techniques, and he helped solve the problem of synchronizing abstract forms with sound. He was an original filmmaker of wit and imagination.

Joie de Vivre

In 1934 Hector Hoppin and Anthony Gross produced a delightful animated film, *Joie de Vivre* ("Joy of Life"). Its use of both the graphic and ballet dancing forms of the arabesque is based on Henri Matisse's 1906 painting of the same title. The film shows Matisse's feeling for the purity of uninhibited behavior through two female dancers placed in a contemporary (1930s) setting. In exploring their playfulness (with a male as well as with each other), this sophisticated black-and-white cartoon puts both the style and the attitudes of the Matisse paintings into motion. In terms of

11.9 *Left:* Matisse's *Joie de Vivre* (Photograph Copyright 1975 by The Barnes Foundation, Merion, Pennsylvania). *Right:* Hector Hoppin and Anthony Gross's *Joie de Vivre* (The Museum of Modern Art/Film Stills Archive.) The style and attitudes of the Matisse painting are put into motion in the animated film.

the use of the arabesque and the relationships between movement and sound, *Joie de Vivre* also predicts the later Beatles movie, *Yellow Submarine* (George Dunning, 1968).

Len Lye

In the late 1930s and early 1940s, British sculptor Len Lye developed techniques that are still being experimented with today. In such films as *Trade Tattoo* (1937), *Musical Poster Number One* (1939), and *Swinging the Lambeth Walk* (1940), Lye showed the expressive possibilities of solarization, of the photographic negative image, of using photographic materials with animation, and of drawing directly on film.

Lye made advertising shorts for the famous GPO Experimental Film Unit as well as for the Ministry of Information. His films showed the importance of commerce, warned people not to tell military secrets because Nazis might hear

them, and propagandized the British postal system. His techniques of drawing on film were studied and further developed by Norman McLaren.

Norman McLaren

In the 1940s, Norman McLaren came from England to work for the National Film Board of Canada. Since then he has made scores of original films. He has used live forms with animated forms; he has scratched the emulsion side of film with pins and razor blades to produce figures as well as sound; he has used pastels; and he has created textures by inserting dustlike material into the grooves made by etching. He furthered Len Lye's technique of painting along the entire length of a film, hence avoiding the structure of single frames.

The artistry of drawing both sound and visuals

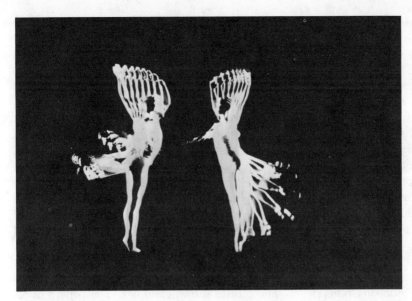

11.10 *Pas de Deux.* (The Museum of Modern Art/Film Stills Archive. Courtesy National Film Board of Canada.)

on film perhaps reached culmination in McLaren's *Synchromy* (1970). This film clearly supports the description a BBC documentary gave to his work, *The Eye Hears, the Ear Sees.* Abstract geometric forms in *Synchromy* change positions with one another as colors of each "panel" modulate and change with the pitches of the melodies and harmonies composed directly on the optical sound track. The joining of the two senses into one perhaps satisfies that fusion of cinema and pure form that abstract filmmakers have long strived for.

Examination of motion itself is apparent in most of McLaren's works and can clearly be seen in *Pas de Deux* (1968). This film attempts to study the beauty of motion. The multiple images, by creating motion in space, hearken back to effects used by the Futurist painters. The content of the film is only secondarily the dance; primarily, it is the examination of movement through optical printing techniques.

The film was shot at forty-eight frames per second to slow down the action. The dancers were back-lit in order to clearly show the contours of the figures when they are multiply exposed and their motions extended through time. The music —Roumanian panpipes—was recorded and re-recorded to fit the pacing of the movements. Originated by dancers, but created from the shooting through many printing manipulations, *Pas de Deux* reshapes original motion into pure cinema.

The Underground Film

Some of the significant directions of experimental films of the last three decades can be found in the evolution of form, technique, and ideas seen in films made mostly by Americans.

Maya Deren and the American Underground Film

Maya Deren, who died in 1961, lived her life by making films and showing them and lecturing about them. She was totally committed to the idea of the filmmaker as artist, as painters have often been so committed—that is, as a person totally involved with and living off works of art. This interconnection between life-style and filmmaking implies a special, sympathetic association between the films and the audiences viewing them. This relationship underlies the so-called underground film, a description that includes not only films, but sympathies expressed toward them by dedicated audiences.

Two of Deren's films—*Meshes of the Afternoon* and, to a lesser extent, *A Study in Choreography for Camera*—provided artistic expression that nourished the works of many later American filmmakers. *Meshes of the Afternoon* (1943) uses distorting lenses, soft focus, unusual camera angles, and imaginative editing to explore relationships between illusion and reality. The story of a young lady who dreams of suicide, then actually commits the act, the film intertwines—and at times confuses—fantasy and actuality in ways that remind us of the French Surrealist films of the 1920s. Its Freudian symbolism, dreamlike imagery, repetition of actions, use of masked figures, and naturalistic portrayal of death embody techniques used for years by European avant-garde filmmakers. The film's suggestion that the psychoanalytic examination of a person was a worthwhile experience for film to explore, though not a new idea at the time, was a breakthrough in American filmmaking. *Meshes of the Afternoon* anticipated the tone of despair and confusion that permeated several post–World War II experimental films, as well as the mood-piece narrative pictures made in America during the 1945–1952 period.

A Study in Choreography for Camera (1945) was quite different. The film shows dancer Talley Beatty in one continuous dance that is carried through several interior and exterior spaces. At the beginning of this short film, pan shots invisibly cut to give the impression of Beatty being in several places at the same time. Then, a cut on action shows him leaping from the woods into a room. Camera movement ceases at this point, and relationships are suggested between the spaces created by motion and the shapes of objects in those spaces. This is all explained visually in the last shot, where the dancer, outdoors again, freezes in a posture that makes his figure a part of the design created by the tree limbs and bushes surrounding him. The pattern of his dance is the structure of the film.

Her deep attachment to dance as well as to the mysticism of voodoo extend the mood of Maya Deren's films into the realm of feeling. The idea that the dead exist as ghosts to be called upon through ritual creates in her films patterns of movement shaped by ethereal motions.

Although Deren felt deeply about things, there is still something self-indulgent about her work. This aspect has been picked up by many filmmakers, especially in their early works, and seems to equal "art" both to them and to their followers. Yet what finally separates her works from the mannered ones is the originality of fusing technique of expression with subject.

From the mid-sixties through the seventies, filmmakers by the score, "turned on" to the medium, made films similar to those of McLaren, Deren, and Brakhage. Particularly popular were psychedelic films, which intermixed the colors of moving shapes, manipulated noncamera processes, and used film to suggest the drug expe-

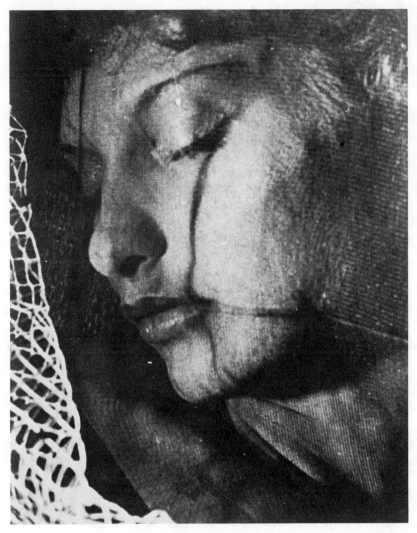

11.11 Maya Deren in her film, *Meshes of the Afternoon.* (The Museum of Modern Art/Film Stills Archive.)

rience. Lacking both technical control of the medium and a knowledge of history, some of these filmmakers made their films and themselves available for rental to mostly college groups traveling and speaking about their films. Many, if not most, of these films were unimaginative. This does not mean that people should not make films concerned with feelings. It is just to suggest that a proliferation of identical works has the impact of a well-worn cliché.

11.12 A continuous dance carried through several places in Maya Deren's *A Study in Choreography for Camera.* (The Museum of Modern Art/Film Stills Archive.)

Kenneth Anger

The experimental film went underground in the late 1940s and in the 1950s to express the values of those who opposed the conventional world and its morality. As in Europe earlier, sex and its attendant patterns of fear, frustration, sacrifice, and erratic behavior was looked upon as a topic for specific exploration. Films began to make public the private nature of sexual urges.

An example was the work of Kenneth Anger. Anger started making films when he was very young, and by the age of twelve he had completed a film on incest. Later, he was to express relationships between violence, fascism, and homosexual ritual. *Fireworks* (1947) is a dream fantasy about a homosexual youth who is beaten up by gay sailors. Explicit phallic symbolism, together with the title's double meaning of violence and ejaculation, foreshadowed directions Anger took in his films.

Anger's themes, and frequently his style, owe much to Maya Deren and Sergei Eisenstein.

Aspects of Deren's surrealism can be seen in his attempts to express his own personal frustrations through visual images; the drive and power of the visual rhythms of sexual violence, sadism, and masochism derive from Eisenstein's theories of montage. Like Deren, Anger is also fascinated with mysticism and ritual. The effect of the idea of death on human behavior pervades his films. His well-known *Scorpio Rising* (1962–64) ritualizes interior frustration and the death wish with Nazi violence and homosexuality, all keyed to the lyrics of pop songs. The famous French underground novel, *The Story of O,* a tale of sadism and sexual possession, was one toward which his impulses naturally led him, and he made a film of the novel in France in the early 1960s.

Calling himself a magician in the tradition of Méliès, Anger forces us to question the reliability of learned experience. What we see may not be so important as how what we see influences emotions.

The retreat into the self to find new visual forms

for personal expression rests in the Surrealist films of the 1920s and 1930s and continues in American films of the last twenty-five years. The fact that motion pictures are a public art form does not hold in relation to films shown to limited audiences. These films often have the power and conciseness of poetry, while at the same time they have the line, color, and contour of imaginative painting.

Jean Cocteau

French poet, playwright, artist, and filmmaker, Jean Cocteau, has had an immeasurable influence on the underground film, including American filmmakers such as Anger. In dealing with the influence of classic myth on modern life, Cocteau shaped surrealism into personal and compelling films.

Orpheus (1950) examines the poetic imagination and problems of human existence. Based on the Greek myth of Orpheus—the supreme poet to whose songs rocks and trees danced—this film uses modern imagery to express the continuing problem of the creative intelligence. In the Greek myth, Orpheus's wife Eurydice died and Orpheus journeyed to the lower world to get her back. He won from Hades the chance to bring her back, on condition that, on ascending, he not look back until safely above and in the sun. He guided Eurydice (with the sound of his lyre) up through the dark, but just before arriving in the sunlight, he turned and looked at her. Eurydice disappeared, and he lost her for all time.

Cocteau made this myth into an allegory in a modern setting that showed that to escape the demands of the everyday world, the poet must travel to the "lower depths"—the St. Cyr section, near Paris. Cocteau thus suggests a new mythology based on the old. For instance, motorcyclists, coming for Eurydice, are a motif throughout the film; they suggest the irrational, those elements in our culture that most of us cannot understand because we are locked into predictable patterns.

If life is not predictable, this film says, then the behavioral patterns formed by ritual through the ages may offer some explanation. *Orpheus* states that life is ephemeral and that the basic human condition, toward which we daily move, is death. The artist's striving for life, he says, is seen in his work, which is more permanent than life. The fantasy quality of this film's images at times suggests that retreat into the nether regions of the mind is not an escape from reality but a confrontation with self-truth, that we find sustenance within ourselves rather than from our contemporaries.

The original ways that Cocteau combined images to give contemporary relevance to historical human experience has affected many filmmakers, and his influence can be seen in many experimental films.

Contemporary Directions

The ideas of "private vision" and Surrealism continued to affect the films of the sixties and seventies. With the rise of the drug culture, there emerged films that tried to show the "trip" experience. These free-flowing juxtapositions of shots associated by line, shape, color, and sound—and only occasionally by a narrative line—often suggested that the psychedelic experience might provide a valid way to see the world.

On the West coast, Bruce Baillie founded the nonprofit Canyon Cinema Cooperative to distribute films of any serious filmmaker willing to submit prints for rent, with the filmmaker receiving two-thirds the rental price and Canyon one-third.

Baillie's own films use various devices of experimental films: compilation footage; montage; strange or unexpected shot juxtapositions; the Mélièsian grab bag of stop motion, reverse motion, slow motion and accelerated motion; overexposed and underexposed footage; and black and white alternating with color. His several pictures are original and very American in theme. *Mass for the Dakota Sioux* (1963–64), for instance, is cut to the form of the Catholic Mass and is a requiem for the vanishing American Indian. It is also a lament for the souls of the white people whose "civilization" replaced that of the Indians. A medieval monks' Gregorian chant accompanies several images that start out and return to a man ignored and dying on a city street. Through the film, television, cars, tunnels, and bridges rhythmically are counterbalanced to each other. The filmmaker shows a civilization dying because there are no values to sustain it.

This theme is continued in *Quixote* (1965), which shows filmmaker Baillie as Don Quixote, searching for the real America. What we see, finally, is an America without a future because of too much concern for ourselves rather than others. We see men at a luncheon eating, then pigs eating; we are shown newsreels from Vietnam, and shots from all over of American cities, farms, workers, and white-collar workers leading their affluent lives free from war or death. The film's rediscovery of America ends in New York City, concluding with a girl twisting either in giving birth or in self-induced sexual ecstasy. It is to this we have come, the film says: America reveling in itself, celebrating itself through its own lust—or, in the larger sense, through its own will for instant gratification. What we give birth to is only our narcissistic values.

The two films parallel each other in style and theme, although *Mass* is more strictly organized. *Quixote,* as the title would imply, is more erratic.

The sound track, for instance, changes quickly from one sort of sound to another, while the shots contrast patterns that show the chaotic images of an America impossible to shape.

Scott Bartlett is an experimental filmmaker who has developed (as critic Gene Youngblood calls it) "expanded cinema." Bartlett's films use video techniques, compilation footage, and optical printing to show a world that is technological to the point of being out of our control. For example, *Offon* (1968) alternates three- to five-frame shots to affect changing patterns of red and blue, set to a beat that moves closer and closer to our own heart beat. The film uses persistence of vision to give a flickering effect that plays directly on our nervous system.

Moon 1969, which celebrates the trek to the moon, uses the ancient elements of earth, air, fire, and water to structure the instinct for discovery around the human urge for exploration.

Moon 1969 has no images at the beginning—only the voices of the astronauts reading from *Genesis* the Christmas eve they circled the moon. The film then cuts into a night view from the cockpit of a plane flying toward a landing strip. The downward floating seems interminable, with a repetitive, pinging sound accompanying it, until the runway lights, superimposed, twist away from each other. Television images show us the astronauts in their spacecraft. Images of the natural world are juxtaposed with electronic images and sounds, and we sense a descent back to earth. Finally, there is a close-up of a beach and a slow zoom shot back to show the beach, a peaceful sea, the sky, and the falling sun. Bartlett's films show that a new world now describes us and defines an existence different from the old world of natural elements. Yet, he shows, it was our reactions to that natural world that began all our discoveries.

This new world is further evidenced in the

films of John Whitney, who has explored the aesthetic possibilities of computer graphics. He has gained fame for such films as *Permutations* (1968) and *Matrix* (1971). In these pictures, geometric shapes interweave like pulses floating to and from each other to give a feeling of visual music.

Jonas and Adolfas Mekas started the journal *Film Culture* in 1955 to put the contemporary *avant-garde* in focus (though also publishing essays on Vertov, Eisenstein, and others of the past). The magazine stimulated serious interest in the filmmaker as artist, suggesting a rich history that otherwise might not have been brought to our attention.

The increased interest in the underground film (which accompanied the growth of *Film Culture* and helped it survive) gave sustenance to potential filmmakers. Although some films were made principally for other filmmakers (and film enthusiasts with specialized knowledge), many people began to see the possibilities the medium had beyond telling a story. One of them was Ed Emshwiller, a former science fiction illustrator, whose *Relativity* (1966) deals with time and space relationships between shapes and people and shows insights into the reality of nature.

The surprising thing is that films—owing so much to the general ideas of relativity—have not before been so specific in showing their indebtedness to those ideas. As *Relativity* jour-

neys through the mind and the cosmos, knowledge is acquired by the speed at which we move in relation to the time it takes us to move. That time is part of the system that is the film: a four-dimensional space-time continuum. Juxtaposing objects and images force us to participate in a world we might not otherwise have experienced. Emshwiller's method shows us that what is outside ourselves depends on the workings of a mind that creates knowledge at any given point of observation; it gives us our world and ourselves as one. All we see are reflections of our capacity to see, and all we experience is located in a time created by our mental response to the flow of images.

The experimental film owes a great deal to twentieth-century art movements and to psychology. Growing up with the great ideas that changed our civilization, and attempting to understand those ideas through their impact on people and the ways that they see, experimental filmmakers have long sought to show us our potential by expanding the limits of the medium.

The word "experimental" can describe many different filmmaking activities. By limiting ourselves to those films and filmmakers that express ideas and passions through an evolving technology, we can more completely understand the diverse activities of the last half century.

Part
Five

Filmmaking
Activities

Preproduction

12

Visual communication requires the film writer to see the dramatic implications of images in motion. This might seem easy for a person brought up in a supposedly visually oriented culture, but theatrical structure and audience reliance on dialogue often results in images being sacrificed to the spoken word. The photographic image is compelling, but so are those aspects that enable film to condense or extend time and to rearrange physical space. These two aspects should be kept in mind when we are trying to find a film idea. One of the creative rewards in making films of originality is that the film's form emerges in the shooting and editing from the images and their relationships suggested in the script.

It is obvious that a film idea should be visual rather than theatrical or literary, but what this specifically *means* is less obvious. Suppose we want to document the activity in a supermarket. We have a potentially good film idea, for the various foodstuffs, their geometric arrangements, the conflicts of color and line and textures among produce and packages can evoke expressive images. These images can be combined with motion: people moving with their carts, different actions everywhere, and the linear possibilities of mobile composition in the long aisles.

But in cinema, we do not tell a story; we show

it. In the supermarket example, the film idea remains alive as long as the occurrences are *shown.* If sound is added, such as the voice of a narrator describing the activity or the voice of a lady the camera is following, the language might detract from the visual impact. When narration provides information, filmmakers then may feel they do not have to show that information. The use of sound for effect is one thing, but in the use of parallel sound the narration can overpower the visuals by allowing words to replace the direct showing of experience. We cannot always show everything, but we can be selective, using what we show to suggest the whole. This can be done by space manipulating space. For example, shooting from a low angle up at a food shelf can suggest cans and packages stacked to an extraordinary height; or shooting food shelves from a high angle with a telephoto lens can "squash" space and make the food shelves appear like mountains. Scriptwriters should know both the limitations and the potentials of the medium. This knowledge rests on the primary rule of writing for film: Whenever you can show it, don't say it.

One problem is that, by necessarily using words when writing a script, writers have at their disposal many literary devices—imagery, figurative language, verbal description, archetypical symbols, verbal rhythms, and other elements of poetry and prose—and these devices almost insidiously impose themselves in writing. Added to this is the long history of creating action through dialogue in theater. The result is that the scriptwriter has a formidable number of literary techniques to work against. To refine the language, through several drafts, to that point where it can convey potential images is one of the most painful tasks of writing for film.

The key to writing film dialogue is to remember that little conversation is significant talk. People are moving most of the time (this includes their mouths), and it is from these movements that the filmwriter selects materials that express their emotions, desires, and psychological conflicts. Cinema not only can show how people look, it can also show what they think. A film idea, then, is *operational* and *perceptual,* as opposed to *verbal* and *conceptual.* The surfaces shown should present interpretable material.

If an idea starts with a unique image rather than with a verbal notion, it may indeed be a film idea. Say we want to make a film of a famous jazz trumpeter. Images come to mind: his horn, jazz club atmosphere, lights, colors. And sounds: crowds, music, applause, music, banter, chatter, rhythm, music. Say, on the other hand, we want to make a film of the musician giving his outlook on life by discussing with other musicians his life's work. Because words are so important here, the filmmaker would almost be forced to furnish simply a historical record (a valid function of cinema, of course, but not one we are concerned with here). The filmmaker may try to add interest to the words by providing various kinds of shots and techniques—close-ups, medium shots, cutting, panning—but the basic concept is not a film idea. We have all seen such films in which the filmmaker tried to save the idea by adding compilation footage or by intercutting shots of the events being talked about. Structure usually is weak here because it is imposed, almost desperately, to create variety.

A film idea is inadequate if it forces the cameraman or editor to provide motion and to vary image. Sound, especially spoken language, can be misused because it is so deceptively easy to use. A film idea offers action by means of image movement rather than by means of explanation. A film idea calls for interpretation through images rather than for the camera simply to photograph what already has been clearly stated.

Director David Lean suggests that a film is a series of shots edited together to give the appearance of continuous action. In a novel or on stage, transitions from one bit of action to another are given by means of description, dialogue, a white space (on the page) or a blackout (on stage). In traditional film continuity these transitions are more or less invisible to the untrained eye. They are made by using cutaways, by cuts on action, by music (which can override cuts to suggest continuous action), by montage, and by such laboratory devices as fades, dissolves, wipes, irises, and freeze frames. Because of the perceptual nature of these devices, it is difficult for the reader of a film script to see the rhythm and pace of a film—elements that in any case are more intuitive than formal. Also, to read a shot description may not take the same amount of time as the actual shot.

From Idea to Script

From idea through the shooting script, the writer refines and enriches the potential film. The script will frequently run through the following order of preparation: (1) the treatment, (2) the rough draft of the script, (3) the stages toward a final script, (4) the final script (which is actually not final), and (5) the shooting script.

The Treatment

There are several ways to approach and prepare the treatment, but we must use the method that seems appropriate to our temperament and to the visual idea we are trying to structure.

The treatment generally expresses the feeling and sense of the anticipated movie. Thus, in writing the treatment, we can linger in figurative language to explore a scene, to elaborate on events, and to draw any dramatic lines. Thus, the treatment can make obvious what might have seemed a good idea by objectifying it for the first time.

The treatment usually either is in sentence or paragraph outline form or is written similar to a short story done in the present tense. Using the present tense is important because, regardless of the historical time of a scene in a film, that scene is projected to an audience in the present. The use of the past tense in a treatment would contradict the immediacy of the final film and would throw the writing back into literature rather than forward into picture.

Treatments are used for all types of films. The example in the inset (pages 242–243) was done by a student for a short personal experimental film.

A treatment can go through several drafts, each version further clarifying movement and unifying the images. The treatment helps the writer extend key themes or shots into potential cinematic structures. It also gives the writer a framework within which to suggest scenes for later amplification. In addition, the treatment helps determine the efficiency of the idea in relation to available locations, actors, crew and sets; or, in the case of an animated film, in relation to design materials, movement patterns, lighting, and rear screen projection.

The treatment can be approached through images, through character, or through atmosphere. If it is written in paragraphs unified by time and place, then each of these paragraphs can each form the sequences in the first rough draft of the script.

The Rough Draft

Part, sequence, scene, and *shot* are the terms that commonly refer to the sections of the script, from the largest and more general to the specific. Depending on the script, part and scene sometimes are not used; and, depending on the style of the picture, sequence and scene are sometimes used interchangeably. Sequence and shot are the more continually used terms.

A *part* is a large section of the script dealing with a variety of actions, often in several locations, and is unified thematically. A part is similar to an act in a play or to a movement in a symphony.

A *sequence* is unified by time and place or by character. It is equivalent to a chapter in a novel. In a script a sequence is usually, but not always, notated by using a capital letter, starting with A.

A *scene* is one of two or more specific dramatic elements of a sequence, and it is unified by time, place, *and* action. The scene is today occasionally avoided in notation, but when it is used it is denoted by a number. The third scene of the fifth sequence would be notated *E.3.*

The *shot,* of course, is the fundamental unit of a film. The second shot of the third scene of the fifth sequence would be notated *E.3.2.*

In going into the first rough draft of the script, it is wise to supply extra sequence letters and, within sequences, extra scene and shot numbers. These additional notations are marked *reserve.* They are extremely valuable in the evolution of the script for they relieve the annoying and time-consuming problem of having to shuffle notations as new ideas are incorporated into new sequences, scenes, and shots. As sequences, scenes, or shots are occasionally deleted, their notation is kept in place and they are marked *reserve.*

Another reason to use the reserve notation is that, during the production phase, the director or writer, in responding to the immediate circumstances of shooting, will see that a new shot is required. Directors always keep in mind potential editing problems, and they will occasionally ask for a new shot or possibly even a new scene "for protection." That is, if they feel that a scripted shot or scene might not work in editing, or that a concept or action can be made better, they will ask for additional material. This is one important reason why the writer should be present during shooting.

Notation is extremely important to have in a film script. The numbers and letters are used to slate the shots and the sound takes. Without these slates, it would be virtually impossible to synchronize sound with film and to keep the shots in order. Without the notation, a shooting schedule could not be made, the day's shooting schedule could not be precisely announced, and, generally, the apparent but hopefully untrue situation that during a production nobody seems to know what anybody else is doing would be a fact.

In the rough draft we begin notation by setting down in sequential order the shots and sequences suggested in the treatment. The rough draft also makes available to us a context for precisely determining the content of specific shots in order to see their relationships through time. The rough draft for a narrative film script is frequently more theatrical than cinematic, especially in terms of dialogue and scenic structure.

Stages Toward the Final Script

A good first step to follow in moving away from the rough draft is to look at each piece of dialogue and ask, "How can I show this?" There are, of course, times where speech works as nothing else can—in a throw-away fashion, or when one

---

Example of a Treatment

The Sorcerer's Revenge*

The Sorcerer's Revenge is a fantasy short subject that will combine stop-motion miniature animation with live action. The action in the film occurs in synchronization with a specific selection of music—the "Uranus, the Magician" segment of Gustav Holst's symphony, The Planets.

It is dusk in a small town in the Midwest. The townspeople are having a square dance and bonfire in the open square of the town. In the background,

we see a small crowd of men pushing a Merlinesque magician; his two small, hunchbacked assistants; his wagon; and his horses to the outskirts of the town. The camera concentrates on this action.

The sorcerer's wagon is of the type one would expect a traveling gypsy's to be, and from the printing on its side, one learns that the sorcerer is a traveling magician. The crowd of men throw the sorcerer and his assistants onto the dirt road, unhitch the horses, and turn over the wagon. The men laugh and leave the three outcasts alone. The outcasts turn the wagon right-side up and pull it away from the town to a nearby graveyard of Civil War soldiers.

Inside the wagon, the sorcerer chants while brewing a bubbling mixture in his cauldron. Here, the music begins. The mixture is dried to a powder, which the sorcerer divides between himself and his

---

*©1973, David Gregory. Used with permission.

of the defining characteristics of a character is his or her manner of talking. It is, however, quite different for a character's speech to be mannered than for all the speech in a script implicitly to convey action, as in stage drama.

In theater, a play's physical action is determined by the director's interpretation of the play's dialogue and any stage directions given in the script. Also, even with the use of selective spot lights and other isolating devices, the theater is always in "long shot"; that is, the audience selects what to look at. In the movies, the director frequently uses selective focus to direct our attention to a particular object or person. Thus, the selection of what we see is made before the actual presentation.

To help substitute images for words, a storyboard rendering might be helpful. The format on page 244—one of many possible—has proved useful to filmmakers and writers. Scores of these can easily be mimeographed or dittoed.

The rectangles are for roughing out sketches of ideas for a shot. If we are filming for a 35 millimeter wide-screen format, storyboard rectangles should be in wide-screen ratio. These rectangles can be used either for the main action of one shot in each rectangle, or they can be used to indicate, in number 1, the framing of the action at the head of a shot; in number 2, the framing of the action in the middle of the shot; and in number 3, the framing of the action at the end of a shot. In this way, each storyboard sheet can be used for one shot.

The smaller rectangles below, as well as the spaces between them, can be used for indicating camera movement, dialogue, special effects, music, close-ups, or whatever else is appropriate.

Storyboards can let us see the possible conti-

---

assistants. They leave the wagon and walk about the graveyard sprinkling the powder on the graves. Upon the sorcerer's sprinkling of powder and voicing of a few chants, a living skeleton pops up out of each grave. Some of the skeletons still wear tatters of their Civil War uniforms, and some still carry swords and medals. There are about twenty-two skeletons, all wild with movement. Three skeleton horses are arisen also.

The hunchbacks bring in rifles and swords. Some skeletons practice marching and drilling with the rifles, while others fence with each other. The sorcerer directs the skeletons to assemble for a march and then points toward the town (where the festivity is still going on). The skeleton army marches toward the town, and upon arriving, kills the entire panic-stricken population in a graphically depicted orgy of slaughter. In the melee, the two hunchbacked assistants are killed. The skeletons spread the bonfire about the town until the whole town is burning.

The sorcerer sits away from the town on a hillside by the graveyard. He watches the scene and sighs, showing a bit of regret for having taken such a severe revenge. He stands up and remains still, looking down onto the burning town. He doesn't see two skeletons with a pitchfork stealthily making their way a distance behind him. They balance the pitchfork between them and, with a running effort, ram the pitchfork through the sorcerer. Once the sorcerer falls dead, the skeletons everywhere break apart and fall to the ground.

When morning arrives, the camera pans the smouldering town. Warm sunrays reveal the disjointed skeleton bones and the bodies of the murdered people. No one is left alive.

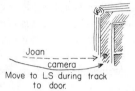

Joan ⟶
camera ⟶
Move to LS during track
to door.

| L.S. Joan. Establishes her in room. | C.U. Joan's face. (Surprise as she hears an unusual noise. She starts to get up.) | M.S. Joan arising. (She starts towards the door. Camera tracks with her.) |

12.1 Format for a storyboard.

nuity of the film. They also can help experimental filmmakers determine the appropriateness of special effects or optical printing devices.

In the short personal film, the writer/filmmaker frequently finds it helpful to write a description of each shot from the rough draft on a three-by-five-inch card. This procedure is useful for at least three reasons. First, the cards can be shuffled so that different shot orders can be viewed in order to sense possible pacing. Second, the cards can show what might be redundant and therefore consolidated with other shots. Third, in writing down the shot in isolation, the filmmaker can sense alternative image possibilities as well as modifications of the action.

The Final Script and the Shooting Script

The evolution of the script toward its so-called (but not really) final form involves condensation,

elimination, and invention. The more problems solved for the director and the editor at this point, the more efficient and less expensive the actual production will be.

Yet, a script is hardly ever completed until the film is in its final form. Even the version settled upon to mimeograph and hand out to participants is called by some the "first final version." Because a film's action, dialogue, and space-and-time arrangements often change during the shooting, the order of shots is frequently changed during the editing. Some shots, scenes, or even whole sequences are omitted in the cutting stage. And, occasionally, films that seem to be finished are changed after a premiere or preview showing.

The first final version of the script can be the shooting script. This can have the form as shown in the inset (page 245); or it can be written so that the action is on the left and the dialogue and sound on the right, as in the second inset, page 246.

Example of Shooting Script with Action and Dialogue

From *America First**

4th Day

103.1   *The kitchen of Royal's house.* Early morning. Al, Sy, and Cal
        have spent an uncomfortable night trying to sleep in the
        kitchen. As it was cold, they begged and stole various mate-
        rials to cover themselves. Sy is already awake. He notices
        that the other two are still asleep. Sensing a chance to escape,
        he drapes himself in an old blanket and silently leaves. The
        camera follows him out of the house. He looks around out-
        side. In the distance Rose Anne seems to be doing a morning
        chore. While he watches, he is grabbed by Al, who holds
        him back.

104.1   Reserve.

105.1   *In a cleared field.* Morning. Edgar squats as he digs small
        holes with his bayonet and plants seeds. Every so often he
        consults Walt's gardening book.

106.1   *Royal's back porch.* Royal shaves. Walt approaches him.
        WALT: Aren't you late for work?
        ROYAL: Ain't going today.
        Royal continues to shave.
        WALT: I got my man out there planting.
        Royal continues to shave.
        WALT: We're gonna need some money.
        Royal continues to shave.
        WALT: Got any?
        ROYAL: Nope.
        WALT: What're you going to do?
        Royal continues to shave.

---

*©1972, Optos Limited. All rights reserved.

Example of Shooting Script with Action, Dialogue, and Sound

From *America First**

4th Day

103.1. *The kitchen of Royal's house.*
Early morning.

Wide-angle shot of Al, Sy, and Cal wrapped in blankets on the floor. Sy is awake.
Pan with Sy as he arises with his blanket.

Muffled train noise heard in the distance.
Humming of an old refrigerator.
Brief gasping snore from Al.

103.2. Track with Sy as he leaves the house.

103.3. MLS. Sy as he exits from the house and looks around. The shot widens to include Rose Anne in the distance carrying a pail.

Early morning bird sounds.
Dogs bark.
Sound of Rose Anne moving through field.

Al enters from frame left and grabs Sy, who has started to move toward Rose Anne.

Sound of Al approaching.

104.1. Reserve.

105.1. *In a cleared field.* Morning. Edgar digs small holes with his bayonet and plants seeds. Walt's gardening book is open on the ground beside him.

Digging sounds. Birds chirp. Far away, behind the hills, a shotgun is fired.

106.1. *Royal's back porch.* MLS. Royal shaving. Walt enters from frame right. Slow zoom in to tight two-shot [shot with two people in it] at last line.

Royal continues to shave, trying to avoid the conversation.

Sound of electric razor throughout.
WALT: Aren't you late for work?
ROYAL: Ain't going today.
WALT: I got my man out there planting. (Pause.) We're gonna need some money. (Pause.) Got any?
ROYAL: Nope.
WALT: What're you going to do?

From the inception of the idea through the first final version of the script, the writer attempts to organize a film through language. While the important process of scripting continues, certain other matters have to be decided upon and certain critical tasks have to be accomplished.

Preproduction Planning

Planning for large feature films made within the industry is carried out by a team of specialists. Increasingly, more feature films are being made by private production companies set up by individual filmmakers. Their methods of operation are usually not as complex as those for large industry-made films. A look at their typical activities shows us how films are planned.

A poet or composer can find pencil and paper almost anywhere. A painter can spend comparatively little setting up a studio. But a filmmaker needs money—and usually lots of it—in order to pay for fairly sophisticated equipment, film stock, editing equipment, and laboratory work.

Formats

The type of movie one makes suggests the most aesthetically effective format. Consider types of film—Super-8, 16, or 35 millimeter.

The Super-8 millimeter format has become increasingly popular among experimental filmmakers. As its sound capabilities become more sophisticated, documentary filmmakers find its versatility and portability highly desirable.

The 16 millimeter format, which has in recent years come into its own, gives the filmmaker the capability for making all types of films, including features, with a versatility and control formerly available only in 35 or 70 millimeter. The process of blowing up 16 millimeter film to 35 millimeter for commercial theaters is now accepted fact. With new film stocks available (such as Kodak 7252 color reversal and 7247 color negative), specialized laboratories can produce 35 millimeter prints with almost no loss in quality. (Super-16 millimeter is another format, used infrequently in America but popular in Sweden and other European countries; it provides a larger image area than regular 16 millimeter and hence more photographic quality for the size.)

The 35 millimeter format, however, is still standard in the film industry, and it is also often used for television series films. This format offers the advantage of having excellent visual qualities. The 35 millimeter film has a smooth look, yet, owing to increased portability of 35 millimeter cameras, is able to achieve the informal characteristics of hand-held shots.

The 70 millimeter film is mostly used for epics needing a feeling of grandeur and expanse, such as David Lean's *Lawrence of Arabia* (1962) or Franklin J. Schaffner's *Patton—Lust for Glory* (1969). Multiple-track sound from magnetic tape on both sides of the film print frequently projects qualities of sound not available with other film sizes. The 70 millimeter format can be shot with 35 millimeter film, using a special anamorphic lens on the camera that squeezes the images on the negative. Another anamorphic lens on the projector expands the image again into Panavision ratio.

Feature films are usually shot in 35 and occasionally in 16 millimeter. Sometimes, depending on the market, the 16 millimeter film is not blown up—especially if its intended audience is in colleges, some art-movie houses, and private showings. Private production feature movies, of course, use either the 16 or 35 millimeter format, depending on accessibility of equipment, funds, and aesthetic qualities desired.

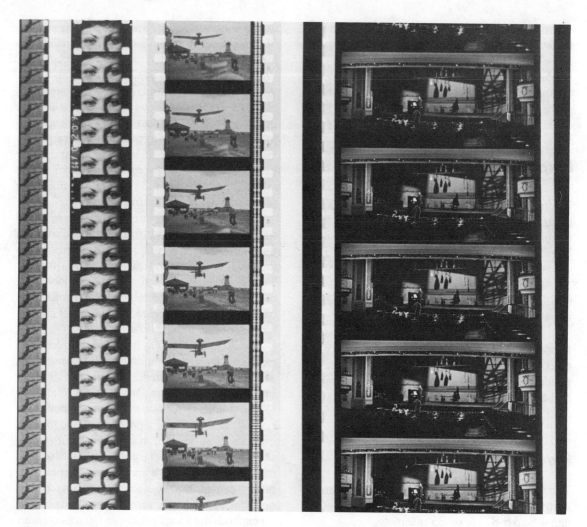

12.2 Film sizes, left to right: Super-8 millimeter; 16 millimeter work print without optical track; 35 millimeter release print with optical track at right; 70 millimeter with multi-sound tracks on magnetic tape to the left and right of the sprocket holes. (Photo by Frank Paine.)

Forming a Film Company and Raising Money

When filmmakers or producers form a private production company, they organize a limited partnership (a small private corporation) for seeking funds for the sole purpose of producing and seeking distribution for a theatrical film. One attribute of private production films is that filmmakers can make the movie in their own area. This helps somewhat with funding, too, for people can be found who are willing to invest in local projects.

In planning a limited-partnership company, the organizers must include activities that predict, for potential investors in the company, successful completion of the project, such as:

1. First final version of the shooting script.
2. Selection of locations.
3. Selection and availability of equipment.
4. Availability commitments from crew and actors.
5. Delineation of jobs and responsibilities.

Once these matters are satisfied, the filmmakers prepare their final budget and form the company. The initial working funds, used primarily for legal, printing, travel, and entertainment costs, are borne by the producers, who contribute the working capital. The limited partnership then issues a prospectus designed to interest likely investors. The prospectus, which typically is attractively illustrated and printed, usually is organized as follows. It first dispels the notion that quality feature films can be made with only large sums of money. It stresses modern production methods, including location shooting, viability of the 16 millimeter format (or increased portability of 35 millimeter format), and commercial and artistic success of recent low-budget, privately made features.

It secondly directs its offer toward the speculative investor and explains that the limited partnership is composed of investors and participants (actors and crew). After film profits have paid back an investor's original investment (with no interest), additional profits are divided into two funds—usually 60 percent for participants, 40 percent for investors.

Participants sign a contract at the beginning of shooting for a certain percentage, which is negotiated between producers and participants to represent a fair share, depending on the participant's contribution (which may include not only talent but also the use of personal equipment such as automobiles and cameras). Percentage figures available are determined by the number of participants (a major crew member or leading actor in a company of thirty people would receive about 5 percent). If participants are not local residents, they may receive free room and board as well as transportation and entertainment costs.

Investors sign a certificate that gives them a profit on their investment according to what percentage of the total budget they contributed. For example, if the film's budget is $100,000 and an investor puts in $10,000, or 10 percent, then after the original $10,000 is returned from the first earnings, the investor thereafter receives 10 percent of all money in the investors' fund.

Thirdly, the prospectus—which should anticipate questions as well as to try to further personal contact—for negotiations—offers information about distribution. This information generally describes the anticipated rating (G, PG, R, or X), the film's primary market, and other distribution possibilities. Each case gives typical figures of profits from private production films.

Fourthly, the prospectus includes a plot synopsis and brief descriptions of the characters in the film. It states the aesthetic nature of the proposed film, including elements of style and techniques not normally used by Hollywood companies. It might give reasons why the film's cost will be comparatively low. It could include a description of any deferred-payment arrangements the company has made with film-equipment rental companies, as well as with processing and sound laboratories. It clearly states the budget.

Finally, the prospectus gives biographical descriptions of the major participants, and the company's (or its chief executive's) address and telephone number, toward which inquiries may be directed.

Budgeting

Filmmakers should have an idea how much they want to spend on a film, then work the materials and people (as determined by the script) to fit that amount. They should consider forming the script around locations in their geographical area. They should consider the number of people in the cast as well as the physical demands for shooting (which determine how large a crew will be needed).

Equipment rental is a major item, and at min-

Example of Preliminary Film Budget

A preliminary film budget—as this sample shows— must take into account preproduction, production, and post-production expenses.

Preproduction

Legal fees . . . . $	300
Printing costs (prospectus)	500
Secretarial (typing script, mimeographing, collating)	500
Travel and entertainment	500
Screen tests (including one day's equipment rental)	300
Processing for above	200
Subtotal	2,300
Add 10%*	230
Total	2,530

*The 10% is always added for unpredictable cost changes and other contingencies.

imum includes the following: camera, lights and reflectors, batteries, camera magazines, lenses, tape recorder, microphones, tripods, dolly, filters, editing equipment.

Items to be purchased include the following: film stock, tape for the recorder, makeup kits, costumes, office supplies, food, expendables, (gasoline, entertainment, and other daily items), accident and hospitalization insurance.

Items that can be made include dolly tracks, sets, and almost anything else except cameras, their accessories, and sound equipment—de-

pending upon the filmmaker's versatility and imagination.

Each of the above items and its cost is listed in in the budget. The number of shooting days, determined by the shooting schedule from the script, is also listed, together with the number of sets or locations to be used. Exact costs are computed from equipment-rental catalogues.

The preliminary budget, therefore, might look as shown in the inset below. This budget does not include any expenditures for crew and actors' time and talents. With a small private production

---

Production

(Ten weeks shooting schedule for company of thirty)

16 mm camera and accessories	3,600
Lighting	1,300
Sound	2,000
Transportation	800
Housing	1,500
Food	1,800
Production-editing equipment (includes synchronizer, sound transfer facility, interlock projector)	2,400
Film	900
Processing and work print	720
Sound tape	200
Insurance	600
Subtotal	15,820
Add 10%	1,582
Total	17,402

Postproduction

(Six weeks' editing)

Editing equipment rental (includes table editor and interlock projector)	4,200
Laboratory fees	1,200
Sound mix	600
Two trial composites (answer prints)	1,600
Blowup	5,000
Subtotal	12,600
Add 10%	1,260
Total	13,860
Grand subtotal	33,792
Add 10%	3,379
Grand Total	$37,171

partnership of this sort, investors and participants alike invest something— time, talent, or money. Such speculation on everybody's part can cut the costs of a film way down. (But if some people are paid, the budget should be increased by whatever fee their salary is.) This film could not be made in large cities where union crews and actors are required. But this sort of filmmaking offers opportunities for young filmmakers who have established a track record with their personal films. The private production film is made primarily close to home. It involves location shooting, willing participants, and flexibility of story and equipment. It is totally autonomous and speculative, both for participants and investors, and financing is controlled by the makers of the film.

The Shooting Schedule

The shooting schedule is made from the script's notated sequences, scenes, and shots. A convenient way to make a shooting schedule is to put each scene on a separate three-by-five-inch card, then arrange the cards in terms of locations and actors.

Movies are almost never shot in sequence. This would be inconvenient and waste time. Grouping the cards in order of locations allows the filmmaker to take all the shots in a particular place during one block of time. If these cards are next arranged in blocks that allow one actor to be present during the whole time, more efficiency is gained.

The number of each shooting day (as opposed to dates) can be enumerated on title cards, behind which the cards for the shots to be taken on that day can be put in order. This arrangement has to have some breathing space, to allow the filmmaker to catch up on shots he or she might have

fallen behind on and to take new shots that might be conceived during shooting. Also, the filming should start out slowly, with possibly three easy takes the first day, then five the next, and so on, until the company gets worked into the routine.

The cards themselves should include the shot notation, the setting or location, the actors needed, and a phrase about the action. A card from the section of the script illustrated earlier would look like this:

> 106.1. *Royal's back porch.* Royal and Walt. Conversation as Royal shaves.

The card then can cue the director into the section of the script in which the shot is placed.

The "Three O'Clock"

This form is taken from the shooting schedule and is posted for the company at three o'clock the day before the shooting it announces. It tells actors and crew what time to report, the costumes needed, as well as special equipment, props, special calls, information for the cooks, and other information (*see inset,* pages 254–255).

Camera/Sound Reports

A record has to be kept for every shot that is taken and for every sound that is recorded. This is so that the editor can find the proper picture and sound takes when he or she synchronizes the film. Of course, each picture and sound take is also slated, the picture by a clapboard and the sound by the tape recordist's voice. In addition, a synch "beep" may also help the editor to synchronize the sound and picture.

The picture and sound may all be on one form. The script clerk or the clapper person may write in information reported by the camera operator and sound recordist.

Each camera take is declared "no good," "hold," or "print" by the director. The sequence number and the take number should be written on each report form, and one page only should be used for each shot. A description of the action should be included, as well as the ASA (the film stock's light sensitivity) being used, the film stock, and the camera operator's name.

The sound take should indicate the sound recordist's name, the quality of the take, the tape roll number, the inches run off for the take, and, of course, the shot and take number.

Release Forms

Release forms are mandatory whenever a filmmaker is using people who have neither signed a contract nor are receiving any salary. Signed by the person being photographed as well as by a witness to the signature, these forms declare that the person gives up in perpetuity all rights of the material photographed to the filmmaker. Sometimes the phrase "for adequate and just compensation" is included and a dollar or two is paid to the person.

Two different forms, one for use with compensation and one for use for no compensation, may be used. Having them printed on different colored paper is helpful. It is best that the filmmaker have a lawyer word the forms.

Property and Equipment Forms

A list of all the properties and equipment the company owns or rents has to be maintained. Each production company can devise forms to meet its own requirements. It is important, however, that the forms be kept up to date and that they show exactly where a piece of equipment or a property is at any given time. While this is especially important for rental equipment, it is also a time-saving device for all other materials. More time can be wasted looking for something that may be under one's nose than most filmmakers like to think.

Locations, Sets, and Properties

Locations can be acquired from friends, or—if a particular location is needed—by contacting owners and paying them rental for the use of the place. Sometimes finding the owner can be difficult. One good way to discover who owns a piece of property is to go to the county courthouse and look it up.

Sets can be built by anybody handy as a carpenter. The rooms of houses can be reconstructed easily using plywood and paint.

Locations and sets usually cannot be used just as they are found, unless one is making a documentary film. Even outdoor locations have to be set with properties, in order to make them look more "real." Yard sales and junk shops offer a good source for properties.

Film Stock

The aesthetic of the picture largely stems from the visual qualities of the image. Film can be high contrast or low contrast; it can be fast to shoot in little light, or slow (and hence more photogenic) to shoot with planned lighting. Both black and white and color film stock has to be lit properly, and certain filters sometimes have to be used in order to achieve the proper qualities of shadow and light, contrast and color.

Reversal film has a positive image, and allows

Example of a Three O'Clock

Date: Location(s):

                               Sequences:

Cast	Costume	Special Report	Special Equipment

Royal _____

Easy _____

Jessie _____

Dahlia _____

Walt _____

Wanda _____

Jeannine _____

Edgar _____

Marvin and Mary _____

Mary Anne _____

Al Krause _____

Cal _____

Sy _____

Rose Anne _____

Cynthia _____

Children _____

Herman _____   *Props*

Seymour _____

Morton _____

Ben Tate _____

Winston _____

Rog _____

Susie _____

Gilbert _____

Kulp _____

Crew	Assignment	Special Calls/Assignments
Lachman		
White		
Helfrich		
Thompson		
Long		
Ceraso		
Davis		
Montgomery		
Mathews		
Mooradian		
Robertson		

Transportation		Lunches Location House
Anderson		
Prince		Snack/Beverage Location
Blumenberg		
Yavelow		
Travellers		Special Meals Location House
Davis		
Lachman		

12.3 Camera Films Available from Eastman Kodak

Name of Film	16mm No.	Availability			ASA Index	
		Super 8	16mm	35mm	Daylight	Tungsten
Eastman XT Negative	7220		x	x	25	20
Eastman Plus-X Negative	7231		x	x	80	64
Eastman Double-X Negative	7222		x	x	250	200
Eastman 4-X Negative	7224		x	x	500	400
Eastman Color Negative	7251		x	x	32*	50
Eastman Ektachrome Commercial	7252		x	x	16*	25
Kodak Ektachrome MS	7256		x	x	64	16†
Kodak Ektachrome EF Daylight	7241		x	x	160	40†
Kodak Ektachrome EF Tungsten	7242	x	x	x	80*	125
Kodak Plus-X Reversal	7276	x	x	x	50	40
Kodak Tri-X Reversal	7278	x	x	x	200	160
Kodak 4-X Reversal	7277	x	x		400	320
Kodachrome II						
Daylight			x		25	6†
Type A (Tungsten)		x	x		25*	40‡
Eastman Color Negative II	7247		x	x	64*	100

*85 filter balanced for 3200° Kelvin
†80A filter
‡85 filter balanced for 3350° Kelvin

the filmmaker to see shots in the actual color they have. Reversal is pretty much standard now in the 16 millimeter format and is always used for Super-8. Kodak's 7252 color reversal achieves acceptable results in 16 millimeter when an internegative (a negative between the original reversal print and the release prints) is made and enlarged to 35 millimeter.

Negative stock, however, is still standard for commercial films. Shooting negative film can result in more release prints of quality. Today the original 35 millimeter negative does not need a positive, then an internegative, struck in order to achieve release prints. A generation is not lost in the printing process before the release print is obtained (as is in the case with reversal film).

The choice of film stock a filmmaker wishes to use depends on several things, including the number and quality of final prints desired.

Today all sorts of films can be made by all sorts of people working outside the organized industry. This is not to say that the industry does not offer opportunities for professional employment. Opportunities for breaking in, however, are scarce in Hollywood, where union personnel themselves frequently find it difficult to get steady work.

The procedures above are not complete or unique, but they should help filmmakers move from idea to script and thence to organizing their own productions.

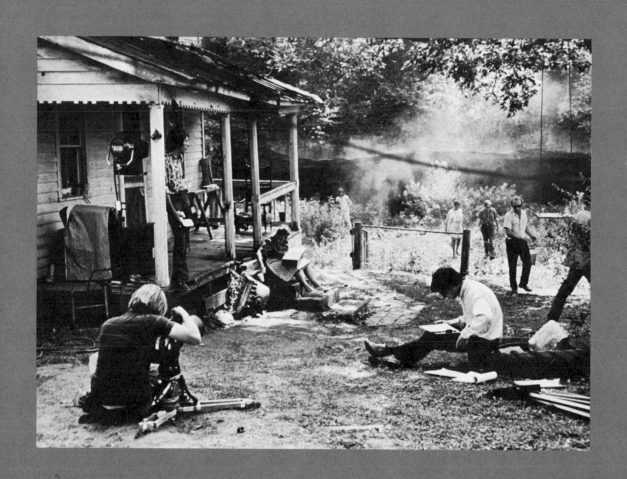

The Production Staff

13

The number of people needed for any production depends, of course, on the scope of the project. This chapter describes the jobs and main duties of key production personnel.

Producer

The producer is the chief executive of the whole production. He or she is responsible for all matters involving the logistics and business of the production, including the job of seeking distribution. The producer also is the one who seeks money for the project and controls the purse strings. Depending on the size of the production, the producer may delegate many responsibilities to staff members such as a business manager, unit managers, and secretaries. The producer, however, makes all the final business decisions.

Director

The director is the chief executive on the set. He or she makes all the artistic decisions and is responsible for the handling and directing of actors, for the types of shots to be taken, and

Opposite page: Production still from J. L. Anderson's *America First.* Courtesy Optos Limited.

sometimes for the final editing. On the set, the director's word is law.

Director of Photography

Sometimes called the DP, the Director of Photography makes all the key decisions about the shooting of individual takes. The DP, in accordance with the director's wishes, chooses appropriate lenses, organizes moving camera shots, decides on filters, and checks the appropriateness of the lighting. The DP works hand in glove with the director, frequently offering suggestions for the director's consideration. In the industry, the DP has not usually been the one to actually operate the camera, although this is changing.

Assistant Director

The assistant director, or AD, protects the director from having to be concerned with other than artistic matters. The AD solves most petty production problems and is the person the director turns to when something is needed.

First Cameraman

The first cameraman frequently operates the camera and, in collaboration with the DP and the director, will physically set the lights. When the DP is operating the camera, the first cameraman will "follow focus"—that is, manipulate the focal length of the lens in order to keep moving characters sharp or to keep characters in focus as the camera moves. When the first cameraman is operating the camera, an assistant will follow focus.

Crew Chief

Abhorred by some, this term describes the special duties of the person responsible for directing the work of the gaffer, clapper person, grips, and "gofer" (the person who runs around after things).

Unit Manager

This person performs the duties of the crew chief as well as manages all details for each production day. When a movie is being shot simultaneously at more than one location, each production unit will have its own manager.

Gaffer

As the electrician on the set, the gaffer maintains the power supply (including batteries) for the camera and lights. On location shooting, the gaffer frequently has to be a wizard in order to arrange outlets, power sources, and wiring.

Clapper Person

This person sees that every shot is slated. When he or she strikes a clapper board at the beginning of every take, the sound of the stick striking the board will allow the editor later on to synchronize the sound with the picture. At the point of striking, the slanted lines are together and lined up, to aid in this process. In addition, the clapper board gives all the essential information: stock used, sequence, scene and shot number, take number, director's name, cam-

13.1 Clapper board about to be clapped. (Photo by Frank Paine.)

era operator, and whether or not sound was used in the take.

Grips

The grips are the laborers of the production. They lay the dolly tracks, carry tripods and other equipment, help physically set the lights, and generally do whatever is needed in the way of hard work. The grips sometimes may also be the dolly pushers during filming, a task not as easy as it looks since the dolly must be pushed slowly and steadily, a job that requires a feel not everyone can master. Sometimes a grip will be the production's carpenter, although in larger productions needing several sets the job of carpenter is a full-time position.

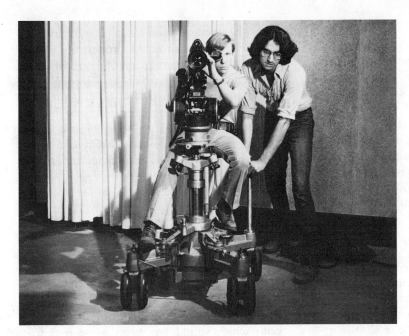

13.2 Elemack dolly with camera operator and dolly pusher. (Photo by Frank Paine.)

Continuity Person

The continuity person is one of the most important on the set. Each shot is taken so slowly and carefully that it is difficult sometimes to remember that one take is going to be cut with another one taken some time ago—or perhaps not yet taken—and that they have to match up. The continuity person is responsible for seeing that clothes, hairstyles, makeup, and character movement are all identical in matching shots. For example, in a scene of an actor chopping a log, in which a low-angle shot will be cut with an overhead shot, the continuity person would be responsible for checking stance; grip on axe; placement of hands, head, and body; and position of log and props in view to make certain all match exactly. The continuity person makes drawings and takes Polaroid photographs of movement and placement.

Prop Person

The person responsible for properties makes sure that they are painted or aged exactly as required by the circumstances. This person keeps an inventory list, so that any property can be gotten on a moment's notice. Prior to the actual production, he or she lists and gathers all properties needed during shooting. Except on larger productions, the properties person today may often be responsible for costumes.

Makeup Specialist

Working with the continuity person, the make-up specialist applies facial and hair coloring for matching shots. This is especially important when much of the shooting is done outdoors, for the sun can tan the skin and bleach the hair of actors. The makeup person also applies and maintains consistency of makeup for any actors who are aged, made youthful, have scars, need wigs, black teeth, false eyebrows, or any of a number of other unique physical characteristics.

Script Clerk

The script clerk stays with the director during the shooting, and carries a script for the director's immediate reference. This individual also marks off shots as they are taken, keeps notes on any peculiar characteristics of a shot (e.g., a left-to-right pan discovering so-and-so on a swing), keeps check on the shooting schedule for the director's reference, and generally acts as an executive secretary on the set. On some productions, the script clerk may double as continuity person.

Sound Recordist

The sound recordist has to find the best position for the microphones, then confer with the DP to see if the sound equipment is going to interfere either with camera movement or with the image. Also, the recordist may set the mike only to discover that the camera, however adequately blimped (covered to prevent camera noise leakage), is too close to the mike and will pick up the camera's motor noise. Each take requires specific solutions to these problems.

The sound recordist also keeps or relays to the clapper person the records of the tapes used. Just before each take, the recordist in-forms the director when the tape recorder is up to "speed" (moving at the proper rate to synchronize with the camera's motor so that sound and image—both of which flow through time —will mesh exactly in the editing process). After the take, the recordist plays back the tape to determine its quality. When there is a borderline problem on the acceptability of a sound take, the director, and sometimes others, will all listen to it in order to determine if another shot (assuming the camera take was a "print") should be taken.

Production Editor

In order for the director and others to see the "dailies," or rushes, a production editor is needed to synchronize the work print with magnetic tape onto which sound has been transferred from the original recording tapes. The magnetic tape and the work print (a copy of the original film) are then "strung out" in synchronization according to the shot order indicated in the script. With two or more "print" or "hold" takes, together with the accompanying sound takes, these string-outs are projected every evening or so by means of an interlock projector, which runs sound tape and film simultaneously. No sound effects are added at this time; there is just the dialogue or the silence if the shot was taken without sound, or "MOS" (which comes from *mitout sound,* a phrase picked up from German directors shooting in America during the early days of sound).

The Writer

If at all possible, the writer should be present during shooting. The director may want to confer with him or her about the meaning of a particular shot, or dialogue may need to be rewritten, added, or deleted. The writer, when asked, can contribute ideas concerning possible positioning of actors, camera movement, object placement, and other matters of style. The writer also is useful to the director after viewing the rushes, especially to act as a sounding board for the director's comments about the artistic integrity of the picture as it progresses.

Each shot is usually taken at least twice; sometimes it is many more times. In a master scene situation, the establishing long shot is taken, with great care observed by the continuity person, who notes every movement and gesture. The close-ups and medium shots are next taken, with actions identically repeated by the actors. The reason that usually multicamera setups are not used is that the lighting has to be adjusted for each close-up, medium shot, and long shot. It is not unusual for a scene that lasts twenty seconds on the screen to be composed of eight shots that took two days to shoot.

Each person on the set has specific responsibilities to help the production move along as smoothly as possible. While one shot is being taken, the crew is usually working on another set-up, so that after the completion of the takes the director can move right along to the next shot on the shooting schedule. Interior sets are kept ready in case bad weather makes outdoor shooting impossible.

Once on a set, many people fascinated with the glamour of behind-the-scenes movie making soon find the experience to be slow and sometimes very boring. The process of shooting motion pictures is quite opposite in pacing to the excitement of the final film projected on the screen.

Postproduction Activities

Postproduction includes the activities of phasing out the company, editing, and distribution negotiations.

Phasing Out the Company

It is not unusual for some actors to be recalled during the postproduction phase. As the film nears its final editing, the editor or director may determine that a new shot is needed to make clear a transition between shots. These matters cannot always be determined during viewing the rushes (although most of them are). It is therefore necessary for the producer to keep an up-to-date availability list on which is listed the location of all major actors and the dates they are free to return for retakes or for new takes.

As sets are taken down and equipment returned to rental companies and equipment rooms, the inventory has to be checked off so that all props, camera equipment, and other items are located exactly in case they need to be used for retakes. Accurate receipts are kept for all equipment returned.

Most productions have a production still photographer who takes hundreds of pictures of the production. Some of these production stills can be used for advertising purposes. The rest are

kept in the archives, which house all the scripts (including the various stages of rewritten scripts), the continuity material, the camera/sound reports after the editors are through with them, the director's notes, clippings from newspapers and journals about the production, memorabilia, and other things. These archives are important for film historians as well as for the director and other personnel to study when preparing for another picture.

Editing

At the beginning of the editing stage, the print takes and accompanying sound takes should pretty well be in order and synchronized. Using an interlock projector as well as the viewing screen on the editing machine, the editor carefully selects which takes to use out of all those that were printed. The film is first rough-cut; that is, each acceptable take is cut at a particular frame at the beginning and at the end to give an impression of pacing and flow.

Tracks of sound taken at times other than during the shooting—so-called wild sound and "buzz" (or atmospheric noise)—is transferred to separate magnetic tapes used in the editing process. Dialogue from one take may be dubbed into the picture from another take.

As this process moves toward the fine (or final) cut, a mixing chart is composed, indicating what sounds are going to be added to each shot in order to broaden and enrich it. Some of these sounds (such as music, animal noises, airplanes

Opposite page: Photo by Frank Paine.

flying overhead—the list is endless) are recorded at this time, if they were not recorded during the production.

When the work print is finally cut, a black-and-white so-called *scratch print* is duplicated from it. This print, which has no splices to possibly break or stretch and hence cause the film to go out of sync, is used during the sound mix. At the same time, if the sound on the editing tapes has deteriorated, the original dialogue tapes are again transferred to new tape so that the quality will remain high for the mix.

At the mix, various tape tracks are orchestrated during a slow projection of the scratch print. A footage counter below the screen allows the sound technician to bring in the required sound at the exact moment. The sounds mixed are filtered, echoed, their timbre raised or lowered, and volume levels set. Sounds required but not prerecorded can now be put on the master tape track with the use of a Moog synthesizer or a machine (called a Mellotron) that contains hundreds of tapes of everything from "footsteps over gravel" to "early morning thrush calls." During the mix one person sits with the master chart and calls out the appropriate track and key number on the Mellotron for the mixer to push. In addition, a dubbing booth may be used for dubbing in sounds and dialogue during this process.

The mixed sound is recorded on 35 millimeter magnetic tape, then transferred to an optical sound track (which most projectors read and transfer into aural), which is printed on the answer print so as to synchronize with the picture during projection.

The answer print (also called a trial composite) is made from the original negative or reversal footage. The individual shots are arranged in separate A and B rolls so that optical devices (such as dissolves and fades) can be added and smoother transitions can be effected without the visual intrusion of splices.

During the printing of the answer print, the levels of light are controlled and filters are sometimes used in order to ensure correct color values. Also, shots can be printed in such a way as to add or decrease the amount of light the image will show, so that a shot taken in daylight or artificially lighted can be printed to give the appearance of night. (It is a standard joke during production that night shots have to be especially well lighted.)

Distribution

The major feature film companies frequently do their own distribution. There are also specialized distributors for all sorts of films—from porno films, to art films, to industrial and educational films. The one certainty about distribution practices is that there is no certainty.

If distribution deals have not been made during production, the producer works hard during the editing stages of a film to find a commercial outlet for it. The producer arranges screenings for distributors who will look at the film on its completion.

Advertising materials, including a preliminary pressbook, should be available to show distributors. The pressbook includes credits, stills, production anecdotes, and the film's story line. It may also include posters, newspaper advertising, and articles about the film from any trade journals that have printed the producer's press releases. After the fine cut is finished, the editors may assemble a trailer from out-takes (takes not used) as well as from duplicated original in the final film.

The producers of a private production film of any sort—narrative, documentary, or experimental—would do well to consider entering the picture in festivals. Film festivals in other countries can open up possibilities for distribution abroad. Also, any invitation screenings, prizes, or critical acclaim accorded the film at these festivals can increase the chances of getting a distributor at home. There are many festivals other than the big ones at Cannes, Venice, Chicago, or New York. For instance, the International Film Festival of Nyon, Switzerland, is devoted to films shot in 16 millimeter. The Mostra Internazionale del Film d'Autore, formerly at Bergamo and now at San Remo, Italy, pays particular attention to *auteur* films. MIFED, in Milan, provides an open market for features and documentaries for television. The Zagreb World Festival of Animated Film, in Yugoslavia, is internationally recognized as a meeting place for distributors and filmmakers interested in animated film. The Mostra Internazionale del Nuovo Cinema (International Exhibition of New Cinema) in Pesaro, Italy, pays particular attention to the films of new filmmakers, as does the Mannheim festival in West Germany. The Edinburgh Film Festival, in Scotland, is an especially good place for innovative and experimental feature films.

Some festivals will consider a film if it has not been screened in the particular country in which the festival is held, regardless of whether or not it has been released in other countries. If a filmmaker selects festivals carefully, they can be of help in securing exposure and distribution.

Patterns and Practices of Exhibition

The producer signs a contract with a distributor. Usually, the producer agrees to pay for or give the distributor a given number of prints. Sometimes, a distribution deal can be made only after heavy negotiation concerning the content and editing of a film. Some distributors are absolutely adamant (and frequently correct) about what an audience will accept or not. It is not rare that part of a distribution contract will require the producer to eliminate certain shots from a film or to reorder shots. The producer usually pays for this work, as well as sometimes for advertising.

Distributors may arrange an advertising campaign that can saturate a community with the film, build word-of-mouth publicity about it, and make it a success. Sometimes they will ask the producer to make available some of the stars of the film or the director for premiere or publicity showings.

If the film is in 35 millimeter, it can play in all standard movie houses. If it is in 16 millimeter, it can play the college circuit, 16 millimeter commercial art houses, as well as private and public educational organizations and clubs.

The contract gives the producer a certain percentage of the money coming in to the distributor from the screenings. The distributor makes a percentage—or sometimes gets a straight rental fee—from exhibitors. Occasionally, the distributor will require a minimum guarantee and a percentage of any money over that. For hot commercial films, it is not unusual for exhibitors to pay 90 percent of their box-office receipts or more to get a first-run showing. In these cases, much of the money they make comes from refreshment sales, particularly from popcorn, which has over a 500 percent markup.

The money the distributor gets from the exhibitors is sometimes used to pay for the cost of prints, for advertising, and for other expenses. After these expenses are taken care of, the agreed-upon percentage is paid to the producer, who uses this money to pay back the original investors. The rest is then divided into the proper funds or is declared as profit.

Typically, on a two-dollar ticket, eighty cents might go to the exhibitor, forty cents to taxes and the motion picture employees' retirement fund, and eighty cents to the distributor. Of his or her eighty cents, the distributor would keep—on a 60–40 split—forty-eight cents, while thirty-two cents would go to the producer.

All sorts of deals can be arranged with distributors. The producers have to watch their step all the way. It is not that distributors are crooks; most of them are fair and honest business people. It is just that, as in any business, a product is acquired in order to make the organization the largest profit possible.

Alternatives to Formal Distribution

Filmmakers and private production companies are increasingly distributing their own films. Actor George C. Scott decided to make his own films and sell prints outright to theater owners, but most filmmakers do not have Scott's reputation or popularity. Still, makers of short films as well as features can put together a pressbook, get together a mailing list of groups geared to the type of film being marketed, and work up sufficient interest in it to rent or sell prints. With suf-

ficient capital, producers can rent a theater for a full week or split-week run, paying also for saturation television and newspaper advertising.

Television is a good outlet for films, and the Public Broadcasting System is continually looking for interesting and informative documentary and experimental films. Learning resource services at schools and colleges regularly buy all sorts of films. Film society and classroom projection of films of all kinds have made the college market sizable.

The chances against a feature film being completed and distributed are very great. Even within the industry, completed films sometimes die in cans in storerooms. Although the odds are overwhelming, the satisfaction and personal rewards of completing a film seen by others is great. One might think that with all the work that goes into any film, there should be sympathetic audiences waiting for it. Unfortunately, this is not always true, although there is always an audience for any good film. Finding that audience sometimes is one of the most difficult aspects of filmmaking.

Epilogue
The Film Revolution

Impresario Ely Landau's American Film Theatre presentations, which have offered filmed stage plays to the American public on a subscription basis only, emerge from circumstances that individual filmmakers have recognized for a decade: that the motion picture entertainment needs of American audiences have changed.

The mass audience of 80,000,000 Americans who regularly attended the cinema every week twenty years ago has fragmented. However much market analysis and great salesmanship it took for Mr. Landau's idea to materialize, it appears that the gamble was at least partly based on the fact that today the weekly American audience attending movies averages 14,000,000 people —and most of them choose the pictures they to go see, rather than simply go out of habit.

The big studios are finally recognizing audience fragmentation. To be sure, in the past there have been *genre* pictures—the Western, the gangster film, the horror film, the musical comedy. And pictures have been made to appeal to certain parts of the so-called general audience—the beach-party picture, the counter-culture picture, black pictures. These frequently resulted, in the last twenty years, from an appeal to audience types by means of content rather than from the erratically successful star system.

The inability to predict the success of a picture is evident even in such big box-office attractions as *Love Story, The Godfather,* and *Joe*—pictures the producers thought might not go. An example of the difficulties of predicting success is shown in the case of a 1973 picture called *Walking Tall,* about a Tennessee sheriff, which was failing in the big cities. This film's first ad campaign touted violence. But when the advertising was changed to emphasize the movie as a love story (although violence is its most definitive attribute), it sold very well. The picture eventually grossed over $15 million because the distributor recognized the importance of the special audience—the black and white middle Americans who look for values common to their experience.

"Hollywood" has more and more become a euphemism for an American film industry of great variety, including filmmakers as different from each other as John Cassavetes, Stanley Kubrick, Paul Morrissey/Andy Warhol, Roman Polanski, Dennis Hopper, and many others who frequently make pictures that are unique rather than imitative of industry formulas.

Filmmaking in America is moving in directions suggested by certain foreign filmmakers. Ideas that affected American feature films emerged from both Italian neorealism and the French New Wave, as well as from the personal and individually styled films of Ingmar Bergman, Satyajit Ray, Akira Kurosawa, and others. American filmmakers became sensitive to the aesthetic possibilities of the *auteur* films, and their "personal" films changed the tastes of their audiences. John Cassavetes's *Faces,* shot in 16 millimeter over a long period of time and completed against overwhelming odds, showed that the private

Opposite page: Photo by Frank Paine.

271

production feature could succeed both artistically and financially. Although millions of dollars are still being spent on Hollywood films to provide spectacles that only money can make happen, the smaller, more individual films have emerged as alternatives for American audiences. The major distributors today are continually looking for private production pictures that they might distribute under their banner.

Such package concepts as Ely Landau's point to the growing importance of the specialized audience. And recent small pictures such as *Billy Jack, Medium Cool, The Rain People,* and *Night of the Living Dead* suggest that these movies will continue to be made and that they will be seen. Because such pictures are produced at costs lower than if they were made within the organized industry, they do not need mass audiences to realize sufficient profits.

These pictures are being made in spite of great odds. In Hollywood and New York, less than 50 percent of all features announced for production ever get to the shooting stage (the figure would be much lower for the private production picture). In one recent year in New York, *no* feature film was completed by the initially announced completion date. Also in New York, about 20 percent of all pictures on which shooting started were never finished; and less than 65 percent of all finished pictures were distributed. Almost in defiance of these odds, large numbers of individual filmmakers without direct access to the organized industry are planning, shooting, and completing pictures, and sometimes they are even getting them distributed.

The United States is in a revolutionary stage in filmmaking. At high schools, colleges, and universities, many students who in past years might have majored in literature, creative writing, art history, or painting are now selecting cinema. Rapid advances in film technology and in film scholarship are continually creating areas for productive study.

From this excitement, as well as from those pictures that have succeeded critically, a private production aesthetic peculiar to the American experience is developing.

We know that, despite the myth, motion pictures do not necessarily have to be expensive to be successful, either aesthetically or economically. One can form a limited partnership, offer certificates to speculative investors, offer contracts to actors and crew for an agreed-upon percentage of any possible net earnings from the picture, offer percentages and negotiate deferred payment contracts with laboratories and equipment rental firms, shoot the picture in the general area where one lives, and come up with a film of quality for a fraction of the cost the same film would bear if shot "professionally." One *can* be a professional outside of Hollywood and New York.

This point must be qualified, but the qualifications are enriching rather than restricting in their possibilities for filmmakers. It is not true, of course, that the picture made in each situation would look the same. One important reason for doing a private production feature is to create a work that represents a personal style rather than an industry look. A private picture shows qualities of form and feeling that arise from a tight-knit group of people, all committed to one goal, living together in a closed situation for the intensive period of production time. This quality has many of the same strengths a repertory company has. It works successfully because of the close interaction of people on and off camera.

Added to this are the ways in which location shooting develops the participants' sensitivity to a film's geographical environment. In such a tightly knit situation, found locations create for participants a personal space, much like one's room or one's home. Because a private production film frequently grows from the special qualities that exist in an area, the film style arises from the actors' and crew's interaction within the locations and among the movie-making paraphernalia. The fiction of the film arises from a real feeling for place and for the project.

Although the style of such films emerges from individual people and places, it has to be consistent with the overall aesthetic written into the script. Usually this aesthetic is not totally prestructured. One important advantage of personal filmmaking is that a person can improvise. One can also take advantage of chance happenings; there are opportunities to catch people (and sometimes they are the actors) unaware. The private production film, then, can capitalize upon its involvement with all the impulses that lead to its creation. It can shape a work that enriches the participants, the viewers, and the film medium itself.

The possibilities for the private production picture indicate the excitement possible for the filmmaker who wants to explore the medium while at the same time investigating conditions of society. This kind of filmmaking is one promising area for work in the evolution of a mature American cinema. As such, it offers possibilities for the further enrichment of all of us.

Appendix:
Careers in Film

The changing industry, and the variety of forms that filmmaking takes, offers to serious people career opportunities in filmmaking. Also, the growth of interest in film studies offers many possibilities for people interested in nonproduction film activities.

Careers in Filmmaking

It is difficult to break into the organized industry, but not impossible. For writers who would like to sell an idea, a scenario, or a full script to the movies or to television, an agent is an absolute necessity. Most agents will look at the work of any writer, for their livelihood depends on constantly discovering new talents and new materials. If a person is unknown, an agent will probably require a recommendation from an established teacher or writer. A brief letter of query to an agent, to see if he or she would be interested in looking at the work, might save a lot of needless mailing. Motion picture agents are mostly located in, or have offices in, Hollywood. Their names and addresses are listed in a yearly publication called *Writer's Market,* which can usually be found in the reference room of any library. Agents who charge reading fees should be avoided.

Small production companies, as well as production companies organized within a large commercial firm, offer possibilities for people starting out. Work in many of these companies requires an all-around knowledge of filmmaking—from shooting, through lighting, scriptwriting, and editing. Anybody looking for a job should have a professional-looking résumé that includes at least the following information:

Name, address, telephone number.

Education.

Work experience.

A list of all film work, including titles of films, any festivals they have been in, dates when they might have been aired over television, and other screenings.

The résumé should indicate that a videotape or a representative reel of the individual's films is available upon request.

At least three references—names, addresses, and occupations—should be listed. These references should be able to testify to the applicant's experience and potential in the field.

A personal letter should accompany the résumé. Names and addresses of companies to write to can be found in the yellow pages of telephone directories of the areas desired, as well as in the files of most film departments in colleges and universities.

Job openings are also regularly announced in such trade journals as *Variety* and *Back Stage* and in magazines such as *Filmmaker's Newsletter, Film Comment, The American Cinematographer* (see the classified ads), as well as in the classified columns of such newspapers as the *Village Voice* and professional organization announcements such as the University Film Association's regular

Digest, which announces openings for film teachers and filmmakers in academia.

People interested in specialized work, such as editing, sound mixing, or processing, can frequently find free-lance work in large cities. Television stations also employ film editors and cinematographers.

What a person eventually gets can stem from who he or she knows. In a university situation, the opportunity to work with filmmakers and to talk to visiting filmmakers can provide opportunities for work in a private production film of one sort or another. People interested in film have a common bond of interest, and the desire to help a talented person is universal. Because the competition is so great—and because there is always someone out there more knowledgeable and experienced—the more expertise one shows through his or her completed works, the better the chances of getting a good job.

While it is not impossible, it is rare for a person to start out as a cinematographer or as a sound recordist, except in a small production company composed of two or three people, who all do everything. A potential professional should not be afraid to sweep floors and carry equipment; in fact, he or she should be eager to do it.

Jobs can be found, sometimes easily, sometimes with much effort. A recent college graduate with excellent recommendations sent out 120 letters and résumés to production companies throughout the country. From these letters, he received three interviews and one job offer. The offer—with a small production company based near Cincinnati—was for a six-month's trial period at good pay. He had to do janitorial work and physical labor as well as load film, sometimes shoot it, set lights, edit, and be generally available. This represents a good way—and a normal one—to get started professionally in film production.

Careers in Film Study

Teaching offers a wide variety of job possibilities. High schools are more and more adding both filmmaking and film appreciation courses to their curricula. It is not unusual for a person interested in teaching film in high school to contact a superintendent in an area whose schools do not yet have film study and suggest a course of study. Also, educational placement bureaus at colleges and universities have lists of such job openings. One should take advantage of them.

College (including junior college) and university teaching usually requires an advanced degree. The American Film Institute issues a *Guide to College Courses in Film and Television,* which lists courses and degree programs in these areas throughout the United States. New film departments and degree programs, both on the bachelor's and on advanced levels, are being instituted every year. In teaching, the more education *and* experience one has, the better the chances for a good job. So many film courses are being taught by instructors of literature, theater, and art that qualified film people are in demand. Opportunities here are bright.

Writing about film, as a critic, reviewer, or historian, cannot make a person a living wage unless one is writing for pay as a staff member for a magazine or a newspaper. These jobs are hard to come by, but one can work toward getting them by writing intelligent essays on film and sending them off to major film journals (listed in bibliography). One should study a journal to determine its needs. In addition, writing reviews for a college or local newspaper can give one material for a portfolio to show potential employers. Good writers, who write about film *as* film, are hard to come by, and the demand for them will increase.

Library work offers interesting employment.

With the growth of scholarly interest in film, many libraries are building film sections. Work as an *archivist* in a film library, or as a *film librarian,* can be interesting and stimulating. Large public libraries, as well as college and university libraries, may have need for such a person.

Other Opportunities

Various agencies of the United States Government, such as the Agency for International Development, United States Information Agency, National Aeronautics and Space Administration, and Central Intelligence Agency, have film production departments and film libraries. Because the job market here as elsewhere changes almost monthly, it is wise to write about not only present openings but also anticipated openings.

Working as assistant manager, manager, or advertising specialist for a movie theater or theater chain can be stimulating. One can inquire about jobs through the manager of any theater, getting the proper name and address of the home or regional office to write to.

The above represent some areas for inquiry concerning work in motion pictures. Because job opportunities are in flux and new positions open up all the time, one should keep in touch with people in the profession to see what is happening. Before any of this, however, it might be wise to have some good films or some published writings under one's belt. Potential is one thing that can be seen in works. It can rarely be accurately determined by talk alone.

Selected Bibliography

During recent years, innumerable film books have been published to meet the growing interest in the field. This bibliography concentrates on those books that are more specialized than a general text and that may provide additional information. These books, then, may be useful for readers who may want to focus their attention on a particular area of interest.

Film Theory, Aesthetics, and Criticism

Armes, Roy, *Film and Reality: An Historical Survey.* Baltimore: Penguin Books, 1974.

Arnheim, Rudolf, *Film as Art.* Berkeley: University of California Press, 1957.

Bazin, André, *What is Cinema?* trans. Hugh Gray. Berkeley: University of California Press, 1967.

Bluestone, George, *Novels into Film.* Baltimore: Johns Hopkins University Press, 1957.

Casty, Alan, *The Dramatic Art of the Film.* New York: Harper & Row, 1971.

Corliss, Richard, *Talking Pictures.* Woodstock, N.Y.: Overlook Press, 1974.

Eisenstein, Sergei, *Film Form and The Film Sense,* trans. and ed. Jay Leyda. Cleveland: World Publishing Co. [Meridian Books], 1957.

Jacobs, Lewis, *The Movies as Medium.* New York: Farrar, Straus & Giroux, 1970.

Kael, Pauline, *Going Steady.* Boston: Little, Brown and Co., 1970.

Kael, Pauline, *I Lost It at the Movies.* Boston: Little, Brown and Co., 1965.

Kael, Pauline, *Kiss Kiss Bang Bang.* Boston: Little, Brown and Co., 1968.

Kracauer, Siegfried, *Theory of Film.* New York: Oxford University Press, 1965.

Lawson, John Howard, *Film: The Creative Process,* 2nd ed. New York: Hill & Wang, 1967.

Levaco, Ronald, *Kuleshov on Film.* Berkeley: University of California Press, 1974.

Linden, George W., *Reflections on the Screen.* Belmont, Calif.: Wadsworth Publishing Co., 1970.

Lindgren, Ernest, *The Art of the Film,* 3rd ed. New York: Macmillan Co. [Collier Books], 1970.

Lindsay, Vachel, *The Art of the Moving Picture.* New York: Liveright, 1970 (reprinted edition).

MacCann, Richard Dyer, ed., *Film: A Montage of Theories.* New York: E. P. Dutton & Co., 1966.

Mast, Gerald, and Marshall Cohen, eds., *Film Theory and Criticism.* New York: Oxford University Press, 1974.

Münsterberg, Hugo, *The Film: A Psychological Study.* New York: Dover Publications, 1970.

Perkins, V. F., *Film as Film.* Baltimore: Penguin Books, 1972.

Pudovkin, V. I., *Film Technique and Film Acting,* trans. and ed. Ivor Montagu. New York: Grove Press, 1970.

Reisz, Karel, and Gavin Millar, *The Technique of Film Editing,* 2nd ed. New York: Hastings House, 1968.

Richardson, Robert. *Literature and Film.* Bloomington: Indiana University Press, 1969.

Sarris, Andrew, ed., *Interviews with Film Directors.* New York: Bobbs-Merrill Co., 1967.

Simon, John. *Private Screenings.* New York: Macmillan Co., 1967.

Stephenson, Ralph, and J. R. Debrix, *The Cinema as Art.* Baltimore: Penguin Books, 1965.

Wollen, Peter, *Signs and Meaning in the Cinema,* rev. ed. Bloomington: Indiana University Press, 1972.

Zettl, Herbert, *Sight—Sound—Motion: Applied Media Aesthetics,* Belmont, Calif: Wadsworth Publishing Co., 1973.

The Narrative Film

Bellone, Julius, ed., *Renaissance of the Film.* New York: Macmillan Co. [Collier Books], 1970.

Brownlow, Kevin, *The Parade's Gone By. . . .* New York: Alfred A. Knopf, 1969.

Geduld, Harry M., ed., *Filmmakers on Filmmaking.* Bloomington: Indiana University Press, 1969.

Gelmis, Joseph, *The Film Director as Superstar.* Garden City, N.Y.: Doubleday & Co., 1970.

Harcourt, Peter, *Six European Directors.* Baltimore: Penguin Books, 1974.

Jacobs, Lewis, ed., *The Emergence of Film Art.* New York: Hopkinson & Blake, 1969.

Macgowan, Kenneth, *Behind the Screen.* New York: Delacorte Press, 1965.

Mast, Gerald, *A Short History of the Movies.* New York: Pegasus, 1971.

Rotha, Paul, and Richard Griffith, *The Film Till Now.* London: Spring Books, 1967.

Solomon, Stanley J., ed., *The Classic Cinema.* New York: Harcourt Brace Jovanovich, 1973.

Taylor, John Russell, *Cinema Eye, Cinema Ear.* New York: Hill & Wang, 1964.

Social and National Film Histories

Anderson, Joseph L., and Donald Richie, *The Japanese Film: Art and Industry.* New York: Grove Press, 1960.

Jacobs, Lewis, ed., *The Rise of the American Film.* New York: Harcourt Brace Jovanovich, 1969.

Jarvie, I. C., *Movies and Society.* New York: Basic Books, 1970.

Jarvie, I. C., *Towards a Sociology of the Cinema.* London: Routledge & Kegan Paul, 1970.

Leyda, Jay, *Kino: A History of the Russian and Soviet Film.* New York: Macmillan Co. [Collier Books], 1973.

Randall, Richard S., *Censorship of the Movies.* Madison: University of Wisconsin Press, 1968.

The Documentary Film

Barnouw, Erik, *Documentary: A History of the Non-fiction Film.* New York: Oxford University Press, 1974.

Barsam, Richard Meran, *Nonfiction Film: A Critical History.* New York: E. P. Dutton & Co., 1973.

Calder-Marshall, Arthur, *The Innocent Eye: The Life of Robert J. Flaherty.* New York: Harcourt, Brace & World, 1963.

Hardy, Forsyth, ed., *Grierson on Documentary.* Berkeley: University of California Press, 1966.

Issari, M. Ali, *Cinéma Vérité.* East Lansing: Michigan State University Press, 1971.

Jacobs, Lewis, ed. *The Documentary Tradition: From Nanook to Woodstock.* New York: Hopkinson & Blake, 1971.

Levin, G. Roy, *Documentary Explorations: 15 Interviews with Film-makers.* Garden City, N.Y.: Doubleday & Co., 1971.

Leyda, Jay, *Films Beget Films: A Study of the Compilation Film.* New York: Hill & Wang, 1964.

MacCann, Richard Dyer, *The People's Films: A Political History of U.S. Government Motion Pictures.* New York: Hastings House, 1973.

Rotha, Paul, *Documentary Film.* New York: Hastings House, 1952.

The Experimental Film

Battcock, Gregory, ed., *The New American Cinema.* New York: E. P. Dutton & Co., 1967.

Curtis, David, *Experimental Cinema*. New York: Dell Publishing Co., 1971.

Madsen, Roy, *Animated Film: Concepts, Methods, Uses*. New York: Pitman Publishing Corp., 1969.

Renan, Sheldon, *An Introduction to the American Underground Film*. New York: E. P. Dutton & Co., 1967.

Sitney, P. Adams, *The American Avant-Garde*. New York: Oxford University Press, 1974.

Sitney, P. Adams, ed., *Film Culture Reader*. New York: Praeger Publications, 1970.

Stauffacher, Frank, ed., *Art in Cinema*. San Francisco: San Francisco Museum of Art, 1947; reprinted by: New York: Arno Press, 1968.

Stephenson, Ralph, *The Animated Film*. New York: A. S. Barnes & Co., 1973.

Youngblood, Gene, *Expanded Cinema*. New York: E. P. Dutton & Co., 1970.

Filmmaking and the Film Industry

Bobker, Lee R., with Louise Marinis, *Making Movies From Script to Screen*. New York: Harcourt Brace Jovanovich, 1973.

Churchill, Hugh B., *Film Editing Handbook: Technique of 16mm Film Cutting*. Belmont, Calif.: Wadsworth Publishing Co., 1972.

Fadiman, William, *Hollywood Now*. New York: Liveright, 1972.

Lipton, Lenny, *Independent Filmmaking*. San Francisco: Straight Arrow Books, 1972.

Malkiewicz, J. Kris, with Robert E. Rogers, *Cinematography*. New York: Van Nostrand Reinhold Co., 1973.

Mercer, John, *An Introduction to Cinematography*, rev. ed. Champaign, Ill.: Stipes Publishing Co., 1974.

Vale, Eugene, *The Technique of Screenplay Writing*, rev. ed. New York: Grosset & Dunlap, 1972.

Film Magazines and Journals

American Cinematographer

Cinema Journal

Film Comment

Film Culture

Film Quarterly

Filmmakers Newsletter

Sight and Sound

Take One

Glossary

A & B Rolls The placing of individual shots of original film on two separate rolls for printing. The shots are alternated, so that even number shots will appear on one roll, odd number shots on the other. Thus the resulting print is made from two runs through the printer.

Abstract film Movie in which the images are non-representational and contain only colors, lines, shapes, or geometrical forms. See also *Pure cinema*.

Accelerated motion Image that moves faster on the screen than it would in actuality; an action filmed at *less than* twenty-four frames per second and projected at twenty-four frames per second, gives the appearance of accelerated motion. Also called *Fast motion* and *Undercranked shot*.

Actual sound Sound taken on location during shooting and kept on the track to provide authenticity to the environment.

Anamorphic Lens used on both cameras and projectors which squashes images on the film and extends them to a Panavision or other wide-screen ratio.

Angle See *Camera angle*.

Animation Single-frame motion picture photography of drawn, painted, or actual forms or of still photographs. See *Cartoon*.

Animation stand Device with camera mounted on it equipped to shoot single-frame pictures of material placed in specified positions. A multiplane animation stand allows several different planes of material to be photographed, moved according to calculations, and photographed for the next frame. This gives the appearance of *Parallactic motion*.

Answer print Print representing first view of the final film, complete with optical track, color correction, and light levels. Also called *Trial composite*.

Aperture Opening that controls amount of light received by the film in the camera.

Archival films Films made to record historical events.

Artifact music Sound track music that originates from a source seen or suggested in the shot it accompanies.

ASA Sometimes called "film speed," it derives from the American Standards Association and refers to the sensitivity of film to light. A fast film can shoot in little light; a slow film needs much light.

Aspect ratio Proportion, or size, of the frame or screen, height to width.

Assistant Director (AD) The executive officer on the set; handles all but directorial decisions and carries out charges from the director.

Associative (associational) editing Cutting together of shots of similar but different events to make a statement; e.g., shot of people being arrested cut with shot of animals being slaughtered. Also called *Relational editing*.

Asynchronism Sound heard just shortly before or after movement is seen that produces the sound.

Audience (1) A mass audience is an unstructured group of people from many different backgrounds attending the same picture. (2) A fragmented or specialized audience is a group of people with similar interests or from similar subculture who attend a particular picture for identifiable reasons.

Auteur theory Critical method that sees movies as result in all parts of one creative intelligence. Suggested in 1948 by Alexandre Astruc in an article, "Le Caméra Stylo," the idea is that one person can control the total creative process of a film, much the same as an author does in writing a novel; a film hence could be evaluated in terms of a director's style as it reveals his personal vision of the world. See also *Cahiers du Cinéma* and *Caméra stylo*.

Autobiographical documentary Film in which filmmaker investigates certain aspects of his own life. Pioneered by Federico Fellini in *Fellini: A Director's Notebook, The Clowns,* and *Roma*.

Avant-garde (1) Phrase generally used to call filmmakers experimental. (2) Specifically refers to experimental filmmakers of 1920s and early 1930s, particularly in France.

Back lighting Lighting object or actor from the rear; can produce strong silhouette effect.

Back projection Still or moving images thrown against transparent screen. Actors photographed from other side of screen appear to be in the setting the images show. Also called *Rear screen projection*.

Black-and-white film Film stock that extends from deep black through intermediate shades of gray to pure white; in such films, color values are translated into specific shades of gray. See also *Color film*.

Blimp (1) Soundproof case or covering for camera. (2) To soundproof a camera.

Boom shot Shot taken from camera mounted on specially designed apparatus that can move vertically or horizontally through wide areas of space. Also called *Crane shot*.

Budget Total cost for a film. (1) Preliminary budget predicts costs in order to help structure film planning considerations. (2) Production budget is cost of shooting and editing. (3) Final budget is actual cost of film after the fact.

Buzz track See *Environmental sound*.

Cahiers du Cinéma Influential French film journal that gave voice to young critics (later directors) François Truffaut, Jean-Luc Godard, and others; started by André Bazin, *Cahiers* in 1950s and early 1960s was a strong voice in support of *Auteur theory*.

Camera Machine that takes motion pictures. Compare *Projector*.

Camera angle Position of camera in relation to the object it is filming. (1) Low-angle shot looks up at object. (2) Eye-level shot looks straight at object. (3) High-angle shot looks down at object. (4) Overhead shot looks straight down at object. See also *Reverse angle*.

Camera/sound reports Forms filled out during shooting to indicate scene and shot number, number of the take, quality of the take, action filmed or spoken, and other matters important for editor to know in selecting and synchronizing shots.

Caméra stylo Literally, "camera pen"; idea espoused by Alexandre Astruc in 1948 essay of same title in which he suggested a film can be made by one author, in the manner of a novelist.

Cartoon Animated forms cast into dramatic or farcical story situations. See *Animation*.

Censorship Action by committee, official, or board which suppresses all or parts of a film on legal, moral, political, or other grounds.

Cheat To use the illusory quality of motion pictures to show something different from how it actually is (e.g., standing a short actor on a box when he is kissing his leading lady so that, filmed as a medium shot, he will appear tall).

Cinema (1) Motion pictures generally. (2) In Europe, a motion picture theater.

Cinemascope Wide-screen process developed in 1953 by Twentieth Century-Fox; its aspect ratio is 1:2.35.

Cinematograph In England, a motion picture camera or projector.

Cinematographer Person who takes motion pictures; the cameraman. Also called *Director of photography*.

Cinéma-vérité (1) Documentary (and occasionally narrative) filmmaking style that frequently uses hand-held shots and does not use elaborate lighting or painstakingly prestructured set-ups. (2) Sometimes called *Direct cinema.* (3) Literally, *Film truth,* term introduced by filmmaker Jean Rouch in his 1961 *Chronicle of a Summer, Paris 1960.*

Clapper board Information board the camera shoots at the head of each take which serves to slate, or identify, the take number, film stock, cameraman, and other information; board on top of the slate, when made to sharply hit the slate, produces a sound that, together with the visual, allows the editor to identify and synchronize sound and picture takes.

Close-up (CU) (1) Limited, near view of an object or person. (2) Extreme close-up (ECU, or VCU for "very close-up") shows part of object or person.

Color film Film that is chromatic, extends from white, and regulates both hue and saturation. Compare *Black-and-white film.*

Commentative sound See *Narration.*

Compilation film Documentary film that in total or in part uses footage not shot for that film; term coined by Jay Leyda in book, *Films Beget Films.*

Compilation footage Film incorporated into a picture for which it was not originally shot.

Composition Visual organization of a shot in terms of framing, line, perspective, and camera movement; in motion pictures, composition involves movement.

Computer graphics Film and videotape made by means of an analogue or digital computer.

Conforming The process of exactly matching original film to shots as cut on the workprint and arranging those original film shots on A & B rolls for printing.

Continuity (1) Logical and sequential arrangement of a motion picture. (2) Job during production of ensuring that all visual information interlocks in shots that are to be cut together.

Contrapuntal sound See *Counterpoint.*

Counterpoint Opposition between an image and accompanying audial information on sound track; also called *Contrapuntal sound.*

Crab Small, versatile dolly that can be easily transported and that can move in tight spaces; the crab dolly can move in any of 360-degree directions.

Crane shot See *Boom shot.*

Credits Information at beginning or end of movie which tells names of all people and organizations involved in making the film.

Crew chief Production person who supervises grips and other junior personnel.

Critical focus Line measured from aperture to sharp object; the object in critical focus is at the center of the *Depth of field.*

Critics (1) Serious critics write for an audience well educated in cinema. (2) Popular critics write for a more general but informed audience. (3) Reviewers react to more superficial aspects of a film, such as acting, plot, and story, to inform the audience about its general appeal.

Cross-cutting See *Parallel action.*

Crowd shot Shot with lots of people in it.

Cubism Art movement developed by Pablo Picasso and Georges Braque in France in the 1910s; has influenced use of decor in motion pictures.

Cut (1) Simplest transition in film: one shot ends and another begins immediately; sometimes called *Straight cut.* (2) To edit a film.

Cutaway Cut to, and back again from, a place different from that of the scene's action; it condenses time and eliminates unwanted space.

Cutting See *Editing.*

Cutting on action Editing and shooting technique that uses shot 2 to complete a movement begun by shot 1, thus giving appearance of continuous action.

Dailies During production, film work-printed and shown the day after it is shot. Also called *Rushes.*

Depth of field Area in seeable focus before and behind the object in critical focus.

Direct cinema See *Cinéma-vérité.*

Director   Chief executive on the set; the person who designs shots, interprets script, directs actors, and is totally responsible for artistic qualities of the film.

Director of photography (DP)   Person on the set in charge of all matters relating to the camera and to cinematography. See *Cinematographer.*

Discovery shot   Provides new information that appears in a moving camera shot. Identified by type of camera movement used to discover the surprising or new element (e.g., "pan discovery," "dolly discovery").

Dissolve   Combination of fade-out and fade-in; as one image disappears, new image superimposes over the old for a moment as it emerges into clarity.

Distorted film   Film whose style suggests recognizable forms; degree of realism in between representational and abstract.

Distribution   Marketing of a film; a film "in distribution" is one that theaters or other commercial houses are showing and that people are paying to see.

Distributor   Company that markets a film commercially.

Documentary film   Film that in one way or another shows actual occurrences as they happen to real people. Also called *Factual film, Nonfiction film, Specialized film.*

Dolly   Device with wheels which carries camera and its operator to produce shots that are smooth-flowing and show parallactic motion. See also *Dolly shot.*

Dolly shot   Type of shot that moves smoothly and shows parallactic motion. See *Dolly.*

Dolly tracks   Rails or boards on which dolly rides.

Double-system sound   System in general use for all but archival and news film which records the dialogue and actual sounds on tape recorder separate from the camera; the two, however, are linked up in synchronization. See *Single-system sound.*

Dramatic film   See *Narrative film.*

Dream balloon   An early device (similar to the dialogue balloon in a comic strip) which used images to show what a character was thinking.

Dream mode   Representation in movies of qualities of the mind such as imagination, dream, fantasy, and anticipation. See also *Surrealism.*

Dubbing   (1) Addition to sound track of dialogue or other sound not taken during shooting. (2) Synchronizing dialogue from another language as close as possible to the lip movement and dialogue of a film's original language.

Dupe   Short for "duplicate"; to make print of film from original film or from another print.

Dynamic editing   Cutting and shooting technique that attempts to create for viewer an emotion similar to that of events portrayed.

Edit   To put a film together after shooting stage.

Editing   General term for the many processes of putting a film together after the shooting stage. Also called *Cutting.*

Editing table.   See *Editor.*

Editor   (1) Person responsible for cutting a film after shooting stage (as opposed to *Production editor*). (2) Machine used to edit film, such as a Moviola or a Steenbeck. Also called *Editing table.*

Educational films   See *Informational films.*

Effects   See *Sound effects.*

Environmental sound   Secondary sound in a shot which gives feeling of place and time (e.g., crickets at night). See also *Buzz track, Wild sound.*

Establishing shot   Opens sequence or scene to let audience know time, place, and setting of the story; usually long shot or extreme long shot.

Exhibition   General term for commercial screening of motion pictures.

Expanded cinema   Term given to recent experimental films that use computers, videographics, and other electronic-age devices to produce images and sounds; term used as title of Gene Youngblood's book, which examines concept.

Experimental film   Usually noncommercial film, frequently personal in nature, that attempts to go beyond the generally accepted limits of the medium.

Exploitation films   Movies of sex or violence which by their advertising seek commercial advantage.

Expressionism   Art movement centered in Germany during 1920s; gave rise to techniques that used decor, lighting, acting, costumes, and makeup styles to assert characters' emotions.

External rhythms   Flow of a film created by editing.

Factual film   See *Documentary film.*

Fade   See *Fade-in, Fade-out.*

Fade-in   Occurs when image emerges from black, or from some other color.

Fade-out   Occurs when image disappears, usually into black.

Fast cutting   Short shots cut together to create an exciting rhythm.

Fast motion   See *Accelerated motion.*

Feature film   Film of any sort that serves as a "main attraction"; often called "feature." See *Narrative film.*

Festivals   Special events at which films are shown for other filmmakers, distributors, and the public. There are festivals for new films (including specialized festivals for animation, documentaries, features, etc.), and there are retrospectives or festivals that show the work of one director, of a genre, or of a particular time period.

Fiction film   See *Narrative film.*

Film   (1) Motion picture, or pictures generally. (2) Strip of emulsified acetate, celluloid, or other substance that, when exposed to light and properly developed, has a series of fixed images that can be projected to show movement.

Film stock   (1) Raw footage to be loaded in camera. (2) Specific type of film, identified by its contrast, ASA, and other technical qualities.

Film time   Emotional time of the play of events in a film, as opposed to the clock time of its running period.

Film truth   See *Cinéma-vérité.*

Final cut   State of an edited print as it is ready for the sound mix.

Fine cut   (1) To select exactly at what frame each shot is to be cut in order to provide maximum effect through rhythm, pacing, and movement. (2) Print so selected and cut.

Flashback   Shot, scene, or sequence that shows events at a time previous to the main time period of the story.

Flash forward   Shot, scene, or sequence that shows anticipated or actual events at a time later than the main time period of story.

Flip wipe   See *Wipe.*

Fluid camera technique   Aesthetic of moving the camera through areas of the action to provide participatory and dynamic feeling for the audience.

Focus   (1) Generally, when object of main attention within the frame is seen sharply. (2) To sharpen image by adjusting lens of projector or camera.

Focus pull   See *Focus shift.*

Focus shift   In viewing on the screen or through lens, to allow sharp object to go soft while bringing into focus an object in front or in back of it. Also called *Focus pull* and *Rack focus.*

Footage   (1) Generally, amount of film shot for particular movie. (2) Specific amount of film shot at certain time.

Format   System being used for filming as determined by the size millimeter film—i.e., 8, super-8, 16, 35, or 70 millimeter.

fps   Frames per second. Twenty-four fps is standard sound film speed, and 18 fps is standard silent film speed. (Original silent film standard speed was 16 fps.)

Frame   (1) Limits outside of which a picture does not exist. (2) To pictorially compose a shot. (3) Single still photograph.

Frame-rate speed   Number of individual frames that pass through camera or projector each second.

Framing   See *Frame* (2).

Free Cinema   Diverse British documentary films made after World War II, sponsored by British Film Institute. Such films show concern for individuals caught in the maze of their culture.

Freeze frame   Repetition of same nonmoving image through several frames; when projected it appears a still photograph. Also called *Stop motion.*

Front projection   System of projecting images on a screen before which actors perform, giving the illusion of on-location shooting, other worlds, or the like. Because the image does not lose quality or light by being projected *through* a screen (as in rear screen projection), authenticity is greater.

Full shot   See *Close-up.*

Futurism   Art movement begun in Italy in 1910s, devoted to expressing dynamism of modern technological world by investigating "motion." Futurists made some of earliest experimental films.

Gaffer   Electrician on movie set.

Gate   Small, restricted passage through which film passes; located in back of aperture of camera or projector.

Genre   Any class or group of narrative films, usually popular, which have identifiable styles, themes, and subject matter; i.e., the gangster film, the Western, the horror film.

Gofer   Person who during production is used as general messenger and lackey.

Golden ratio   Aspect ratio of 1-1.33, which was standard before advent of wide screen.

GPO Film Unit   British General Post Office film unit, headed in 1930s by John Grierson.

Grip   (1) Film crew member who does physical work of laying dolly tracks, carrying equipment, and the like. (2) To do such work.

Hand-held   (1) As "hand-held shot," describes image created when camera is moved about without tripod, usually by cameraman. (2) As "hand-held camera," describes lightweight, portable camera.

Head   (1) Beginning of film or reel of film. (2) Beginning of any shot.

High angle shot   See *Camera angle.*

Holography   Method, using laser light, to project object in three dimensions without screen.

Hue   Particular tint or shade of color.

Image   Photographic representation of actual, distorted, or abstract forms.

Image manifest   Name for film aesthetic used when image itself (what is shown in single shot) assumes burden of presenting information, frequently through camera movement.

Image manipulative   Name for aesthetic used when events and actions in movie are composed and related to each other by means of editing.

Industrial films   See *Informational films.*

Informational films   Documentary films made for industry or education, designed to provide specific knowledge for special audiences.

Integral shot   Any shot that is complete scene in itself without cutting.

Intercutting   See *Parallel action.*

Interlock projector   Projector that synchronizes sound tape and movie film for screenings during editing stage.

Internal motion   See *Internal rhythms.*

Internal rhythms   Created through image manifest by means of camera and object movement, framing, lighting, decor, color contrast, and others. Also called *Internal motion.*

Intertitle   See *Titles.*

Iris   Circle, diamond, pentagon, or other geometric form that encloses an image.

Iris-in   Closes border around character or object.

Iris-out   Withdraws border from character or object.

Jump cut   Type of editing that omits space through which character or object moves, thus giving audience feeling of discontinuity, frustration, or anxiety. Also used, with accelerated motion, for comedy. Compare *Pixillation.*

Key light   See *Lighting.*

Kino-Eye   Theory of documentary filmmaking espoused by Dziga Vertov in 1920s and 1930s. With its accompanying theory of *kino pravda* ("cinema truth" in English, *"cinéma-vérité"* in French), *Kino-Eye* was forerunner of contemporary *cinéma-vérité.*

Kuleshov workshop Group formed around Lev Kuleshov in Russia after the 1917 Revolution. The workshop people were influential in developing theories of editing, composition, and the uses of other manipulations in narrative filmmaking.

Lap dissolve Short for "overlap dissolve," which has become shortened to "dissolve." See also *Dissolve.*

Leader Blank film used at the beginning (head) and end (tail) of a reel of film. Also used during editing to fill in spaces between shots in order to keep synchronization. Head leader is frequently blue, and tail leader is frequently red. Universal leader has the "countdown" sequence.

Lens The camera's "eye," through which the events photographed are translated onto film. (1) The wide-angle or short focal-length lens gives a wide field of view; (2) the normal lens sees things pretty much as our eye would see them; (3) telephoto, or long focal-length lens gives a narrow field of view. See also *Zoom shot.*

Lighting (1) *Key light* gives the main source of illumination to an object; (2) *high key lighting* provides a more than normal amount of light to the object; (3) *back lighting* illuminates an object from the rear; (4) *low key lighting* provides a less than normal amount of light to the object; (5) *fill lighting* brightens dark areas created by key lighting.

Lip sync See *Synchronize.*

Location shooting The filming of a motion picture outdoors or away from a studio set.

Long focal-length lens See *Lens.*

Long shot (LS) Complete view of an object with some surrounding area seen above and below it. An extreme long shot (ELS, or VLS for "very long shot") shows the object as well as more of the environment or setting the object is in. See also *Establishing shot.*

Loop (1) Film with head and tail spliced together so that it runs through the projector continuously. (2) A loose piece of film formed in a half circle above and below the gate of a projector and camera. These loops prevent the film from being damaged by the action of the pull-down clamps, which change the frames twenty-four times a second in a sound film.

Lyrical documentary Type of documentary film that asserts subjective truth through experimental sound, editing, and camera techniques.

MacGuffin See *Weanie.*

Magnetic stock Perforated sound tape of the same size as the film format; used to synchronize, edit, and project sound movies before the first trial composite.

Magnetic track Strip of magnetic sound tape that runs at the edge or edges of a print. Most sound films, however, have optical tracks. See also *Optical track.*

Masking Blocking off a portion of the image in order to reproduce another image in that space. Used by Méliès, and in films since that time, to combine miniatures or animated forms with live action as well as for supernatural effects.

Master scene technique Shooting and editing method that breaks a scene down into long shots, medium shots, and close-ups. The shots are usually cut with each other on action to give the appearance of continual flow.

Matching action Type of cutting on movement which creates a geographical space that does not necessarily exist in reality. See also *Cutting on action.*

Medium shot Using the human body as reference, a view of the body from the waist.

Millimeter (mm) (1) Types of lenses are described by their length in millimeters. (2) Film is described by its width in millimeters: 8 mm, 16 mm, 35 mm, 70 mm.

Minimal cinema A direction of recent experimental film, minimal cinema does not permit any camera, lens, or editing manipulations to interfere with the action photographed.

Mise-en-scène (1) Literally, "staging"; now a part of on-location shooting aesthetics and, within that context, means atmosphere. (2) In France, *mise-en-scène* means "direction."

Mix   Orchestration in a sound laboratory of all the various sounds in a film.

Montage   (1) Editing techniques based on the theories and practices of Sergei Eisenstein and other Russians. (2) Different sorts of shots juxtaposed one with another. (3) Popularly, any fast cutting.

MOS   Literally, "mit-out-sound"; a shot taken during production without any sound being recorded during the take.

Motion Picture Association of America, Inc. (MPAA)   A movie industry organization that suggests regulations and provides information about movies and industry practices to the public.

Moviola   *See Editor* (2).

Multi-cam   Short for "multiple cameras." Technique of taking a shot with more than one camera at a time. Typically, this technique is used to get a variety of angles for a scene where only one take is possible, such as in the destruction of an expensive set or in a vigorous fight where matching action shots would be difficult to achieve.

Multiple exposure   Three or more shots taken on the same piece of film. *See also Superimposition.*

Narration   Audial information or observations made by voice that speaks over the picture; in England, called "commentative sound."

Narrative film   Motion picture that tells a story. Also called *Dramatic film, Feature film, Fiction film, Story film,* and *Theatrical film.*

Negative   A print in which light and dark areas are in reverse.

Negative film   Stock in which light and dark areas are reversed; after processing, this "original negative" is used to get positive prints.

Neorealism   Phrase coined by Umberto Barbaro in 1943 and used to identify those Italian films of social consciousness made from about 1945 until 1952.

Newsreel   Documentary form such as *Fox Movietone News* and *The March of Time,* which presented current events.

New Wave   (1) Category of French filmmaking *(Nouvelle Vague)* in the late 1950s and early 1960s. (2) Grew out of *auteur* criticism and was made possible by the development of lightweight, portable cameras (which could be hand-held), lighting equipment and sound recording equipment, as well as the invention of the zoom lens and faster film stock. (3) Films showing on-location shooting, the use of film as an eclectic medium, and experimentation with narrative structures.

Nonfiction film   *See Documentary film.*

Noninvolved documentary   Factual movie that does not attempt to manipulate unreasonably the truth of the events shown. Also called "objective documentary."

Nonstructured documentary   *See Noninvolved documentary.*

Nonsynchronization   No apparent connection sensed between the image and the sound.

Normal lens   *See Lens.*

Nouvelle Vague   *See New Wave.*

Offscreen   Indicates action sensed beyond the limits of the frame; for example, offscreen noise.

Optical printer   Device that, using a projector and a camera, prints a film one frame at a time and that can be manipulated to provide many effects, including superimposition, stroboscopic-like movement, and enlargement or reduction of prints to different formats.

Optical track   Most motion picture sound is produced by a track of visual patterns which runs along the edge of the film, next to the frame. This optical track is read by a light that transfers the visual patterns into audial ones. *Compare Magnetic track.*

Out-takes   Shots taken but not used in the final picture.

Overcranked shot   *See Slow motion.*

Overexposed shot   Shot that appears very light owing to too much light entering the aperture during shooting.

Overhead shot   *See Camera angle.*

Pacing   Forward movement or flow of a film as created by editing.

Panorama shot   Early name for *Pan shot;* in the early 1900s, it referred to films that slowly panned cities from rooftops.

Pan shot   (1) Any horizontal movement of the camera while it is on a fixed base. (1) A *swish pan* is a very rapid horizontal movement of the camera on a fixed base; the viewed results are blurred forms.

Parallactic motion   Phenomenon observed when new lines of sight and shifting planes come about because the camera is moving through space.

Parallel action   Shots cut together of two or more different actions taking place simultaneously at different locations. Also called *Parallel montage* and *Cross-cutting.*

Parallel cutting   See *Parallel action.*

Parallel montage   See *Parallel action.*

Part   (1) Role an actor plays in a movie. (2) Large section of a script, subsuming sequences, scenes, and shots.

Persistence of vision   Quality of the human eye to retain an image for a split second after that image has disappeared. In film, this allows us to see fluid movement. The process of changing single frames lasts for about a thirtieth of a second; during this time, our retina retains the image just presented to it.

Pixillation   Technique seen when a series of short shots, frequently jump-cut together and sometimes single-framed or undercranked, provide a fast-paced presentation by severely condensing time.

Plot   Organization of events in a narrative film.

Polemic documentary   Factual film that uses camera, editing, and sometimes sound manipulations to comment on the subject photographed. Sometimes called the "subjective documentary."

Positive   (1) A print in which light and dark areas are accurate. (2) Positive film (called "reversal") is film that has a positive image in the original.

Postproduction   Last general phase of filmmaking. Editing is the primary postproduction activity.

Postproduction script   Detailed playscript made from a movie after its completion. Most movie scripts published commercially are postproduction scripts.

Preproduction   First, or planning, phase of filmmaking.

Preview   See *Trailer.*

Print   (1) Motion picture film, ready for projection. (2) To duplicate film from the original.

Private production film   Feature film made outside the organized industry.

Producer's system   Industry-based system that evolved during the 1920s and 1930s. A top-level industry executive, assigned to produce a film, has strict control over all creative and business matters, including the final cut.

Production   Phase of filmmaking during which the picture is actually shot.

Production editor   Person who, during production, strings the dailies together, synchronizes them, and makes them ready for projection.

Projector   Machine that throws film images against a screen or reflective surface during viewing. Compare *Camera.*

Properties   Furnishings and personal possessions that embellish a set and a character; also called *props.*

Pure cinema   Term that evolved during 1920s to indicate film that does not use representational images and that relies solely on techniques of the medium to create movies.

Quick cutting   See *Fast cutting* and *Montage.*

Rack focus   See *Focus shift.*

Ratio   See *Aspect ratio.*

Rear screen projection   See *Back projection.*

Reel   Holder for film, which can be attached to a projector for projection.

Registration   Exact relationship between images and their shape in the projected picture.

Relational editing   See *Associational editing.*

Release forms   Legal forms a person being photographed signs to give the filmmaker all rights to the pictures taken.

Relief   Visual quality given to objects as different light values provide shadows and illumination.

Representational film   Nonabstract and nondistorted film whose images appear authentic versions of reality.

Retake   During filming the photographing of a shot already photographed once or more.

Reversal film   Film whose original gives a positive print.

Reverse angle   Line of sight 180 degrees opposite line of sight in previous shot; if camera is eyes of person looking into a room, reverse angle would show person as seen from within the room.

Reverse motion   Movement of an object in a direction exactly opposite its original movement.

Reviewers   See *Critics.*

Rewind   (1) Device with handles to which reels are attached in order to edit film. (2) To reverse the direction of a print by placing it on rewinds or by rewinding it on a projector.

Rhythm   Visual flow of the film as it creates patterns of movement; created both by editing and by internal movement.

Rough cut   An intermediate stage in editing where there is only one take for each shot in the workprint.

Rushes   See *Dailies.*

Saturation   In relation to color, vividness of hue; also the degree of difference from a gray of equal brightness.

Scale   (1) The relative size of objects in the frame to each other. (2) The size of the object photographed as it appears to the viewer.

Scenario   General written sketch of plot and story for a motion picture not yet scripted. Compare *Treatment.*

Scene   Self-contained unit of dramatic action, structured by time and place. See also *Sequence.*

Scratch print   Duplicate of final workprint; usually black and white and used for sound mix.

Screen   (1) Reflective surface against which a projector throws motion picture images. (2) Movies generally. (3) To project a film.

Script   Extended written account of a movie yet to be shot. The script includes all dialogue, some camera movements, descriptions of action when appropriate, and list of characters and settings.

Script clerk   Sometimes called the continuity person, the script clerk is the secretary on the set during production, working closely with the director.

Semiotics   As applied to film, a study of motion pictures as a complex system of signs; also called "semiology."

Sequence   A major section of a motion picture, roughly equivalent to a chapter in a novel. A sequence is structured by time, place, and action, or by character.

Setup   (1) Final organization of props and furnishings in a setting in which action is to be photographed. (2) Positioning of the camera in relation to the action, as in camera setup.

Sharp focus   Appearance of an image the outlines, textures, and forms of which are clearly distinct. Such an image is also called "sharp."

Shoot   To take a movie shot.

Shooting   Process of photographing motion pictures.

Shooting schedule   Organizational scheme for shooting a movie; indicates what shots are to be taken during particular days and times, what actors or other personnel are to be available, and what props and special equipment will be needed.

Shooting script   Written description of action, camera movement and placement, dialogue, and other sounds, which filmmakers use as a basis for shooting a movie.

Short focal-length lens See *Lens.*

Short subject Brief motion picture, usually a travelogue, other type of documentary, or cartoon, which is shown with a feature film in a movie theater.

Shot Any amount of footage given by one single run of the camera; the basic unit that builds motion pictures.

Shot-change A cut.

Silent film (1) Generally, a film in the era from about 1895 to 1927, when almost no commercial film had a sound track. (2) Any film without a sound track.

Single framing Process of shooting "live" action one frame at a time to give the appearance of pixillation, or of condensing time. Compare *Animation* and *Animation stand.*

Single-system sound Used mostly for news film; records sound magnetically or optically on the film being shot. Compare *Double-system sound.*

Slow cutting Refers to shots fairly long in duration which are edited to create a melancholic rhythm.

Slow motion Any image that moves slower on the screen than it would in actuality. An action when filmed at *more* than twenty-four frames per second and projected at twenty-four frames per second gives the appearance of slow motion. Also called *Overcranked shot.*

Soft focus Appearance of an image that is not sharp; such an image is also called "soft."

Solarization Positive image that includes some negative forms.

Sound effects Noises or other sounds artificially created and added to a sound track.

Sound film Any motion picture that has an optical or magnetic sound track.

Sound mix See *Mix.*

Sound reports See *Camera/sound reports.*

Sound track Strip of magnetic tape or optical patterns which runs next to the frames along the edge of a print and contains the sound for the picture.

Sound transfer Process of duplicating recorded material from quarter- or half-inch original tape to 16mm or 35mm magnetic tape for purposes of editing sound with picture.

Space-time continuum Ongoing intersection of space and time elements that run through a motion picture and give it its own sense of reality. See also *Film time.*

Special effects Usually preplanned, methodical uses of contrivance, such as small explosives in wood to create bullet holes, the use of fog filters, or the burning of a miniature city, which create on the screen an appearance of reality.

Specialized film See *Documentary film.*

Spectacle Movie that presents epic events on a large scale.

Speed (1) *Camera speed* is the frame rate speed. (2) *Projector speed,* except in specialized machines, refers to eighteen (silent speed) or twenty-four (sound speed) frames per second. (3) *Film speed* refers to sensitivity of film to light (see *ASA*). (4) *Lens speed* refers to the capacity of a lens to let in high or low amounts of light. (5) "Speed" is a phrase used by the sound recordist to let the director know that the tape machine's motor is running at the same rate as the camera's motor.

Splice (1) Point at which two shots are joined together during editing either by cement or tape. (2) To join two shots together.

Splicer A machine used to join two shots together during editing. (1) A *tape splicer* uses transparent tape specially made for the job. (2) A *hot splicer* speeds up the process of drying cement splices.

Split screen Occurs when two or more separate motion picture images, resulting from different shots, appear within the same frame.

Star system Marketing procedure for selling motion pictures through commercial exploitation of the actors starring in them.

Static camera shot Image viewed when the camera does not move.

Stop motion   Technique of stopping the camera, changing the action without moving the camera, then starting up again to provide supernatural or magic effects of appearance or disappearance.

Story film   See *Narrative film.*

Straight cut   See *Cut.*

Structural cinema   Experimental film movement that examines the parameters of the cinematic medium through motion pictures; for example, a forty-five minute zoom shot, a 360-degree pan shot, or a stationary camera overlooking a street would offer material for studying the potential uses for the zoom lens, for the speed of panning, or for the uses of framing.

Structuralism   As applied to film, a study of motion pictures in terms of their construction, shapes, and proportions.

Studio constructivism   Phrase used to identify the settings of those German motion pictures of the 1920s which were shot entirely in the studio; since that time, the phrase describes the settings of any such pictures.

Studio system   See *Producer's system.*

Subtitle   See *Titles.*

Superimposition   When two or more overlapping images are seen at the same time.

Surrealism   (1) Art movement developed in 1920s which asserted that subjective and physical reality could combine to form a super reality. (2) Surrealistic film usually employs fantasy through time and space manipulations which would appear illogical if in the physical world.

Swish pan   See *Pan shot.*

Synchronize   To exactly line up dialogue and other sounds with the image. The test for this is called "lip sync," which shows an exact conformation between lip movements and the sounds they produce.

Synchronizer   Machine used by editor to exactly line up the sound tape track with the picture track.

Synchronous sound   In a movie, when there is an exact one-to-one relationship between picture and sound.

Tail   (1) End of a film or reel of film. (2) End of any shot.

Take   One run of the camera as it shoots action; during production, takes are classified as "no good," "hold," and "print."

Take-up reel   Reel used on projector to receive the film after it has run through the projector.

Telephoto lens   See *Lens.*

Texture   Distinguishing qualities of the surfaces of objects; for example, skin pores, grains of sand, smooth silk.

Theatrical documentary   Factual film that, though using real people, has a dramatic structure that expresses conflict, action through dialogue, rising action, climax, and falling action.

Theatrical film   See *Narrative film.*

Thesis film   Narrative film with all elements arranged to explore or support a premise.

"Three o'clock"   Form used during production and posted at 3 o'clock, to tell next day's shooting schedule.

Three-shot   Shot with three persons in the frame.

Tilt shot   Any vertical movement of the camera while it is on a fixed base.

Time-space continuum   See *Space-time continuum.*

Titles   Any written information inserted either below images (subtitles) or between images (intertitles).

Tracking shot   Particular type of dolly shot which occurs when the camera moves parallel to a moving object it is following.

Trailer   Short film that advertises a movie soon to play the theater; also called "preview."

Traveling shot   Any moving camera shot except the pan or tilt.

Treatment   Description of a movie's action, written in the present tense. The treatment precedes the first version of the script and is written for the purpose of getting the story on paper as completely as possible.

Trial composite See *Answer print.*

Tromp l'oeil Appearance of three dimensions on a two-dimensional surface.

Trucking shot In England, a *Dolly shot;* sometimes, any *Traveling shot.*

Two-shot Shot with two persons in the frame.

Undercranked shot See *Accelerated motion.*

Underexposed shot Shot that appears very dark owing to too little light entering the aperture during shooting.

Underground film Name given to recent American experimental films.

Unit manager Person who manages the production on the set. When more than one location is being shot at once, each production unit has its own unit manager.

Variable-focus lens See *Zoom shot.*

Videographics Art of using television techniques for making motion picture or videotape presentations.

"Weanie" (1) Object on which the plot turns—for example, the uranium concealed in the wine bottle in Alfred Hitchcock's *Notorious* (1946). (2) Called a "MacGuffin" by Hitchcock.

Wide-angle lens See *Lens.*

Wild sound Sound taken by tape recordist when no camera is present; usually *Environmental sound* to be added to track during mix.

Wipe (1) Action of new image from one direction or another pushing old image off the screen. (2) *Flip wipe* occurs when old image turns around, bringing viewer new image from other side.

Workprint Duplicate print of original footage which editors use in cutting a film.

Writer Person(s) responsible for final script of a movie.

Zoom shot (1) Shot wherein the view changes from a telephoto to a normal or wide-angle composition or vice-versa. (2) The lens used for this type of shot is called a *variable focus* or *zoom* lens.

Index